DESCANT.
LABORARE
QUE STUDERE
ORARE

# Variety Without Disorder:
# St Columba's School, Kilmacolm
# 1897-1997

Plato puts his finger on the weakness of the democratic form of government, when he speaks of it as 'a charming form of government, full of *variety* and *disorder* . . .' *Our* endeavour must be to achieve variety without disorder.

Miss MacArthur, Prizegiving speech, 1949

# Variety Without Disorder:
# St Columba's School, Kilmacolm
# 1897-1997

Susan Milligan

ISBN 0 9534347 0 2

*Published by*
St Columba's School

*Printed by*
Garthland Print,
Glasgow

# Foreword

Variety! This book is packed with it.

The title of this history of the first one hundred years of St Columba's School comes from the Prizegiving speech, made in 1949 by Miss MacArthur, the Head at that time. She, like all her predecessors and successors, was responsible for the introduction of new ideas and fresh approaches to enable the school to respond positively to the changing social, economic and educational conditions and trends of the day, and of a century.

And so, in orderly fashion, St Columba's has developed, preserving the ethos and standards set by the far-sighted Glasgow businessmen responsible for its establishment in 1897, retaining and living the motto 'orare, laborare, literisque studere', but growing and diversifying to become the modern, co-educational and highly successful academic school it is now in 1998.

This is a book which chronicles remarkable changes in attitude and educational opportunity, courage and daring on the parts of Heads and Governors, and commitment and dedication by countless staff over one hundred years. More important, however, it tells the tale of a much-loved school seen through the writing and pictures found in the school archives, and recounted today when memories of school days are shared at Former Pupil events and reunions. It is a book which will interest, stimulate, educate and amuse its readers

I believe that the author has firmly captured the essence and spirit of St Columba's. I am honoured and pleased to commend this book to you. Enjoy the rich variety of St Columba's.

Helen M Laird

# Acknowledgements

My primary sources for this book have been, in chief, documents and publications held by St Columba's School. My principal sources of information were the St Columba's School Magazine, 1907-1997, and the Minutes Book of the Girls' School Company. There are, in addition, the School's Jubilee Book (a slim volume entitled *St Columba's School, 1897-1947*), several prospectuses, beginning in 1926-27, and boarding prospectuses from 1927 and 1928. *The Story of Shalott*, a compilation of writing and photographs by the boarders of 1966, was of use for Chapter Eight, and there are various other albums and scrapbooks, notably some two dozen scrapbooks compiled by former Headmistress Miss Clark. Another former Headmistress, Mrs Caldwell, kindly let me see the texts of all her prizegiving speeches.

I am most grateful to the many former pupils, teachers and other associates of the School for their willingness to let me interview them for the book. The dozens of hours spent in this way provided me with a mass of useful material, and much pleasure besides. Several former pupils provided written accounts of their memories, which I have been able to use, either as a source of information, or as quotations in the book. Miss Jean Nicol has been most helpful in passing on accounts sent in to the Former Pupils' Association, and in providing information about the Association's recent activities.

I should like to express my thanks to Mrs Evelyn Hood for giving me the transcripts of two interviews which she conducted before I took over the task of writing the book, and for her kindly interest in the progress of the work. I am grateful to the following for making documents available to me: Laurel Park School, Glasgow, for *The Park School 1880-1930* ; Glasgow University Archives, and Ms Lesley Richmond in particular, for documents relating to early women students; Ms Clare McGread, Archivist at Glasgow School of Art, for similar documents in her care; Mrs Maureen Lochrie for drawing my attention to her interview with Lady Stansgate, and Mr David Roberts, Keeper of Archives at Paisley Museum and Art Galleries, for making available the transcript. I have also consulted many publications held by the Glasgow Room of the Mitchell Library.

The task of research and writing would have been almost impossible without the assistance of two people in particular. Miss Kathleen Weir and Mr Parker Nicol gave me the results of their previous research and made their knowledge of the School available to me as a resource which I frequently drew on. In addition both have read the text, from its earliest draft onwards, and have made many helpful suggestions and comments. I am also very grateful to Mr Andrew Livingstone and Dr Helen Laird for their guidance and interest in the work, especially in its later stages.

Mrs Rosemary Reeves (Sim), the School Librarian, has at all times been a willing and efficient colleague in the many tasks which have been asked of her, and especially in collaborating on the selection of illustrations to which she has devoted many hours. Her assistance with the considerable job of captioning the photographs has been invaluable.

I am grateful to Mr David Craig for drawing the plan of the main building showing its historical development. The postscript chapter, 'The Centenary Year', was written and compiled by Adrian Miller, Head Prefect 1997-98, with the assistance of Mrs Lindsey Duncan. Several staff, including Mr Alan Rodger, helped with the preparation of the lists at the end of the book.

I should like to thank the many former pupils and staff who have lent photographs and helped to identify the people in them. Thanks are due to the following bodies for permission to reproduce certain photographs in their possession: the Glasgow Room of the Mitchell Library, for the photographs in Chapter One of Professors Young, Lindsay and Jack, John E Watson, Robert Murdoch and Frederick Moir; Kilmacolm Civic Trust for the three early photographs of Kilmacolm in Chapters One and Eight, and the Red Cross photograph in Chapter Six; and *The Herald* for permission to use the photograph of Winifred Drinkwater in Chapter Six.

# Author's Note

I have followed the convention used by the school magazine when naming married former pupils, in giving the maiden name in brackets after the married name. Every care has been taken to cite names accurately in their up-to-date form, but it has not always been possible to check for recent married names.

Information about honours awarded to former pupils has come mainly from the FPs' section of the school magazine: where lack of information about such matters may have led to omissions, this is regretted.

In captioning photographs, a few names have proved elusive, despite the greatest possible effort to identify them.

# Contents

1 1897 Original red sandstone building.
2a 1905 Assembly hall with stage.
2b Between 1905 and 1908 Attic floor of main building developed to provide science laboratory and music rooms.
3 1923 Main building extended northwards to double the number of classrooms.
4 1928 New gymnasium with art room and music rooms above. A corridor and cloakroom area links with the hall.
5 1936 Main building again extended northwards to give a new science laboratory, domestic science room, new kitchen, servery and dining room, as well as extra classrooms. Eredine, a house fronting onto Gryffe Road, was purchased and demolished to provide playground space.
6 1965 Science block with three laboratories and a general purpose room (later developed into a lab) built on west half of Eredine playground.
7 1968 Part of middle playground converted into extra cloakroom space, which in 1982 was further developed to give the boys a cloakroom and toilet accommodation.
8 1975 Cargen Lodge purchased for art, music and diction classes (mainly).
9 1988 New kitchen built with direct access to the hall which was now used as the dining room. Old kitchen, servery, and dining room converted into technology room, computer room and Transitus classroom.
10 1996 Roof of science block raised to make room for two new labs.
11 1996 Gymnasium divided to make Transitus classroom and cloakroom. All PE classes now held in the games hall built in Shalott grounds, opened in 1993.

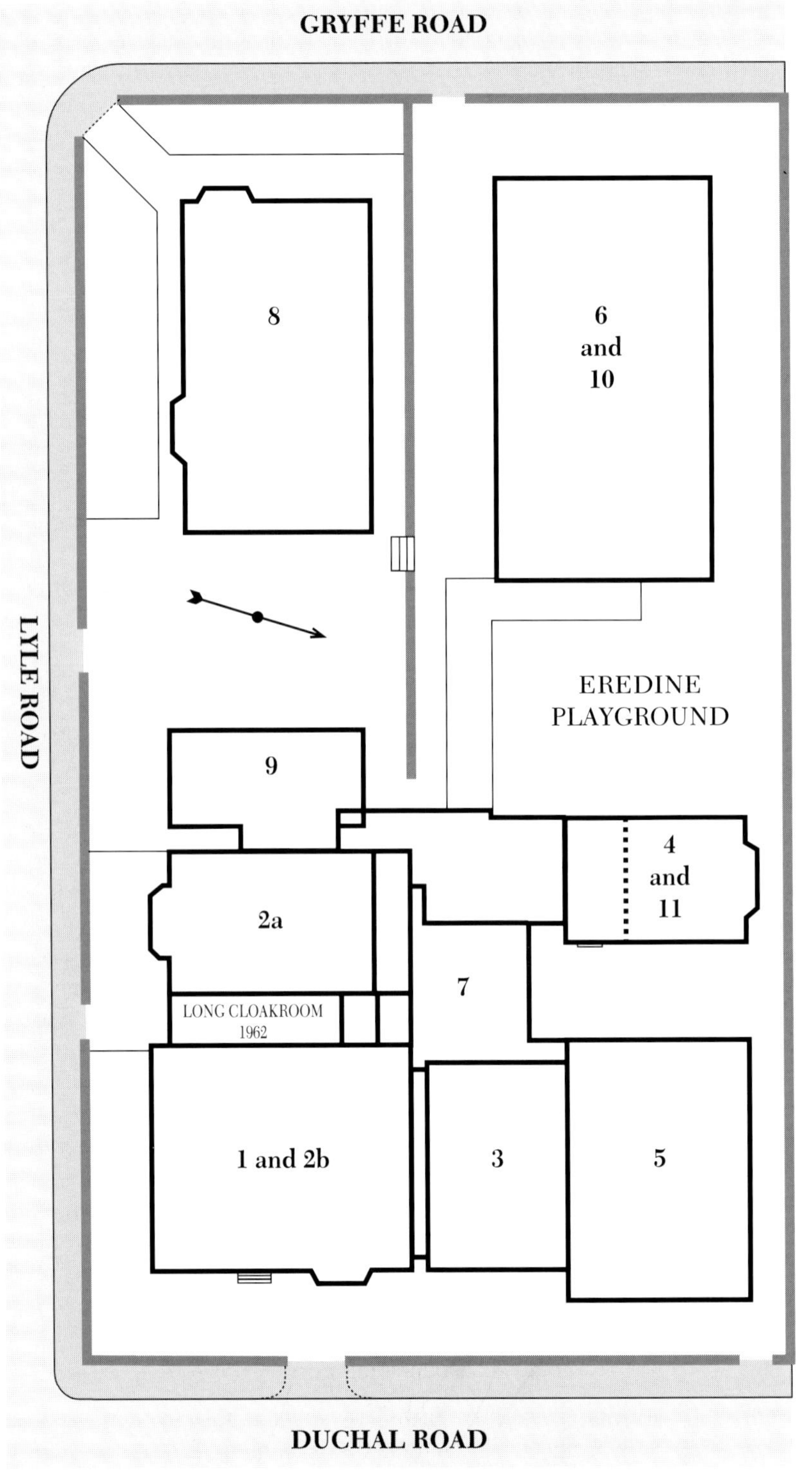


*Plan of the School showing the development of the main building*

*Chapter One*

# Beginnings

> Everywhere the fact that the pupil is to become a woman, and not a man, operates upon her course of study negatively, not positively. It deprives her of the kind of teaching which boys have, but it gives her little or nothing in exchange. It certainly does not give to her any exceptional teaching adapted to her career as a woman.
>
> (J G Fitch, *Report to Schools' Enquiry Commissioners*, vol. ix, 1868, p. 290)

The education of girls in the late nineteenth century could be a haphazard affair. The frustration felt by intelligent girls at the huge gap between their learning and that of their brothers is a well-known theme of Victorian novels and biographies of Victorian women. But in the second half of the century more and more voices were raised in the demand for equality of opportunity in education for women, and the movement to admit women to universities – and allow them to graduate – and to prepare them for higher education by sound and serious schooling, steadily gathered momentum.

The family of eight-year-old Georgina Kinnear had moved to Glasgow from Edinburgh in 1834. Georgina was an exceptional child, who formed the habit at an early age of getting up each morning at five o'clock to read, well wrapped in a shawl, in the attic of her family's house in Clarence Place, near the Sauchie Haugh, as it was then. She never went to school, and gained her education in languages from her brothers' tutors, and in other subjects largely by her own efforts. In 1880 Georgina Kinnear was appointed first Headmistress of Glasgow's newly established Park School, and for the next twenty years she devoted her considerable energies to introducing the hundreds of girls who passed through her school to the great possibilities offered by a liberal education. It is thanks not only to her, but to the gentlemen Directors of the Girls' School Company who appointed her, and to those who were a few years later responsible for the opening of a sister school in Kilmacolm, that many fortunate young Scottish girls of those days received an education not inferior to that of their brothers.

## The Girls' School Company and Glasgow's pioneers of women's education

The Girls' School Company was formed in 1879 by a group of Glasgow businessmen, professional men and academics, with the object of founding a school or schools for girls where they could receive a sound and liberal education. To understand the significance of this venture, it is necessary to know a little about the persons involved, the reasons for their involvement, and the nature of the need which they set out to answer. Of particular interest is the connection between the Girls' School Company and the provision, through Queen Margaret College, for women's entry to Glasgow University.

Georgina Kinnear must have had an influence on the early days of St Columba's School, in particular because, when she was consulted about the appointment of its Headmistress, she nominated Miss Young, who had been at the Park School first as her pupil, and then as a member of her staff. When Miss Kinnear retired from Park, Miss Young succeeded her, and another Park teacher, Miss Waugh, took over at St Columba's. In the early cross-fertilisation between the Park School and St Columba's, Miss Kinnear's influence was very great.

***Miss Kinnear, from the portrait by Sir James Guthrie***
With thanks to Laurel Park School

Georgina Kinnear was a most remarkable woman. The second half of her life was devoted to the education of girls in Scotland, in which she was one of the little group of women pioneers. In her early days she had travelled in Europe, spending some years in Russia where she was tutor to the children of a would-be reforming Minister of Tsar Alexander II. On her return to her own country she spent a couple of years teaching at Cheltenham Ladies' College under the famous Miss Dorothea Beale. She was then asked, in 1877, to be one of the four original teachers at St Leonards School, St Andrews, under Miss (later Dame) Louisa Lumsden. This school was very important for private education in Scotland, in that it was the first to be set up on the model of an English public girls' school. Of these there were two prototypes: Cheltenham Ladies' College and the North London Collegiate School. In England the latter school, headed by the renowned Miss Frances Mary Buss, had served as the model for a string of private girls' day schools, under the umbrella of the Girls' Public Day School Company (later Trust), and the movement took only a few years longer to make an impact in Scotland by the establishment of the school in St Andrews.

Miss Kinnear made a deep impression upon all who worked with her or studied under her. She was a woman of great learning and true scholarship, but it was the originality of her mind that marked her out as extraordinary. A Liberal and a reformer by political inclination, she was something of a radical in her educational thinking even among the company of these early champions of women's education. She disliked examinations, believing them to encourage cramming and to give an inaccurate picture of the state of a pupil's true knowledge of her subject. However, she was enough of a realist to know that exams must figure in the preparation of girls for higher education. Her own teaching was over the heads of some of her pupils, but she was fond of telling them: 'You are not here to learn, but to learn how to learn.' All forms of pettiness, small-mindedness and complacency were completely foreign to Miss Kinnear. A pupil of hers, Margot Wells, recalled that:

> Her sudden and startling 'Whys' would set our dull minds groping for a reason for actions hitherto taken as a matter of course. Her constant battle cry 'Think for yourselves' had its effect deeper and more far reaching than any mere drilling of facts into reluctant small minds.
>
> (Joan Lightwood, *The Park School 1880-1980*, pp. 32-33)

Miss Kinnear, in her years as Headmistress of the Park School, used to be invited to tea every Sunday at the home of Professor John Young, two of whose daughters, her pupils, recalled:

> . . . the breathless way in which she would tear off her gloves and dolman, dropping them on the drawing room floor and plunging into conversation as if she had not a minute to spare from such an entertaining pursuit.
>
> (Lightwood, *Park*, p. 25)

*Professor Young*

Professor Young, father of five daughters, occupied the Chair of Natural History at Glasgow University, and was an ardent supporter of women's education. He gave lectures to women two years before they were officially admitted to university lectures. These lectures for women led to the establishment of an Association for the Higher Education of Women (in 1877), which was in 1883 incorporated as Queen Margaret College. Professor Young was on the Council of this College from the beginning and in 1890 was made first Dean of the College's own Medical School. Two years later the Honorary Secretary of Queen Margaret College, Miss Janet Galloway, succeeded in getting women admitted to the University proper for the first time, by obtaining the affiliation of the women's College to the University. When she died in 1909 Miss Galloway was remembered with affection by the girls of St Columba's:

> She took a real interest in our school affairs, and often came to see us, and was always very kind to those who passed on to the University.
>
> (School Magazine, Easter term 1909, p.29)

*Professor Lindsay*

Professor Young and another participant in those early lectures for women, Professor Veitch, were two of the founding fathers of the Girls' School Company.

The Reverend Professor Thomas Lindsay, often known as Principal Lindsay, one of the original Directors, was Chairman from 1883 until 1914, and an influential figure in the setting up and early years of St Columba's. Like Professor Young, Principal Lindsay was an energetic supporter of the movement for the higher education of women, and, with his wife, helped in the establishment of Queen Margaret College.

The Company employed the services of a Secretary, John Spens, of Maclay Murray and Spens, who later accepted a directorship. The Treasurer was David Hill Jack, accountant, who later became Secretary and Treasurer and then, in 1909 a Director, in what was to be more than half a century's association with the Company.

**The original Directors of the Girls' School Company**

**J L K Jamieson**, J P (the original Chairman), engineer and shipbuilder
**Professor John Young**, M D, Professor of Natural History at Glasgow University
**Professor John Veitch**, LL D, Professor of Logic at Glasgow University
**Professor William Jack**, LL D, HM Inspector of Schools in Scotland, Professor of Mathematics at Glasgow University
**The Reverend Doctor James Dodds**, DD, Minister of St George's Parish Church, Glasgow
**J M Cunningham**, General Manager of the Clydesdale Bank
**William Galbraith**, lawyer
**J B Wingate**, of Black and Wingate, cotton manufacturers
**Robert Laidlaw**, of R Laidlaw and Son, gas and water engineers
**James Dunn**, of David Dunn and Son, provision merchants
**The Reverend Professor Thomas Lindsay**, DD, LL D, Professor of Church History at the Glasgow College of the Free Church (Chairman 1883-1914)
**John E Watson**, partner in a firm of chartered accountants
**Robert Murdoch**, Councillor, of R Murdoch and Co, iron and steel merchants
**Alexander A Ferguson**, wine and spirit merchant

The last four, together with **A M Lindsay**, lawyer, a Director from 1893, were those most actively involved with the Company at the time of the setting up of the School at Kilmacolm.

*Professor Jack*

*John E Watson*

*Robert Murdoch*

## A need fulfilled

The Company, in establishing a school in Glasgow, and in due course, in Helensburgh and Kilmacolm, filled a significant gap in the educational needs of this area. There already existed private establishments which imparted genteel accomplishments, generally showy but superficial, to the daughters of gentlemen, but where serious education in academic subjects was not to be expected. Sound education was the aim of the Education Act (Scotland) of 1872, which committed the State to providing schools for all children aged between five and thirteen. But it was elementary schooling which was thus revolutionised, while secondary education, far from being promoted by the Act, was relegated to second place. It is true that public schools which taught advanced subjects in addition to the three Rs, were permitted to be taken under the authority of the new school boards, but the funding of such schools was haphazard, depending partly on endowments, fees and donations. With a few exceptions, they did not flourish, and the way was open to competition from private establishments. Secondary education in this period came more and more to be left to schools outside the public system. As for the education of girls, the shortcomings of the public provision were even more serious. In 1883 the School Board of Glasgow reported that:

> . . . in Public Higher Class Schools the provision for girls is very restricted compared with that for boys . . .
>
> (Circular (55) on Higher Education.
> Reply of School Board of Glasgow to SED, 1883)

In response to this Garnethill School had by 1894 been turned into a senior school for girls, and after considerable early success it became the High School for Girls.

But in the West of Scotland in the 1870s there was scant provision for the serious education of girls of middle class families, and when on 19th December 1879 a public meeting was held in Glasgow 'in connection with the establishment of a school or schools for girls' a committee of about fifteen gentlemen was quickly formed, and soon afterwards set up the Girls' School Company. Enough shareholders came forward to invest in the project to enable the committee to buy the fine building at Lynedoch Street, up till then occupied by a boys' school, and by May 1880 the curriculum of the new school had been drawn up and Miss Georgina Kinnear appointed as Headmistress, at an annual salary of £400. From the outset this establishment set itself high aims, and it was Professor Young who insisted that it should not be described in the prospectus as a school 'for the daughters of gentlemen'. His daughters later described his wish that the school produce:

> . . . educated women fit to give the school a cachet far beyond mere ladylike accomplishments.
>
> (Lightwood, *Park*, p. 17)

The Park School flourished and did indeed, under the guidance of its Directors, prepare girls for higher education. By October 1881 there were 179 pupils and eleven staff. Pupils were examined by the University Examining Board. In the School's fourth year a chemistry laboratory was built, a great source of pride for the School. Many of the girls went on to have successful university careers, at Oxford, Cambridge and London as well as the Scottish universities.

Such was the success of the Park School, and of the Company, that when in 1895 a school was offered for sale in Helensburgh, the Directors and Miss Kinnear decided in favour of buying the property and opening a branch school. The Charlotte Street School, later named St Bride's, opened in September 1895 with forty-eight pupils as a day school for girls, run along the same lines as Park, and Miss Renton was transferred from the Park School staff to be its Headmistress. As the number of pupils grew, other properties were purchased to accommodate them.

## A school for Kilmacolm

Before the railway came to Kilmacolm in 1869 the adult population of the parish was less than 400, much of it outside the village on the farms. The village in those days consisted of a cluster of thatched cottages around the Old Kirk. The coming of the railway led to an expansion, gradual at first, then increasingly rapid, of the size and amenities of the village. A gas works was built in 1873, and five years later water was supplied and drains laid. In the meantime new arrivals had built around ten villas and half a dozen smaller houses. In 1880 a 'hydropathic establishment' was opened just outside the village and Kilmacolm's reputation as a health resort was begun. In 1887 a public school was built, well equipped by the standards of its day. The growing population, standing at about 1200 by 1889, and increasing to 2000 by 1900, soon made the water supply inadequate and new waterworks were put in place at the turn of the century, and a more efficient drainage and sewerage system completed in 1903. Electric light was supplied in 1904, and public lighting grew from about ten gas lamps in 1876 to about 100 in 1907. By the 1890s a good many of the handsome villas that characterise present-day Kilmacolm had been built.

With the arrival of the families who built these houses came the demand for a school for girls. The Minutes Book of the Girls' School Company records, on 17th April 1896, that interest had been expressed by certain gentlemen from Kilmacolm in the opening of a school there by the Company, that a suitable site could be secured, and that it was proposed to raise £3000 of capital for the school. The Directors discussed this application and decided in favour of it, provided that the £3000 of capital could be raised by local subscription. They also expressed a desire to include representatives from Kilmacolm on the board of Directors, and approved a draft circular to be distributed in the neighbourhood. At the next meeting, on 19th May:

***The Old Kirk, Kilmacolm, 1870***

. . . the Secretary introduced a Deputation of gentlemen interested in the Proposed School at Kilmacolm consisting of Messrs Fred. L M Moir, Frank Burnet and David Todd.
(Minutes Book, 19 May 1896)

*The Cross, Kilmacolm, c 1900*

The meeting was assured that the sum of £3000 was guaranteed, and accordingly agreed to issue shares to this amount. The next thing to be done was to acquire half an acre of ground, and commission plans and estimates for a building. This last task was put in the hands of Messrs Frank Burnet and Boston, Architects. David Todd, of Bridge of Weir, and Frederick Moir were appointed as Kilmacolm representatives on the Board of the Company. By September the plans for the school were ready, and duly approved, and soon afterwards estimates totalling £2175 for the building costs were accepted. A year later, on September 13th 1897, the square red sandstone building at the corner of Duchal Road and Lyle Road was ready for opening. The grounds had not yet been put in order – that was attended to (for the sum of £36) the following year.

Frederick Moir and David Todd thenceforth regularly attended the Girls' School Company meetings in Glasgow, demonstrating a real commitment to the development of the school. Frederick Moir, born in 1852, was a philanthropist whose sphere of influence extended far beyond Renfrewshire. He was an African trade pioneer who had in his younger days responded to David Livingstone's dying appeal to Britain to 'heal the open sore of Africa'. As Director and Secretary of the African Lakes Corporation, he was one of those who carried on the famous explorer's work of wiping out the slave trade by opening up Central Africa to trade and civilisation. The Corporation, which had been formed as a shareholding company with a primarily humanitarian objective, explored, traded, planted stations and opened up the rivers and lakes of the Zambesi Basin with steamers. It achieved its main aim, ending the slave trade in the Lake Nyasa area in twelve years, and, like the Girls' School Company, also succeeded in paying its shareholders. In 1891 the African Lakes Corporation handed over to the British Government the treaties it had made with the African chiefs and a British Protectorate was proclaimed. Frederick Moir came back to Scotland and was active in numerous social and church projects until his death in Glasgow in 1939.

*Frederick Moir*

Frank Burnet (1846-1923) was a well-established architect by the time he helped to found the School. He had worked for Glasgow Corporation and travelled on the Continent, in Egypt and the Holy Land. He was particularly proud of his designs for improved artisans' dwellings, of which he built many,

***Frank Burnet***

***A T Taylor***

and on a grander scale he was responsible for several buildings in central Glasgow. He built himself a magnificent house, Earlston, in Kilmacolm, and sent his daughters Daisy and Dorothy to St Columba's and his son Frank to the preparatory department. Frank inherited the family business and the firm went on to design most of the later additions to the School. (He married one of the daughters of A T Taylor, Margery, and their daughters Margaret and Mary Rose were pupils at the School in the 1930s. Daisy Burnet had three daughters, Frances, Joan and Elspeth MacRobert all of whom went to the School, and Joan later taught games there.)

A T Taylor (1873-1953) later Sir Alexander Taylor, KBE, was one of the original subscribers for the Kilmacolm school. Twenty years later he became a Director of the Company and then, in 1944, Chairman of the local Directors for St Columba's. He moved to Kilmacolm when he married, and bought the house which he named Shieldhall, which was later sold to the School as a boarding house. He was one of the founders of Kilmacolm Golf Club, and he went on to become one of the most prominent men of public affairs in Renfrewshire, sitting on the County Council for very many years, and its Convener from 1944 until 1949. He became Chairman of Glasgow Royal Infirmary and was knighted for political and public services in 1938. His business was sugar importation, and during the War he was a consultant to the Ministry of Food, particularly in the matter of sugar rationing. A good and modest man, he loved children, and he used to tell of an encounter with a young pupil one day when he was tired and ill, walking up the hill from the station and feeling rather depressed:

> In his hand he carried a despatch case full of business papers. He met a little girl from St Columba's and spoke to her. She said to him, 'I see you take music!' And he went on his way, completely cheered up.
> (School Magazine 1952-53, p. 16)

In March 1897 Miss Kinnear attended the Directors' meeting at which the appointment of a Headmistress for the Kilmacolm School was discussed. She recommended Miss Margaret P Young, a teacher at the Park School, and the meeting agreed to appoint her at a salary of £200. It is a matter for speculation whether any of them guessed that Miss Young would only occupy the post for three years, and whether they knew that in their making of the choice, the Directors and Miss Kinnear were ensuring for the new school, not yet known by the name of St Columba's, a foundation upon solid rock.

*Chapter Two*

# Margaret P Young 1897-1900

> The days of inferior educational advantages and facilities for study given to women in comparison with those offered to men are in Scotland a thing of the past. From the Infant School up to the Honours Classes and Degrees of the Universities, all possibilities of education are open to them.
>
> (Janet Galloway writing in C S Bremner's *Education of Girls and Women in Great Britain*, London 1897)

What satisfaction it must have given Janet Ann Galloway to write these words! She had devoted herself to an unpaid career in advancing the cause of women's education in the West of Scotland, and by the date of writing she had seen the first thirteen women graduate from Glasgow University, three in Arts and ten in Medicine. And so 1897 was an exciting year for the opening of a new school for girls.

But, exciting as it was for the schoolgirls who aspired to something more than 'staying at home to help mother' and for the women students working for their degrees, the struggle of society to come to terms with the strangeness of the change in the expectations of women was to continue for a while yet. One of Glasgow's female graduates wrote, of the graduation ceremonies of the late 1890s, that:

> . . . each woman as she approached the rostrum was singled out for outbursts of wild catcalls and vigorous cheering as if she were something from another planet.
>
> (Euphemia Gray, 'Through College Windows' V, *The Glasgow Herald* 19 March 1955, p. 3)

Even among supporters of the higher education of women, there were many who viewed with alarm the risks to the prevailing order in society, especially regarding family life, if middle-class women were to migrate outside the sphere of domesticity which had been reserved for them throughout most of the century. In 1896, at a meeting of the Glasgow Branch of the Teachers' Guild, Dr R M Wenley, Dean of the Faculty of Arts in Queen Margaret College and Lecturer in Philosophy at Glasgow University, described the radical agenda of the 'New Woman' as 'an attack upon the family'.

The doors, however, had been opened – at first in some places only to be firmly slammed shut, in others just enough to admit a determined foot – but, by 1897, opened they certainly were. But uncertainty remained. How should girls' schools be organised? What *was* the distinctive form of education useful and suitable for females? For what were girls being educated? – for only a minority would actually go on to a university. The working out of the answers to these questions in practice took several decades. Meanwhile the newly recruited Mistresses at Kilmacolm had to get on with the job.

## The first day

The sun shone on Monday 13th September 1897, when the red sandstone school at the corner of Duchal Road and Lyle Road opened its doors to its first pupils. Fifty-four pupils had enrolled for the first term of the new school, and the first thing they did was to assemble in what was then the hall (a room which served a triple purpose as hall, form room for the youngest pupils and dining room) and was later made into the library. One of the girls on that day, Katherine Wood, later gave a description of the scene:

> We stood in rows, facing the window, grouped rather according to height than to age – some fifty children of all sizes from tinies to big girls, sixteen years old. Miss Young, our Head Mistress, stood behind a leather-topped table, facing us, and the Assistant Mistresses present included Miss Burton the Kindergarten Mistress, Miss MacKay and Miss Amanda Meyer, although we did not know their names till later.
>
> After Prayers, the calling of the Roll, and a short address, Miss Young bade Fräulein Meyer take my row, nearest the door, to the chrysanthemum room. Feeling as if our doom were sealed, we faced round, and walked away, anyhow, up the stairs, preceded by the strange little teacher who spoke in broken guttural English. (But she very soon used our language astonishingly forcefully and well!) At the top of the stairs she ushered us into a classroom which we saw was divided from another one by sliding doors. No chrysanthemums grew in pots, none adorned the window ledge, but quantities sprawled artistically across the wallpaper. We scrambled into places behind empty, new, green desks with creaking lids, and white china inkwells filled with nice blue ink. Examination papers and pens were distributed and from the written results our classes were determined.
>
> (School Magazine 1933, p. 32)

***Miss Margaret P Young, from the portrait by Sir James Gunn***
'She had a quiet dignity that one would expect of a daughter of the Manse, and a whimsical humour that came naturally from a cousin of J M Barrie.'
(School Magazine 1952-53, p. 12)

Another pupil, Elsie Holgate (Linford), who was later to return as music teacher, remembered the smell of new varnish and floor polish and the thrill of opening the very first unblemished green desk in Form II. She wrote:

> The little group of mistresses was regarded with the veneration due to authority and their advanced ages (they were all probably under 25!). At the cloakroom door stood Miss Burton, in a cheerful scarlet shirt-blouse, asking our names as we entered. 'Hello! you're English,' she cried, on hearing mine. 'Shake hands!' And thus, auspiciously, began five happy years at St Columba's.
>
> (*St Columba's School, Kilmacolm, 1897-1947*, henceforth referred to as *Jubilee Book*, pp. 10-11)

As at the Park School, boys were enrolled into the youngest classes, officially called Kindergarten, Transition and Form I. These three year groups were, however, initially taught together, not merely in the same room, but actually by the same teacher – Miss Burton, the 'Initiatory Teacher' – so that they are sometimes referred to at this period as the Initiatory class or Kindergarten. In those days it was usual for a child to start school at the age of six and most children were ready to leave this part of the School at the age of eight or thereabouts. From Form II upwards the School was for girls only.

All the teachers were women. An all-female staff was something which the private schools for girls in Scotland had in common with their English counterparts, and which distinguished them from state schools and endowed schools, even those few such schools which existed for girls only. Hutcheson's Grammar School for Girls and Glasgow's High School for Girls, for example, both had male head teachers at this period.

## The first Headmistress: Miss Young

Margaret P Young was already sixteen or seventeen years of age when her father took her along to the Park School on the first day of enrolment in September 1880. As things happened, they left disappointed that day. As they waited in the ante-room they overheard an exhausted Miss Kinnear declare, 'I won't interview another parent today.' But the Reverend Mr Young and his daughter came back and not only was Margaret among the pupils on the first day, she was made Head Girl. The most important influence that she was to carry away from her time as a pupil was of course that of Miss Kinnear. She later recalled:

> Miss Kinnear herself was the greatest experience of all. Many schoolmasters and mistresses we had seen, but she was a new type.
>
> (*The Park School of Glasgow 1880-1930*, henceforth referred to as *Park 1880-1930*, p. 39)

Margaret Young was remembered with affection by her schoolmates as a bright and lively personality, and by her teachers as that rare creature, a natural scholar. On leaving school she went to the Maria Grey Training College to train for teaching, and thence to Oxford where she taught for two years at the Oxford High School for Girls, one of the schools founded by the

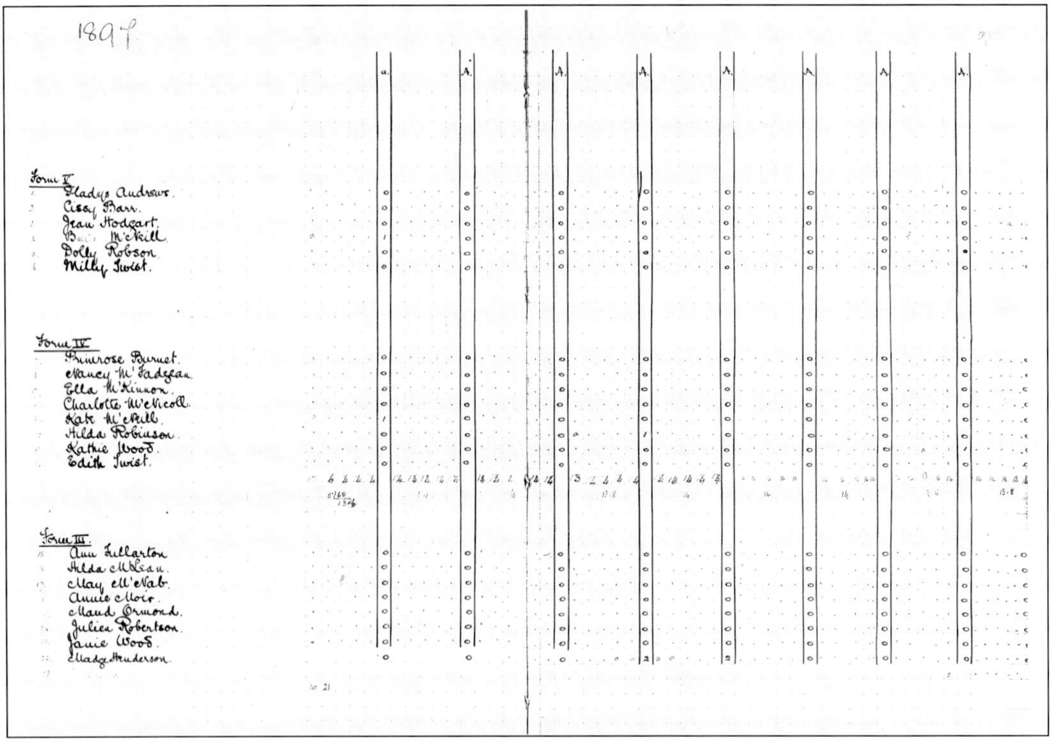
1897
Form V
Gladys Andrews.
Cissy Barr.
Jean Hodgart.
[illegible] M'Neill.
Dolly Robson.
Milly Twist.
Form IV
Primrose Burnet.
Nancy M'Fadzean.
Ella M'Kinnon.
Charlotte M'Nicoll.
Kate M'Neill.
Hilda Robinson.
Kathie Wood.
Edith Twist.
Form III.
Ann Fullarton.
Hilda McLean.
May M'Nab.
Annie Moir.
Maud Ormond.
Julia Robertson.
Janie Wood.
Madge Henderson.

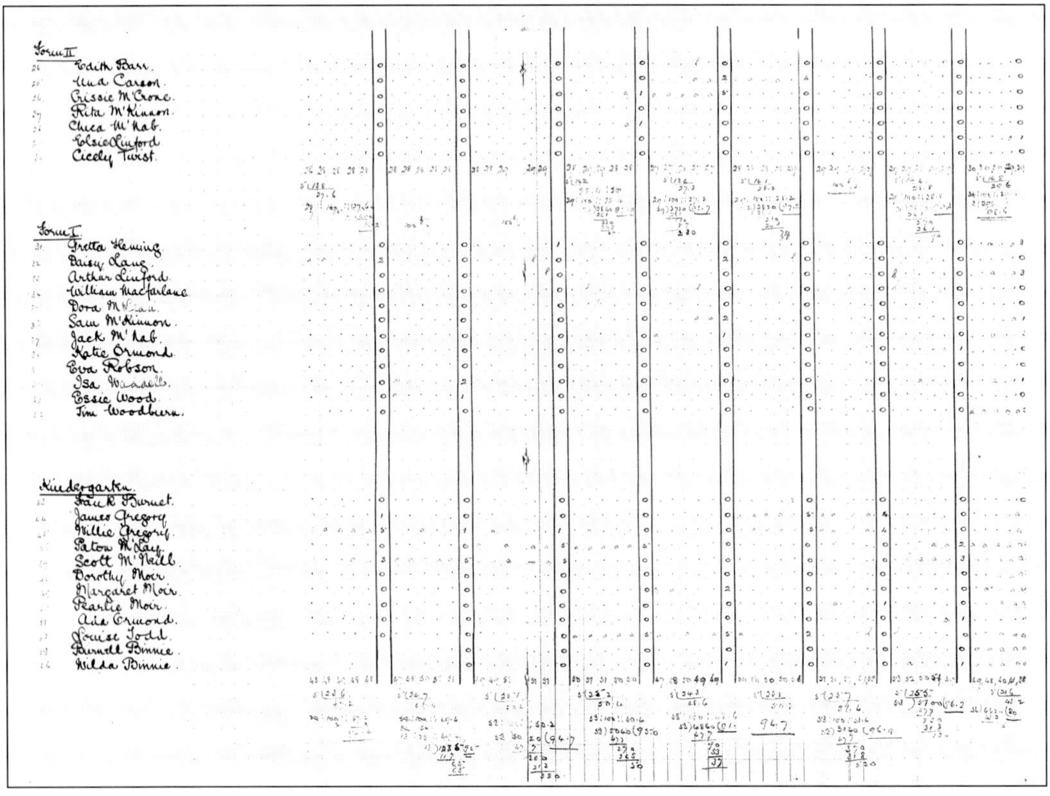
Form II
Edith Barr.
Una Carson.
Crissie M'Crone.
Rita M'Kinnon.
Chica M'Nab.
Elsie Linford
Cicely Twist.
Form I.
Gretta Fleming
Daisy Laing
Arthur Linford.
William Macfarlane
Dora M'Lean.
Sam M'Kinnon.
Jack M'Nab.
Katie Ormond.
Eva Robson.
Isa Waddell.
Essie Wood.
Tim Woodburn.
Kindergarten.
Frank Burnet.
James Gregory
Willie Gregory
Paton M'Lay.
Scott M'Neill.
Dorothy Moir
Margaret Moir.
Pearlie Moir.
Ada Ormond.
Louise Todd.
Burnell Binnie.
Hilda Binnie.

*Opposite: Register 1897-98*

Girls' Public Day School Trust. She then came back to the Park School as an assistant Mistress in 1886, where she soon became one of the best-loved and most respected of the staff. According to reminiscences of Park School pupils from those days she taught English, mathematics and Latin. There is no comparable account of her teaching style from her Kilmacolm pupils a decade later, so it is worth quoting here some of those tributes. Margot Wells recalled:

> Even in those early days she was a great figure, blithe and gay, imparting unconsciously to us so much more than the English she so richly taught us.
>
> (*Park 1880-1930*, p. 48)

The same former pupil also remembered:

> From the first she possessed the born teacher's powers of making the dry bones of a subject live, of interesting even obtuse minds. Some of us, to whom the mathematics hour had always been a dreary sort of purgatory, began under Miss Young to see some light emerge out of the shadows, possibly helped by the sound of her sudden delicious laugh, bubbling up irrepressibly in the midst of the serious business of the hour.
>
> (*Park 1880-1930*, p. 46)

Even Latin lessons she managed to enliven for Katie MacMillan:

> As far as I can remember we were not advanced in this subject . . . the book we read was Cicero's *De Senectute* and it must have been heavy work to drag us through those polished periods. Yet I do not recall one severe look or word from beginning to end of that year in her Latin class. Instead I remember our tasks being considerably lightened by Miss Young's amusing stories and racy comments.
>
> ( Ibid.)

Rita Macindoe, later to play an important part as music Mistress at St Columba's, was younger than these girls when she first encountered Miss Young:

> We liked Miss Young very much. If we were good and attentive she told us stories, and how well she told them. Also if we had two classes in succession with her we were allowed to go quietly downstairs and run round the hall a few times to refresh us. She used to play Prisoners Base with us between periods, as two periods without a change of room was rather trying.
>
> (Ibid., pp. 45-46)

This was the teacher, lively, sympathetic, progressive, whose task it was to recruit a staff for Kilmacolm and launch the new school on its course.

## The curriculum and staff

All was not plain sailing at the start. Additional teachers were required within the first two years, but it proved difficult to find suitably qualified people. Miss Meyer and Miss Burton remained for only three and four years

*A form room*
Room 13, in the 1923 extension

repectively. By June 1901 the only original member of staff still at Kilmacolm was Miss MacKay.

By this time, of course, Miss Young herself had left Kilmacolm: in 1900 Miss Kinnear announced her decision to retire from the Park School, and Miss Young was the Company's choice to replace her. The new Headmistress for the Kilmacolm School was again appointed from among the staff of Park, and Miss Janet Waugh took up her post in September 1900. Despite the rapid turnover of staff in these first years, the school roll achieved an increase from an initial fifty-four pupils to a total of seventy-one by September 1901 (although the roll had dipped in the session 1900-1901).

From the few accounts that have come down to us, it seems to have been a happy place for the pupils. Eliza Donald (Hodgart) recalled that:

> The high-light of my day was the lunch hour which we shared with the Staff and Miss Young. At our end of the table we were listeners only, but she opened up fresh realms for us as she discussed all manner of subjects, with spicy comments on the latest meetings of the Browning Society.
>
> (School Magazine 1965, p. 81)

The dining room (later to become the library) was also the assembly room and the classroom for the youngest pupils. Eliza's contemporary, Katherine Wood, described the uses of the other rooms:

> The Art room with its plaster casts and plaques was next the office; the room to the south of the side entrance was a music-room; and that completed the class accommodation downstairs. At the top of the stairs, a little passage and glass door to the right shut off the Mistresses' room and a music-room; while between them a wooden stair led up to the living quarters of our much-loved cook-housekeeper, Mrs Cameron, and her capable daughter, Lizzie. These two splendid women

*Miss Macindoe*

represented the kitchen staff and kept the school in perfect order. Their kitchen along from the office lay beneath the Mistresses' room, and many a mothering was given to an ailing child by the kindly woman. Many a tea biscuit and cup of milk or cocoa were consumed at the kitchen door in the lunch interval, while Mrs. Cameron delighted us with some funny story; and many a prank did we play on her by way of gratitude!

(School Magazine 1933, p. 33)

The art room mentioned here is now the Rector's room, and the present main office was the kitchen. One of the small rooms between them was the original office. The top-floor living accommodation of the housekeeper was extended some ten years later and now contains small classrooms.

Although there exists no prospectus of the School for Miss Young's period, the above accounts of the School's accommodation and staff provide evidence as to subjects taught. Miss Young taught Latin, history and English: the school magazine of 1965 recalls that Miss Young 'gave her lessons in History and English Literature in the form of lectures', which was the usual format of the time. Miss Meyer taught French and German,

*Miss Young and Assistant Mistresses, 1899-1900*

Back: Miss Meyer, Miss Burton, Miss MacKay; Front: Miss Young, Miss Robertson, Miss Crabtree

***Miss McIntyre***

and Miss MacKay taught arithmetic, mathematics and botany. Two music teachers, Miss McIntyre and Miss Macindoe, were shared with Park School (see Chapter Three). They taught at St Columba's for many years, and were of great importance to the School in establishing what was to become a formidable reputation for musical studies.

Needlework was taught, but we do not know by whom. The art room has been mentioned, with its plaster casts, which, typically of this period, were the subjects for drawing. The art Mistress was engaged on a part-time basis. It was common at this time for mistresses to teach more than one subject, and to be able to turn their hand to teaching various age groups. This is illustrated by a story told by Miss Burton (she was by then Mrs Auld, having left in 1901 to get married) about her time under Miss Young:

> We were a very happy family party and would willingly undertake anything she asked us to do – for in those days we had to be 'jack of all trades'. As Kindergarten mistress, I had to do games and drill as well, and once when it was found that the time of all the other mistresses was more fully occupied than mine, Miss Young said, with her sweetest smile, 'So Miss Burton, I know you will undertake the VIth Form Geography,' and no one would have dreamed of my refusing. It was an alarming thought, for there was a very clever girl in the VIth who was far more competent to do it than I was, but Miss Young helped me along, arranged a syllabus, and all was well.
>
> (School Magazine 1953, p. 12)

Gymnastics was in those days referred to as drill, and the particular form becoming popular at the time was Swedish drill. It was introduced at the Park School around 1897. The Kilmacolm girls, too, marched and swung their arms, and practised stretching, bending and turning under the eye of Miss Burton. It was a type of military drill, done to music, which involved alternating between moving the whole body and parts of the body. One of its advantages was that it was possible to perform it without equipment, in a large empty room, and it was not necessary to change into special gym clothes. In the school magazine of Easter 1908 there is a mischievous poem entitled 'Directions for Drilling' which contains the lines:

> Never keep in time to the music – it's wrong—
> Ignore the accompaniment (as you would in a song);
> The reason the piano is played on is only
> That the mistress who's drilling you shall not be lonely.
> If you find you're not doing the exercise right,
> Don't alter your method – a difference so slight
> Will not matter at all to the teacher or others.
> After all, what is method? Yours is as good as another's.

This kind of physical exercise was aimed primarily at benefiting the girls' health and providing them with an antidote to mental overstrain, which was, in the early days of serious education for females, deemed to be a real danger to them. It was not really designed to teach them gymnastic skills.

As for the academic side of the curriculum, the subjects taught in those days were not exactly those offered at private schools for boys. In the early days of academic education for women, there were many objections and anxieties to be overcome, and some of these anxieties were focused on finding subjects suitable for females to study. The concern was in part that womanly qualities might be sacrificed in the quest for learning. In 1877 the group of learned gentlemen who met to discuss the setting up of an Association for the Higher Education of Women (from which Queen Margaret College grew),

***'We were a very happy family party.' 1899-1900***
(The identity of the interloper is unknown)

had chuckled at Professor Nichol's comments on the curriculum he deemed suitable for women students, who were different from men in their tastes as well as in other respects:

> Certainly, he held, if a lady found more interest in the differential calculus than in the works of Beethoven, or . . . in the formation of a beetle than in the study of Shakespeare, she should study the calculus and the beetle, and not Beethoven and Shakespeare, but he confessed he would rather be associated with the admirer of Beethoven and Shakespeare than the other lady.
>
> (*Glasgow News* 4 April 1877)

Subjects traditionally regarded as masculine were English grammar, Latin, Greek, science and mathematics. A typical curriculum for a girls' school would have included grammar and Latin, but also offered French, arithmetic, history, geography, and of course drawing and needlework. History, having begun as a feminine subject in the days before women could enter a university, was for years to come generally taught not by a specialist teacher, but as a teacher's subsidiary subject, and it was not given its own examination, but appeared as an adjunct to the English paper. If science was to be taught to girls, botany was considered more appropriate than chemistry. The Girls' School Company in fact dared to step outside these boundaries by including chemistry on the curriculum of the Park School, and building a laboratory there in 1886. But Kilmacolm did not have a science laboratory until 1908, and botany was offered there instead.

During the 1870s and 1880s the traditional male/female divide in educational subjects was in many areas broken down, so that it was quite usual for girls to be taught mathematics and Latin, but change in some subjects was slow to come. A two-way traffic, though, had begun to operate, and under the influence of the curriculum taught in girls' schools, that of boys' schools, and indeed of the universities, was widened. In some areas of the curriculum, girls' schools such as those of the Girls' School Company had a head start on their male counterparts. And the best of the girls' schools, among which the Company's schools aspired to be, by the turn of the century surpassed many of the boys'. If only Professor Nichol had known, three decades after the historic meeting, he might have found, in Kilmacolm, intelligent appreciation of the beetle, calculus, Shakespeare and Beethoven united in one feminine mind.

In the teaching of music and physical education, girls' schools marked themselves out as different from both schools for boys and mixed schools. One of the attributes of the Victorian ideal woman was accomplishment in singing and playing the piano, but at St Columba's these skills were taken much further than this. In physical education for girls the newly founded schools were breaking new ground, and, although there was, in Kilmacolm at least, probably no conscious desire to challenge the Victorian concept of woman's place in the world, the taking up of vigorous and competitive team games was a significant element in the preparation of women for the very different world of the twentieth century. It was a challenge in which the early headmistresses allied themselves with their eager pupils.

For the first three years Miss Young had successfully steered the new school, and she handed it over to her successor, Miss Waugh, in good shape. It was not until April 1902 that the Directors decided to name the Kilmacolm school St Columba's (and the Helensburgh school St Bride's). In Miss Waugh's twenty-eight year headship the School took on its distinctive personality, so to speak – a set of characteristics derived very much from the personality of the new head teacher herself.

***Staff and pupils in 1904-05***

Back row: E Black, W Crawford, D Reid, P Handley, M Renfrew, D Hunter, C Guthrie, M Crawford, M Brown, E Wood, M Hendry, M Sloan, E Brownlie, L Woodburn
Second back: W Binnie, H Twist, G Fleming, N Mowat, M Ward, M Mann, E Bird, N Hendry, L Clarke, H Rae, D Lang, M Hewit
Third back: A Fullarton, E Grieve, K McCracken, C MacNab, C Leask, C McCrone, M MacNab, M Brydie, M Martin, I Waddel, J Burnet, C Twist, F Hendry, A McCrone, M Mann, D Dyche, W Graham

Third front: J Blair, J Wood, H McGeachy, Miss Macindoe, J Maclay, Miss Pirret, J Maclay, Miss McIntyre, Miss Waugh, P Graham, Miss Rigold, A MacNab, H McNiell, Miss Taylor, M Rae, Miss Robertson, D Burnet, Mlle Lacaille, J Mowat, H Davidson
Second front: G Scott, M Taylor, M Parker, M Rhodes, J Thomson, D Brownlie, P Dewar, C Woodburn
Front row: J Gregory, J Cuthbertson, K Wood, E McInnes, M Holmes, D Todd, J Guthrie, H Hislop, O Farquhar, R Todd, H McNiell, I Wood, F Buchanan, M Paterson, E Todd, J Cuthbertson, D Lelean

***The 1923 extension, from the north, looking onto the playground, which was used for games***

*Chapter Three*

# Janet J B Waugh 1900-1928

## The challenges of the first quarter-century

The three schools of the Girls' School Company expanded steadily over the first quarter of the century, a success story which brought its own problems, principally of accommodation, in its wake. The only failure of the Company took place early in this period, when in 1908 a school was bought in Queens Park, Glasgow (named St Aidan's) to be run along the same lines as the others. It did not attract enough pupils and it was closed four years later. The building was let, and eventually sold, to Glasgow Corporation.

The First World War of course caused great financial difficulties for the whole country, and meeting the requirement for salary increases in its aftermath proved quite a struggle for the Company. But by 1919 the Company had realised its ambition of paying shareholders a dividend of five per cent. (It had been three per cent for most of the organisation's history.)

In 1907 William Hill Jack, son of David Hill Jack, was appointed Joint Secretary to the Company, together with John A Spens, the original Secretary. Over a period of many years the Secretaries financed the requirements of the Company by means of cash loans at moderate rates of interest, which they renewed from time to time. In 1905 David Todd resigned and was replaced as Director by Frank Burnet, the architect, who remained for eight years.

In 1915, after the death of Professor Lindsay, Professor George Gibson was asked to become a Director to advise on matters pertaining to education, and soon afterwards he agreed to take up the Chairmanship of the Company. He was Professor of Mathematics at Glasgow University and had a wide knowledge of educational systems in Britain and elsewhere. He was Chairman until 1929, and resigned when his health was failing, only a few months before his death.

The other highly significant appointment to the Board of the Company in this period was that of Alexander Peden Fyfe of Kilmacolm, a prominent Glasgow solicitor and a man of wide interests and deep knowledge of music and art. He was one of the founders of the Scottish National Academy of Music, which later became the Royal Academy of Music. He was to serve the Company most diligently and effectively, both as a Director and later as Chairman, from 1921 until his death in 1944.

During the first quarter of the century the workload of the Directors increased to such an extent that it became necessary to appoint sub-committees to deal with certain matters. The Directors grouped themselves into three sub-committees to deal with business particular to each of the schools; these were the local boards, or local directorates. In 1916 Archibald D Ferguson and A T Taylor were invited to become Directors of the Company, and joined Dr James Parker as the local directorate of St Columba's. Dr Parker was also medical adviser to the School. After the deaths in 1921 of Mr Ferguson and Dr Parker, Peden Fyfe and A T Taylor were the Kilmacolm local directorate.

By 1925 such was the pressure of business that, in addition, the Company set up an executive committee to deal with day-to-day matters to do with buildings, staff and finance, comprising Professor Gibson, Mr Anderson (of Helensburgh), Mr Peden Fyfe, and David Hill Jack (the original Treasurer of the Company, made a Director in 1909). Thereafter the gentlemen of the executive committee met monthly, keeping in close touch with the Headmistresses, and only every third meeting was a meeting of the full Board of the Company.

The Education (Scotland) Act of 1918 invited schools in the voluntary sector to transfer their schools to the local education authority. At this time the Roman Catholic schools did so, but most of the private schools stayed independent. The Act also required all schools to standardise salary scales for teachers. The Directors had given full-time staff a ten per cent salary increase in 1916, and they were increased again in 1917, 1919 and 1920. (The annual salary of an ordinary assistant Mistress rose from a maximum of £120 in 1908 to £230 in 1921; salaries were paid termly until 1926.) Financing the needs of the schools in these years was a struggle, but despite the difficulties all three schools continued as fully independent establishments, financed by fees.

*The school hall*

Fees, of course, had to go up. There were increases in 1916, 1917, 1919, 1920 and 1921. At prize-giving in 1920 A T Taylor reminded his audience of the financial struggle that independent schools now faced, and the need for more capital for St Columba's:

> If we did not expand *now* to accommodate our growing numbers, we should be losing a great opportunity, and might even imperil the existence of the school.
>
> (School Magazine 1920, pp. 4-5)

## Expansion upwards and outwards

The only previous expansion of the accommodation at Duchal Road had been in 1905, when Miss Waugh and Frederick Moir had represented to the Board 'the crying need' for extra music rooms and a larger hall. In the summer of this year the hall was built at the rear of the original building. It has served many purposes over the years: originally it was used as a gymnasium too, with wall-bars on the stage. The music rooms were 'redeemed out of the present roof' by extending the attic rooms with large dormer windows. In 1908 the School's first laboratory was created in the largest of these attic rooms.

By 1916 the number of pupils had risen to about 110, and plans for an additional wing were proposed. But with the other strains on the Company's resources, especially the increases in salaries and the acquisition of Shieldhall in 1918 as a boarding house, the Directors found it necessary to shelve the plans. The purchase of Allanbank for the kindergarten in 1919 relieved some of the pressure on the School, and the new wing was eventually built, at a cost of around £4000, by the end of 1923. It contained the School's first purpose-built gymnasium, with windows facing north and east. It also doubled the classroom accommodation:

> The new class rooms are gloriously light and airy and the long wide corridors make the school much less crowded during the intervals than formerly.
>
> (School Magazine 1925-26, pp. 3-4)

By 1926 the pupil numbers had grown again, and some minor alterations, such as the removal of a partition between two classrooms, helped only a little. At the end of the year, Mr Peden Fyfe reported to the Directors that 'generally the school was very congested and teaching was being carried on under great difficulty'. The Board approved a scheme to build a large new art room, a new gymnasium and four music rooms, at a cost of about £3000. The opening ceremony, performed by Sir Robert Bruce, the Editor of *The Glasgow Herald*, in March 1928 was one of the last functions of the school attended by Miss Waugh in her capacity of Headmistress. The new Headmistress, Miss McMurtrie, was there too:

> Tea was served in various parts of the School, and many people were given an opportunity to speak to Miss McMurtrie. Gymnastic teams gave a display in the course of the afternoon, and several of the large gathering were heard to remark at the close of the proceedings that they had never before enjoyed a function at St Columba's School so much.
>
> (School Magazine 1927-28, p. 25)

***The 1928 extension***

The architects for all these alterations and expansions were Frank Burnet and Boston, and they ensured a homogeneity of scale and style with their original building. The elder Frank Burnet had retired in 1913, and it was his son, who had himself attended the school as a small boy, who was responsible for the latest additions. The 1923 wing adjoins the original building to the north, and it was to be further extended in the same style in 1936, making a continuous frontage onto Duchal Road. The 1928 extension was built to the west of the original building, linking up with the hall; in 1996 the gymnasium it contained was divided and transformed into a Transitus classroom.

## Miss Waugh

> Janet Waugh was a woman of outstandingly strong personality. Though in herself unassuming, gentle and kindly, she was inflexible in her regard for principle, and inveterate in pursuit of the ideals she saw clearly before her. The hall-marks of her character . . . were devotion to principle, courage of conviction, appreciation of culture, perfect candour, and indefatigable industry.
>
> (Revd Foster Franklin, *Jubilee Book*, p. 30)

***Miss Waugh***
'She was so august in presence, yet withal so kindly in expression, that even a small child could not help being at once awed and reassured' (Jubilee Book, p. 31)

Under Miss Waugh's headship the School expanded from an establishment of sixty-one pupils to one of over two hundred. From around 1908 onwards a steady stream of girls was sent on to higher education, many making successful careers for themselves and gaining distinction in the universities and music academies. It is clear that Miss Waugh had the confidence of Directors, parents and staff throughout her twenty-eight years. Yet she was much more than an efficient administrator and educator. Time and again those who attempted to recall her distinctive qualities came back to one thing, whether they called it 'inspiration' (Elsie Holgate [Linford]), or 'her deep and abiding sense of beauty in Life, Art and Literature' (Miss McIntyre).

Janet Waugh had obtained the degree of L L A (Hons), Lady Literate in Arts, from St Andrews University, the qualification awarded to women by that university before 1895, when females were at last permitted to graduate with the same degrees as men. The possessor of a fine singing voice, she went on to study at the Royal Conservatorium of Dresden. Miss

***The staff 1900-01***
Miss Abel (?), Miss Robertson, Miss Burton, Miss Mackay; (seated) Miss Waugh, Miss Taylor

Waugh's deep appreciation of culture set the school on the course it was to follow for the future:

> She valued fine scholarship and she loved beauty. Much that is pleasing today in our School buildings and furnishings owes its origin to her, and it was she who set those high standards of artistic appreciation and performance in music, art, literature and drama which we still try to maintain.
>
> (School Magazine 1946-47, p. 8)

She it was who chose the School's motto: *orare, laborare, literisque studere* – 'to pray, to work and to pursue learning', from the Rule of St Columba.

## From kindergarten to sixth form

> I was just six years old when the postman brought me a letter. It said that Miss Waugh (whom I had not yet met, as I was to join the school in the following term) requested the pleasure of my company at a party, and that of – oh joy! – my favourite doll. Her party for the neophytes was a triumphant success and when, a few weeks later, we found ourselves part of the School, we met our Headmistress not as an ogre or an avenging fury, but as a friend who had played Twos and Threes with us.
>
> (Anne Mowat, *Jubilee Book*, p. 31)

For the first few years of Miss Waugh's headship, Kindergarten, Transition and Form I were still taught in one room, at first on the ground floor, and then on the floor above, in what is now the staffroom. As the department

***The kindergarten in 1910 with Miss Rigold***

Back row: Rita Burnside, Margery Reid, Dorothy Denham, Joe Russell
Second row: Norah Hislop, —, —, Allan Macdonald, —
Third row: Jean Jackson, Mamie Galbreath, —, —, Jeanette Todd, Miss Rigold, Alan Service, Lenore Wardrop, Janet Macdonald, Enid Hewit
Front row: —, Marion Crawford, Jean Fullarton, Norman Sanderson, —, Alec Biggart, Mabel Cuthbertson

***Allanbank: the Preparatory School from1919 until 1930***

grew, more room was needed, and in 1919 the Directors purchased Allanbank, a semi-detached house in Duchal Road, near St Columba Church. Here the three youngest classes had more space. Most children started at the age of five or six, and they did not necessarily spend a whole year in each division. Most were ready to move to the Lower School at the age of eight.

When Margaret Holmes, who married the MP William Wedgwood Benn and later became Lady Stansgate, began her schooling at St Columba's in 1904, she spoke fluent French and English but had had no formal education. Since she could not read, she suffered the humiliation of being put into Kindergarten 'with the babies of five years old':

> I was nearly eight and could hardly squeeze into the little seat. I had to begin at the beginning and try to make sense of the picture of a cat beside which stood mysterious symbols reading C A T. I dreaded going to school.
>
> (Margaret Stansgate, *My Exit Visa*, 1992)

Looking back over the years, both in her autobiography and in an interview given ten years before its publication, it was Miss Waugh's Scripture lessons which stood out in her mind:

> The Headmistress, Miss Waugh, was interested in the pupils, and I remember especially how very inspiring her Scripture lessons were, and . . . when you are that age you don't really listen unless you are interested. She'd just been to the Holy Land, which was quite an adventure in 1904, and I remember she said, 'Well now, I hope every one of you will go there one day.'
>
> (Interview recorded by Mrs Maureen Lochrie for Paisley Museum, 1981)

There was something in Miss Waugh's way of teaching Scripture ('I can still hear the commotion in her soul', wrote Margaret Stansgate) that evoked a powerful response in her young pupil, whose own spiritual awakening was already beginning. She made up her mind that she too would visit Palestine one day. Not only did she do so, but she studied theology at London University and developed a lifelong scholarly interest in the Judaeo-Christian tradition. In 1975 a library in the Hebrew University in Jerusalem was founded and named after Margaret Stansgate.

Bible stories, along with reading, writing, spelling, and arithmetic were the usual subjects in which children began their education. The St Columba's prospectus for 1928 also lists sand modelling, handwork, drawing and painting. The methods used in the preparatory classes were based on those pioneered by Friedrich Froebel, and gave a central educational role to play and learning by doing. A training college to teach the method had been opened at Bedford in 1882, and from then on kindergarten teaching was seen as an attractive occupation for middle-class girls. It was from Bedford and other Froebel training centres that Miss Waugh recruited her preparatory mistresses, and she in turn sent many of her senior pupils to train there. For a few years from 1905 onwards, some of them were taught the first part of the Froebel course at the School, and took the Elementary Certificate of the National Froebel Union examination at St Columba's. This course took two years, and some girls attended St Columba's, as Froebel students, for these two years only; the practical part of the course was done in the School's preparatory classes.

The Lower School began with Form II (until 1931 when Form II became part of the Preparatory School); this was the equivalent of modern Primary Four. Next came the third form, IIIB followed by IIIA, equivalent to Primary Five and Six; the top five pupils in IIIA skipped IVC and went straight into IVB (but later everyone spent a year in IVC). The fourth form, IVB and IVA, was equivalent to Primary Seven and Senior One. A little French was begun in the third form, and in the fourth form they began Latin, mathematics and a little laboratory work. On leaving the fourth form pupils were ready to progress to the Upper School, starting at the level which is today known as Senior Two.

*Miss Pirret with Form IV A, 1904-05*

Back row: Essie Wood, Mary Mann, Frances Hendry, Dorothy Dyche, Isabella Waddell
Front row: C Grey, Agnes McCrone, Miss Pirret, Lily Woodburn

***Miss Taylor with Form III A, 1904-05***
Back row: Winifred Crawford, Nancy Hendry, Margaret Renfrew, Doris Hunter, E Black
Second row: Jenny Maclay, Miss Taylor, Ethel Guthrie
Front: Hester Twist

***Miss Robertson with Form II, 1904-05***
Back row: Hamish Davidson, John Gregory
Second row: Edith McInnes, Miss Robertson, John Blair, Margaret Hewit, Jack Mowat, Katherine G Wood
Front row: Bryce Graham, May Rhodes, Jean Cuthbertson

In the summer term of 1913 some senior pupils had the unusual experience of standing on the other side of the desk:

> During this term, owing to the unfortunate absences of two of our mistresses, the Sixth Form have sometimes made small experiments in teaching. The experience is generally illuminating, sometimes humiliating. A question hurled by an infant at your supposed superior intelligence may be answered boldly at the moment, but afterwards with what fear and trembling is the dictionary, or some other authority, consulted!
>
> (School Magazine, summer term 1913, p. 3)

The Upper School consisted of the fifth and sixth forms, V B, V A, VI B and VI A. The curriculum was academic (with classical leanings – 'Latin or German, Greek or Science') leading to the Higher Leaving Certificate, but girls in the sixth form not intending to go on to higher education could instead take a domestic science course, which was, in Miss Waugh's day, fairly limited. Some girls, especially those preparing for Oxford and Cambridge entry, stayed on for a further year in the Upper School, in the Ex-VIth form.

## Music teaching at St Columba's

In one respect at least St Columba's under Miss Waugh exemplified something that was true of most girls' schools of the time, namely that only if the headmistress were keen on music, did music tend to flourish into something more than the obligatory drilling of class after class of young ladies in pianoforte. Music was one of Miss Waugh's great passions in life. According to Jean Graham (Jackson), 'She used to walk up and down the rows when we were singing hymns in Assembly, beating time with her hands, and listening to our voices. I dreaded if she came near me, for I was no singer.'

Miss Waugh taught class-singing, and was remembered as having drawn out performances from her pupils that surprised even them. Anne Mowat counted herself as one of those people who:

> . . . had no voices worth mentioning, but who, because they possessed a reasonably good ear, were given the real excitement of learning to sing an under-part.
>
> (*Jubilee Book*, pp. 32-33)

And Elsie Holgate (Linford), who was very musical, recalled that:

> Tone and attack and expression all had to be as nearly perfect as might be, and in the end we sang really ambitious part-songs with very much more than the average school choir finish.
>
> (School Magazine 1927-28, p. 10)

Even those who were destined never to become proficient at singing or playing were taught to listen to and enjoy music by Miss Waugh, something which they carried away with them from their time at St Columba's and lasted them through their lives.

Miss Martha McIntyre, LRAM, and Miss Margaret (Rita) Macindoe taught until 1914, having accompanied each other on the twice-weekly train journeys between the Park School and St Columba's for seventeen years. Along with her devotion to her pupils and to music, Miss Macindoe had a great interest in drama. Like her colleague, she kept up a close connection with the School for many years through the St Columba's School Society, and while in London around 1930 she hosted the meetings of the London branch in her flat. Miss McIntyre was remembered as an enthusiastic teacher and a most gifted musician. She joined the staff of the Royal Scottish Academy after she left the schools.

***Miss McIntyre with music pupils, 1904-05***

Back row: Daisy Lang, Janie Wood, Edith Grieve, May MacNab, Cicely Twist
Front row: Anne Fullarton, Winifred Crawford, Miss McIntyre, J (Daisy) Burnet, Chica MacNab

At St Columba's much more was done in musical education than in most schools. Playing an instrument was not compulsory, but those who did learn – and in this period only the piano, violin and (in later years) 'cello were offered – had the opportunity to train to a very high standard indeed, high enough to enable some of them, as Miss Waugh proudly said, to take their LRAM examination during the year after they left school, and for some even to make careers for themselves in music. There were three features of the musical life of the school, all of them directly or indirectly owing to Miss Waugh's interest, which made St Columba's very special in this department.

The first was the early formation of a Musical Association. Miss Waugh was Honorary President from the start, and Miss McIntyre, Miss Macindoe, Miss Linford and other music Mistresses were active in the Association for very many years. Miss McIntyre was made Honorary President of the SCSMA after her retiral and she continued to give lectures and recitals and to arrange programmes for the Association. It was very well supported by pupils and former pupils, and an interesting and varied programme of recitals

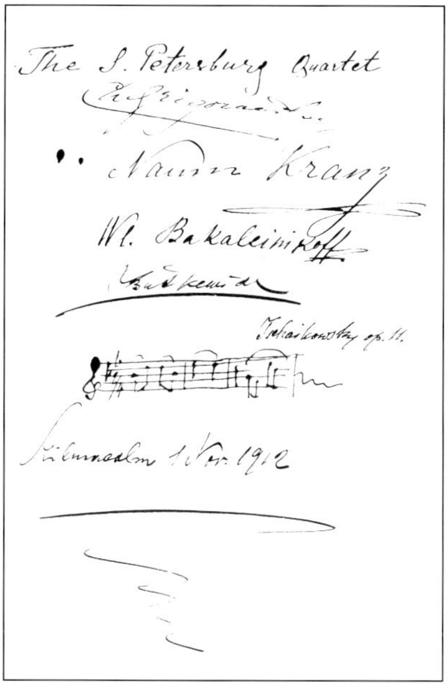


A page from the Autograph Album

was arranged each year. The School concerts too came under the auspices of the St Columba's School Musical Association and the standard of performance in the annual senior concert was often very high, with as many as a dozen individuals performing solos and duets, and choral pieces as well. For a school of its size, such a talent base is impressive.

Secondly, the institution of Subscription Concerts fostered musical appreciation at the school even further. Every year, usually several times a year, musicians distinguished in the national and international arena were invited to give concerts in the school hall, which has good acoustics. The concerts were formal, and parents and friends came in evening dress. Mr Peden Fyfe was one of the promoters of these concerts from the beginning. He had contacts with the Royal Academy of Music in London and was one of the founders of the Scottish National Academy of Music in Glasgow, and he was therefore in the position to invite artists of international standing to make a detour to Kilmacolm during their concert tours. After 1914, when the Concert Committee was dissolved and the SCSMA took over responsibility for the Subscription Concerts, Peden Fyfe's interest was of great help to the School in keeping the concerts going, with eminent names such as Donald Tovey (the great musical scholar and future Professor of Music at Edinburgh University), Sir Walford Davies (singer and composer), and Myra Hess, who gave a piano recital in 1920 at which, unfortunately:

> . . . there was a very small audience and a deficit of 16s. 6d. was the monetary result. However, those who were present will not soon forget this memorable concert. The music was beautiful, the rendering was beautiful, and Miss Hess won all hearts by her simplicity and sincerity. In the school autograph album she has written, 'Thank you for a lovely evening'.
>
> (School Magazine 1920, p.20)

Myra Hess came back in 1925 and 1929 and delighted rather larger audiences.

On 12th March 1915, after a concert of chamber music by a string quartet from the Scottish Orchestra, the third outstanding feature of the School's musical life was unveiled. The Silver Tablet was, and is, an award set up in honour of Miss McIntyre and Miss Macindoe for pupils who reached the very highest standard in music. The standard of playing for both piano and violin were set out at this time and included the performance of seven or eight pieces of music. The programme would last about an hour,

*From the Autograph Album, 1920*

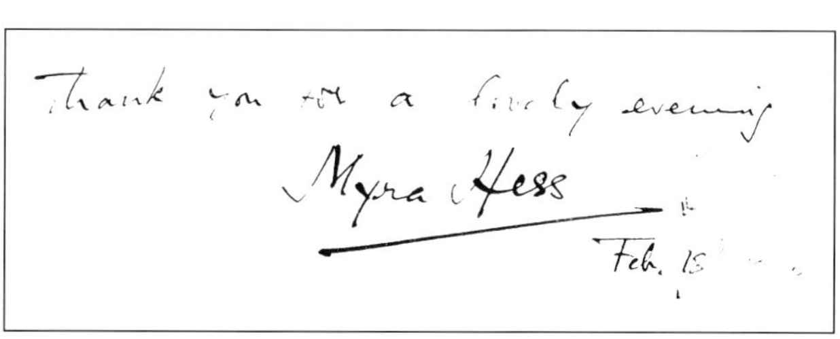

in front of the whole school. The first to have her name inscribed, in 1917, was Margaret Harper (Peggy McConechy), who went on to study at the Royal Academy of Music in London, where she gained great distinction. During the next ten years another five girls attained the standard. In 1922 Lilias Cook (McCallum) played a programme of seven pieces entirely from memory. In later years, too, it was usual for performers on the school stage to play without the music score.

When Miss McIntyre and Miss Macindoe resigned in 1914, the first visiting male teacher joined the staff of St Columba's, and for the next fourteen years Mr Edgar Barratt divided his time between his private pupils in Glasgow and his school commitments at Kilmacolm, teaching his pupils to acquire great sensitivity of touch. Miss Waugh herself enjoyed listening in on his lessons whenever she had the time, and said that she had learned more from him than from any other teacher of piano. He was a composer of some distinctively Celtic piano music, and he accompanied many of the great musicians of his day, some of whom he brought with him to the Subscription Concerts, as the Autograph Book testifies.

In 1912 one of St Columba's original pupils fulfilled her ambition to return to teach at the school she loved so much. Miss Elsie Linford had been a talented pupil; she became senior pianoforte Mistress in 1914. Her creative contribution to the School was outstanding, she was a brilliant teacher and her pupils loved her. In 1922 she composed an operetta especially for the School, for which her own junior pupils wrote much of the music, including some two-part songs. She left to get married in 1926, and as Mrs Holgate continued to be a stalwart of the St Columba's School Society. It was after her marriage that she composed the music for the school song, for which the school Chaplain, the Revd Foster Franklin wrote the words.

The longest-serving member of the music staff, Miss Elizabeth (Lizzie) Renton, taught violin at Kilmacolm, Glasgow and Helensburgh from very early days and retired in 1945, aged sixty-nine. She had a wide reputation as a highly gifted and successful teacher. She was eccentric, not to say chaotic, in appearance, which may have had something to do with her poor eyesight, but utterly devoted to music and a most effective teacher. She used to wander around the room as her pupil played, playing an imaginary violin herself, and *buzzing* the tune under her breath. Suddenly she would swoop upon her pupil, her pencil darting down, not always with entirely accurate aim, to mark something on the score. Her pupils adored her, and after they left and during the holidays, she wrote to them, encouraging them and advising them on what they should be practising. She introduced the teaching of ensemble playing and chamber music in the School.

*Miss Linford (Mrs Holgate)*

The first known pupil from Miss McIntyre and Miss Macindoe's period to go the Royal Academy of Music in London was Agnes (Nan) Ferguson, who was there from 1914 until 1916. She won the bronze medal in 1914 and the silver in 1915.

Margaret Harper (Peggy McConechy) was at the R A M in London from 1917 until 1920. She had a very successful career at the Academy, being awarded the bronze medal for singing and piano, and the Certificate of Merit, the highest award conferred by the Academy. She went on to train for teaching.

Joyce Barr (Nicol) was, in 1926, the first violinist to be a successful Silver Tablet candidate, and the first to be awarded the gold medal presented by the SCSMA for her Silver Tablet performance. Joyce won the Royal Academy of Music's silver medal in 1921 with the second highest marks in the British Empire in the Intermediate Examination.

Avril Leventon (Wright) left school in 1926 and by 1932 was Sub-professor of music at the Royal Academy of Music in London. She returned to the School in 1975 and 1976 to give recitals. Several others went on to study music at the Royal Academies of Music in London and Glasgow after leaving school, and some later became teachers.

## Art teaching at St Columba's

Miss Norah Neilson Gray was visiting teacher of art at St Columba's from 1908 until 1918. She had studied and taught at Glasgow School of Art, and by 1910 had her own studio and held her first one-woman exhibition in Glasgow. She was a brilliant portraitist in oils, but also made an important contribution to contemporary Scottish landscape watercolour painting, and was elected a member of the Royal Scottish Watercolour Society. Like many shy people, she had a particular affinity with children, and she was very good at holding their attention while they were sitting for her:

> At the end of a sitting, if they had been particularly good, they were allowed to paint in a few strokes of the background – a much-coveted honour!
>
> (School Magazine 1931, p. 9)

*Miss Waugh by Norah Neilson Gray*

Miss Gray set her classes to draw not classical busts, but natural subjects. She was appreciated for her patience in helping those whose artistic gifts were not great:

> . . . she helped many a lame dog over the stile of the Intermediate, and taught us all some appreciation at least of the beauties of form and colour.
>
> (School Magazine 1918, p. 4)

Norah Neilson Gray had her first picture hung at the Royal Academy when she was only twenty-one, and she painted Miss Waugh's portrait for the School on her retiral.

During the War she produced some remarkably powerful paintings, notably *The Belgian Refugee*, held by Glasgow Museums and Art Galleries. Perhaps she found the subject for this picture in Kilmacolm, for some Belgian refugees were settled in houses in the village. At Easter 1918 she left the school for VAD work in France, at the Scottish Women's Hospital in the French Red Cross Hospital at the Abbaye de Royaumont, at a time when the hospital was frequently bombed. After her work on night-duty, she used to paint and sketch the soldiers and the nurses in the setting of the cloisters, which were used as a ward. She used the material she had collected there for her picture, *The Scottish Women's Hospital*, which she was commissioned to paint for the Imperial War Museum.

After the War she became the first woman invited to be a member of the Hanging Committee of the Royal Glasgow Institute of the Fine Arts, and shortly afterwards she was awarded first the bronze and then the silver medal of the Société des Artistes Français. She continued to work in Glasgow and Helensburgh until her death. (See *Glasgow Girls: Women in Art and Design 1800-1920*, edited by Jude Burkenhauser, 1990, pp. 201-206.)

In those days the numbers of students at Glasgow School of Art were very small, and gaining an Art School Diploma was still quite an unusual distinction. Norah Gray's first pupil to enter Glasgow School of Art was probably May Crawford, who in 1915 gained the Diploma after only four years' study, having specialised in metal work, and winning several prizes. Winifred Gentleman (Harrower) also distinguished herself at the Art School, gaining her Diploma there in 1918 after only three years instead of the standard five.

The sisters Alison and Winifred McKenzie were taught by Norah Neilson Gray and Helen Lamb (see Chapter Four) before leaving St Columba's in 1921 to go to boarding school. Winifred, in a recently published book of reminiscences of the sisters' lives, recalls loving the art lessons, even though they were at that time held in the hall which also served the purpose of dining room and gymnasium. This meant that they grew used to working amid the lingering aroma of boiled vegetables, and:

> . . . at each lesson everything had to be dug out, arranged and put away at the end.
>
> (Aylwin Clark, *The McKenzie Sisters*, 1996, p. 48)

Winifred was introduced to colour woodcuts, with which she was to become highly successful, by Chica Munro (MacNab), who taught at Glasgow School of Art in the 1920s, and who had left St Columba's in 1906 to go to Art School – possibly the first of Miss Waugh's girls to do so. Winifred took the Diploma in 1927, and Alison, an artist of great power and originality, gained the Diploma, in design and decorative art, in 1929, and was awarded the Newbery medal for the highest distinction in the Diploma examination. Alison's posters for the London and North Eastern Railway, particularly her 'Yorkshire Coast' and 'Norfolk Broads', became classics of poster art. The sisters moved to St Andrews and taught at Dundee College of Art (Duncan of Jordanstone College) where they established the department of printmaking.

## Science teaching

Miss Nellie Turnbull came to the School in 1907 to teach science and mathematics, the year in which the Scottish Education Department began to insist on the teaching of science in every school under its influence. It was in this year that St Columba's developed its science department and equipped a laboratory for teaching chemistry and physics. A graduate of Edinburgh University, Miss Turnbull threw herself with enthusiasm into the fitting out of the new laboratory, and trained her pupils and the domestic staff to help her keep it in order:

> She spent many hours of her own time in preparing her lessons, and in adjusting apparatus, and polishing and dusting it. It was only when a maid had proved herself to be worthy of the responsibility of working in the Laboratory, that she was permitted to enter its locked door.
> (School Magazine 1927-28, p. 12)

When Elinor Rutherford (Jackson) went up to Newnham College, Cambridge in 1919, she contrasted the College's labs unfavourably with Miss Turnbull's domain:

> At first I felt rather scornful after the beautifully-kept lab at school, where everything is of the best, for here they provide you with cheap inaccurate balances, and poor apparatus.
> (School Magazine 1919, p. 11)

The undergraduates, she explained, were not expected to treat the equipment with much respect.

Science was examined in the Leaving Certificate from the start of the century. Learning by discovery was not a method used at this time, the one exception being the observation and collection of botanical specimens. At St Columba's prizes were occasionally given for nature study or collections of

*Miss Turnbull with science pupils in the laboratory*

*The laboratory*

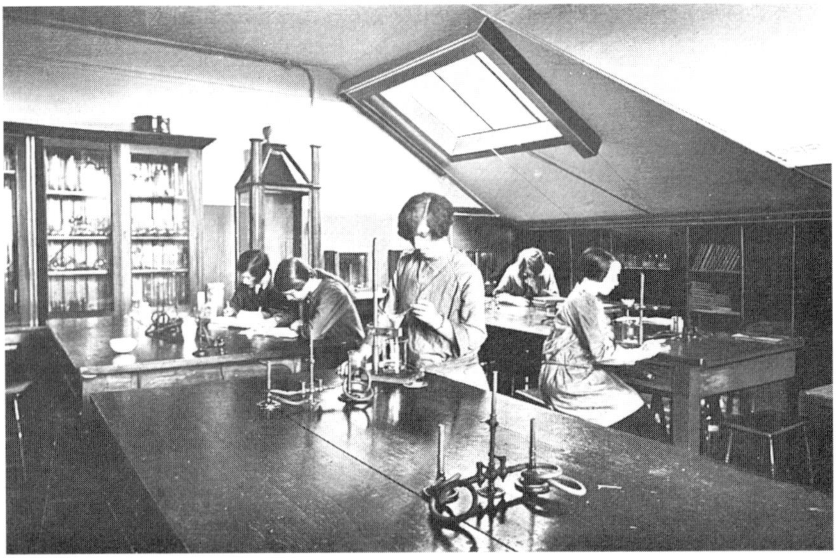

wild flowers. Chemistry at this period was taught by means of experiments dictated by the teacher without any noticeable relationship to each other. Textbooks were not used, but science notebooks had to be compiled and illustrated, and after meticulous marking by Miss Turnbull they were kept for years and used for reference and revision. Miss Turnbull left in 1923 and was succeeded by Miss Jarvis.

Dorothy Jackson (Jackson) was the first pupil at the School to pass Higher Science. One of Miss Turnbull's first pupils to distinguish herself academically was Winifred Bruce (Crawford), who spent her last couple of years at the Park School, entered Glasgow University in 1911 and graduated in medicine in 1916.

## Physical education

It was said of Miss Young, that when she returned to the Park School as Headmistress in 1900, and some of the girls applied to her to be allowed to play hockey, their Headmistress had to ask to be shown what a hockey stick looked like. Hockey had not been played at Kilmacolm in Miss Young's day, and indeed to be allowed to play it was a privilege not to be taken for granted in those days. At the Park School in 1902 a meeting of staff and some senior pupils was convened, at which the pros and cons of hockey were discussed. To the anxious girls desperate to be allowed to play they seemed 'mostly cons'. 'Hockey is a very rough game.' 'It makes girls coarse.' 'It is also dangerous – teeth may be knocked out, or an eye blackened.' 'Perfectly devastating to good looks withal.' There was 'only one pro'. 'It will be good sport.' (*Park 1880-1930*, pp. 89-90)

But with Miss Young this argument was permitted to carry the day, and the Park School Hockey Club was formed. St Columba's too probably began to bully off in the 1902-03 session.

One of the Park girls had recalled how in those days hockey was played in dress of sufficient length that, if you bent your knees, you could stop the

Back row: Julien Robertson, Violet Black, E McKinnon, Elsie Marshall, Anne Fullarton, B McIntyre,
Front row: Katherine Wood, May MacNab, Edith Twist (Captain), Janie Wood, Edith Grieve

***Hockey XI, 1902-03***

ball with your skirt. The demands of propriety had to be met, even if they conflicted with the requirements of play and in fact also with the new ideas about the roles in life for which the schoolgirls were being prepared. The women who emerged from the new schools for girls would be made fit for more active and independent roles than their mothers had filled. The benefits to health and physical stamina conferred by playing games such as hockey were an important part of their education. But there was many a quiet struggle in schools throughout Scotland and England between those who wanted hockey to be played and those who saw the game as a threat to femininity.

It was difficult to get trained gymnastics mistresses in those days, and when the Park School succeeded in obtaining a 'physical culture' mistress in 1904, she was shared with St Bride's. But since there seemed no hope of finding such a teacher for Kilmacolm, Miss Waugh arranged for a pupil, a Miss Muir, to give instruction in return for a twenty-five per cent reduction in her fees. It was probably in 1908 that Miss MacPherson was appointed games Mistress, and this side of school life was put on a more organised footing. Dorothy Ford-Young (Burnet) described the weekly timetable in the magazine:

> Monday and Wednesday are the hockey days, when we go down to the field about half-past three o'clock. We have not yet been able to challenge any other school, but we hope that, with much hard practice, we shall soon be able to do so.

If the hockey days are wet, we have games in the hall. There is a great variety in the games played. Among some of the favourites are: the bean-bag game, hand football, and twos and threes. Sometimes we have vaulting, which is much enjoyed.

We play basket-ball on Fridays, and as the sides are very evenly matched, there are a great many exciting games.

Saturday morning is set aside for the boys. They are working hard at basket-ball, and are going to challenge the girls to play them soon.

(School Magazine, Easter Term 1909, p. 11)

She does not mention badminton, which was also played. The following session the Kilmacolm girls were playing (and winning) basketball matches against Beltrees School, Greenock.

*Drill in the school garden, c 1926*

*Riding on the moor, Kilmacolm*

Over the next few years swimming was taken up, at the baths in Greenock, in water from the Clyde: it was thick, green and very cold. Tennis matches were played against Old Girls, Old Boys and staff, as well as other schools. Netball was taken up in place of basketball, and some girls had riding lessons, side-saddle at first, at a riding school in Paisley. Hockey matches were played against Park School, St Bride's, and other schools. The St Columba's pupils started playing lacrosse and cricket in 1917.

In 1925 the lacrosse team played their first matches, against the 2nd XIIs of Renfrewshire Ladies and Glasgow Ladies, losing both but not too discreditably. An enduring drawback to playing lacrosse was that only one other school in the Glasgow area played the game, Craigholme School in Pollockshields, so that all other outside fixtures had to be played against ladies' teams. Despite this, however, and despite great enthusiasm and some success for hockey in the early 1920s, the announcement was made in 1926 that lacrosse was to be adopted as the school game, and that hockey would now only be a subsidiary game. The switch to lacrosse later gave rise to a story that there had been a fatal accident on the hockey pitch, but this has no basis in fact. The channelling of resources into lacrosse paid off: the team won all six games played that year, all against ladies' teams.

Until 1916 hockey was played on grass at the public ground of Birkmyre Park, and other games were played in the school grounds, which had not yet been built over. In that year ground was rented as a playing field for the School off Gryffe Road, and the Company defrayed the expense of access and fencing. But the Company did not see the purchase of playing fields for its schools as a priority, and it was understood that the schools would try to raise most of the money themselves. It was not until 1921 that the field was levelled and tennis courts were laid out, the Company agreeing to meet one fifth of the cost. The School meanwhile set to work with a will to raise funds. The former pupils organised a subscription dance and a gymkhana, and Miss Ferguson, games Mistress from 1920 until 1924, produced a fairy play. Miss Linford, most ambitiously of all, produced her new operetta. But the efforts of the entire school, and many Old Girls and parents, culminated in the

*The school playing field, c 1926*

***The old gymnasium, in the 1923 extension***
(now divided: part of it is the present Room 2)

***The gymnasium of the 1928 extension***
(now converted into the Transitus classroom)

School Fair, an event long remembered for the creative thought and originality which went into the many stalls and other attractions. The combined events raised a most gratifying £692 7s. 8d. But, as the editor of the magazine acknowledged, it was the generosity of a benefactor that ensured the acquisition of the Ashes, as the grounds came to be called:

> But for the kindness of Sir Hugh Shaw Stewart, our ambitions . . . would not yet be fulfilled. As it is, the playing fields bid fair to become the centre of attraction at Kilmacolm, as the numerous spectators at the Sports . . . testified.
>
> (School Magazine 1922, p. 4)

The hard pitch for playing hockey and lacrosse was not in fact finished until the end of 1926. (The Park School did not acquire playing fields of its own until 1924, when Professor Gibson, Chairman of the Board, put up a sum of money of his own and persuaded the reluctant Directors that no school could now afford to be without its own facilities for games.)

It was especially fitting that in 1923, the year following the grand efforts in aid of the playing field, a new athletic shield, designed by P W Davidson of Glasgow School of Art, was instituted, to be awarded each year to the girl who showed the greatest all round skill in games, gymnastics and swimming. In 1925 a silver cup was given to be awarded to the form which excelled in gymnastics. Drill stripes and coloured girdles were already established as rewards for individual success.

The first source of women teachers of physical culture, as it was then called, was the Bergman-Oesterberg training college at Kingsfield near Dartford. The college opened in 1885, at least fifty years before any such establishment for men. It was Miss Waugh's practice to visit the college in order to select games mistresses for the School. The school also sent a steady stream of girls to Kingsfield – Jean Davidson (Cuthbertson), Mary White (Rae) and Dorothy Jackson (Jackson) were among the first from St Columba's to go to Dartford to train.

## Miss Waugh's achievement

Miss Waugh was an unforgettable influence on every pupil in the School, from the young ones in the preparatory school Scripture classes to those in the top form English class. One pupil recalled that Miss Waugh's English literature lesson was the highlight of her week:

> It was then that Poetry became a live thing and ceased to be regarded merely as 'two more verses for Tuesday night's prep'. But most of all we loved the digressions that led to talk which, though we did not realise it, encouraged originality and also our immature powers of criticism.
>
> (Elsie Holgate [Linford], School Magazine 1927-28, p. 10)

Miss Waugh's wide interests and great mental powers and range made her an outstanding educator. Anne Mowat, one of her most gifted pupils, recalled:

> I do not remember being 'taught' anything by her, after I was about thirteen. But I do know that I learned an amazing lot, much of it far

beyond the scope of the usual Sixth Form syllabus. I think Miss Waugh's genius lay in guiding us to teach ourselves.

(*Jubilee Book*, p. 32)

The staff headed by this remarkable woman was scholarly and professional. It included some outstanding individuals, who successfully prepared many girls for university and who had a lasting influence on the lives of many more (see Chapter Six). Among them, for a year or two during the War, was a young classics graduate, Miss Beatrice McMurtrie. When the time came for Miss Waugh to retire, she was in no doubt whom to suggest as her successor.

***Miss Waugh with senior girls, 1917***

Back row: Dorothy Whyte, Mabel Cuthbertson, Jean Fullarton, —, Anna Whyte, —, Jean Jackson, Elinor Morrison, Peggy Kerr
Second row: Lilias McCallum, May Todd, Margery Reid, Joyce Friend, —, —, Winifred Howie, Miss Patton, Enid Hewitt, Jessie Lawther, —, Alice Jackson, Norah Hislop
Front row: . . . Macdonald, Miss Turnbull, —, Miss Hagart, Nell Pearson, Miss Waugh, Kitty Todd, Mamie Galbreath, Minnie Pearson, Doris McCrone

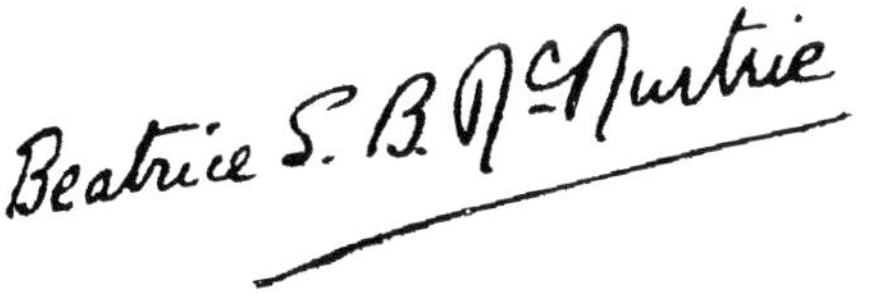

*Chapter Four*

# Beatrice S B McMurtrie 1928-1945

When Miss McMurtrie left the staff of St Columba's during the First World War to serve as a volunteer in France, she was bidden farewell with regret, although she had been at the School such a short time. She wrote to the school magazine about her work for the Sécrétariat français des Villages Libérés, scratching together from the ruins of the war-devastated villages of the Aisne and the Marne a one-roomed school and teaching, with makeshift equipment, the village children who had suffered terrible losses and privations during the German bombardment and occupation.

***Miss McMurtrie***

Beatrice McMurtrie obtained a first-class honours degree in classics from Edinburgh University in 1904, to which she added the Cambridge Teachers' Certificate from Maria Grey College, London. After the War she resumed her career teaching classics in Hertfordshire and Edinburgh, and by 1928 was Deputy Headmistress of Edinburgh Ladies' College. Here she had thrown herself into extra-curricular activities, particularly those which involved social service outside the school, and had introduced the teaching of Greek to the curriculum.

An outstanding scholar, Beatrice McMurtrie had many other interests in life. Like Miss Waugh, she loved to travel, and had been all over Western Europe. She liked to take walking holidays, and had a great love of the hills and the sea. She valued an understanding of international affairs, so vital to her generation. There was nothing of the educational snob in her, for all her scholarship: she loved to observe children at work and play, and she understood the tastes of children and young women who did not love academic things and she thought of ways of making lessons interesting for them.

The economic conditions of the 1930s made it a difficult time for all fee-paying schools, but under Miss McMurtrie the School maintained stability in staffing and reasonably steady pupil numbers. Her last six years were of course the most testing, and she was always remembered for having done a splendid job in keeping the life of the School beating away quietly despite all the upheavals of War. Her pupils at the time took for granted that their

*The Preparatory School at Shieldhall, c 1931*

*The Eredine garden, 1939*

*Part of the playground before 1936*

studies would go on calmly, and only later thought of the efforts of organisation and strength of spirit required to ensure that:

> . . . not a single day's teaching, even during the raid weeks, was missed or broken into from the beginning to the end of the war.
> (School Magazine 1943-45, p. 15)

## The Company: keeping the ship afloat

The 1930s were difficult years from the point of view of economic survival, and there was a general decrease in numbers in all three schools of the Company, but especially in Park and St Bride's, until 1939. For most of the decade St Columba's numbers hovered around the 200 mark, but in the session 1938-39 they dropped to a rather low 170.

Meanwhile the cost of maintaining – and extending and improving – several buildings in each of three locations was a considerable drain. The Government recommended a cut in teachers' salaries during the national financial crisis, which left the Company's salaries at a higher level than those paid by Local Education Authorities. In 1932 the Directors reluctantly took the step of asking all staff to accept a five per cent cut in salary, to bring them into line with government recommendations for Local Authority schools. The Headmistresses were asked to advise the Directors of any cases in which hardship would result. All the salaries received a restoration of two and a half per cent in September 1937, and in 1939 it was decided to restore the remainder for each teacher five years before her retiral date was due, in order not to reduce her pension.

The most far-reaching change in the financial affairs of the Company in this period was its conversion from a share-holding company into an Educational Trust. This was the achievement of Mr Peden Fyfe, who noted that the Company could be exempted from income tax (which, over the past five years, it had been paying at the rate of around £1200 per annum) if it devoted its entire profits to educational purposes. To this end the Company was in 1932 wound up as a shareholding company, and set up under the same name as a new company operating as an Educational Trust. The shareholders were asked to accept debentures, which would pay cumulative interest at five per cent, or, if they did not wish to do so, to sell their shares. The new Girls' School Company Limited was registered on 6th June 1932, everything carried on as normal both in the St Vincent Street office and in the schools, and Mr Peden Fyfe could be well satisfied with the fruits of the considerable amount of work he had personally undertaken.

The saving on tax was not nearly enough to compensate for the gap between income from fees and required expenditure. In common with most independents, the Girls' School Company had to borrow to finance the requirements of the schools. In 1937, for example, the Directors negotiated a loan of £17,000 from the Scottish Temperance and General Assurance Company over ten years at four and a half per cent, secured by a bond over the Company's fifteen properties in Glasgow, Helensburgh and Kilmacolm, in order to reduce the bank overdraft, and in 1947 they renegotiated it at three and a half per cent, increasing it by £4800 in order to repay loans at five per cent from Miss Waugh and Mr William Hill Jack.

***Prefects, 1938-39, in the Eredine garden***
Back row: Dorothy Robertson, Pat Wilson, Kathleen Weir, Diana Cunningham, Xaveria Fyfe
Second row: Clare Little, Janette Turnbull, Betty Watt, Muriel Phillips (joint Head Girls), Constance Bridge
Front row: Joan Hairs, Doris Millar

***The new laboratory, 1936***

Clockwise from left: Flora Macdonald, Katherine Mackintosh, Janet Lambie, May Bruce, Isobel Cochrane (standing), Miss Millar, Margaret Howie, Katherine Broadfoot

After a decade in which the Company's receipts of fees had more often than not produced a loss, the Directors decided in 1939 to apply for grant-aided status, in the first place for the Park School. These grants were made by the Government on the recommendation of the Local Education Authority, and were based on the loss incurred by schools in any one year, with a maximum amount per scholar resident in the Authority's area. A condition of the grant was that representatives from the Local Education Authority join the Board. The application for Park was successful, and it was followed by similar applications on behalf of St Columba's and St Bride's. St Columba's received its first grant-in-aid (of £350) in respect of the year ending July 1938, and the Revd Foster Franklin, the School Chaplain, made a welcome appearance on the Board as the representative of Renfrewshire Education Authority. By 1945-46 the grant had been increased to £2500.

## An expanding School

The purchase of Shalott in 1930 for £6500 as a boarding house large enough to take all the boarders was to be offset by the sale of Allanbank and Craigrowan. Meanwhile the Preparatory School moved from Allanbank to Shieldhall, which was altered to accommodate them, and Form II went with them to become part of the new Preparatory School. Allanbank and Craigrowan were put up for sale, but the housing market was depressed and they failed to sell. Craigrowan was eventually let in 1932 and Allanbank in 1933. It was fortunate that Allanbank was not sold, as things turned out: it was used for a year as boarding accommodation for senior pupils from the Park School who transferred to St Columba's at the outbreak of war. In 1941 Allanbank was let to Miss Jean Mackenzie, visiting teacher of German at the School, who agreed to run it as a hostel for members of staff who needed accommodation in the village. On the expiry of this lease in 1945, the house again failed to sell, and it was let to the new modern languages Mistress, Dr Sheila Macdonald. Craigrowan, which needed quite a bit of work to make it suitable for sale as a family house, was instead sold as it was, at a considerable loss, in 1938.

In 1935 the house occupying the plot to the west of the main school was available for sale, and Mr Peden Fyfe told the Directors that:

> . . . the acquisition of this house would relieve considerably the present congestion in the school.
>
> (Minutes Book, 18 September 1935)

Eredine was bought for the sum of £800. The next year it was demolished to give space for a sunny playground and garden. The garden was much loved and school fetes were held there. (Now it is mostly occupied by the science block.)

The new playground was needed as the original had by then almost disappeared under the various extensions, and most of the remainder was to go in 1936, when the final extension to the frontage was built. Together with some internal rearrangements, it cost around £5400: the architects were Burnet and Boston. It contained a new kitchen (now the technical classroom) and servery (to link up with the dining room, which was later divided into

Rooms 1 and 2), more classrooms and cloakrooms, a new science laboratory and a domestic science room equipped for cooking (which has still the same use). In 1938 the old dining room was converted into a handsome new library, the gift of the St Columba's School Society (described in Chapter Twelve).

## The Directors

Mr Peden Fyfe, made Chairman in 1929, and Mr A T Taylor were joined on the local board of St Columba's in 1930 by Mr John G Kerr of Greenock (see Chapter Seven). The final living link with the origins of the Girls' School Company was broken with the death in 1935 of Mr David Hill Jack, the original Treasurer and Secretary and a Director since 1909. Of him the school magazine said:

> Although nominally Secretary, Mr Jack was virtually General Manager, and there can be no doubt that the success of the Company was largely due to his sound judgement and untiring energy.
>
> (School Magazine 1934-35, p. 4)

His son William Hill Jack, who had been Secretary since 1907, having been involved in the Company's work ever since entering his father's office as a young man, retired in 1938, and was then appointed to the Board as a Director. The new Secretary was Mr John Sutherland, who gave nineteen years' service to the Company. A Master of Works, Mr James Stewart, was appointed in 1933, and for the next thirteen years he relieved the Headmistresses and Directors of work relating to the properties.

The first female Director was invited onto the Board in 1927. Miss Maude G May, MA, a former pupil of the Park School, was a lecturer in English at Glasgow University and an Adviser of Studies. It was thought appropriate to have a woman in such a position especially for the interest she would take in girls wishing to enter the University. The next lady Director to be appointed was Lady Hetherington, the wife of Sir Hector Hetherington, Vice-Chancellor of Glasgow University, who served from 1937 until 1952.

## Mr A Peden Fyfe

The contribution of Alexander Peden Fyfe to the Girls' School Company and St Columba's in particular can hardly be overestimated. He was a Director for twenty-five years and Chairman for fifteen, and his death in 1944 came as a sad blow for St Columba's. He had been uniquely well-placed to enhance the musical reputation of the School. On the administrative side, his greatest achievements were in having the status of the Company raised to that of an Educational Trust and in securing grant-aided status. He did not spare himself in his work for the schools, and, as Miss Waugh wrote:

*Alexander Peden Fyfe*

> . . . the only thing that, so far as I know, Mr Fyfe really disliked doing for the School was speaking from the platform in the Hall. But even that he did not refuse to do for us when occasion required.
>
> (School Magazine 1943-45, p. 12)

A man of strong feelings but great self-restraint, he had his own method of dealing with matters which he felt to be important:

> He would write a fulminating letter to *The Glasgow Herald*, then put it in the fire, and go and play a Bach prelude or a bit of Debussy. Then he would settle down quietly to plan and move toward what he had in mind, tactfully and patiently, but not necessarily directly, for he was a master of indirect approach and of apparently incidental achievement.
>
> (Revd Foster Franklin in School Magazine 1943-45, p. 13)

Peden Fyfe was a sympathetic man, concerned to treat the staff of the Company's schools as handsomely as possible, and responsible for many acts of personal kindness. So unobtrusive and self-effacing were his efforts, that over the years everyone had come to take him for granted, and there was a deep sense of loss at his death.

## The War Years

As early as November 1938 the Directors were planning that, in the event of war, they would evacuate the pupils of the Park School to the schools and boarding houses of Kilmacolm and Helensburgh. It was anticipated that the Government would requisition these properties for the billeting of evacuees from Glasgow, unless they were so occupied. By transferring St Columba's preparatory department to the main building and using Shieldhall as a boarding house for Park pupils, full use could be made of the Kilmacolm properties. Parents of Park School pupils were informed of the plans and it was suggested that pupils living on the north side of the city be transferred to St Bride's and those on the south to St Columba's. Boarding facilities were offered to those who did not have friends or relatives able to put them up.

The preparations were timely:

> 'Children are to be evacuated tomorrow,' said the bold headline of the evening paper on Thursday, August 31st, 1939.
>
> Plans were hurried forward – beds and blankets and the black-out were immediately urgent. There was furniture to clear, there were wardrobes to move upstairs and down, there were mysterious labelled bundles for unknown people, and the telephone kept going all the time.
>
> On Friday, September 1st, St Columba's School opened its doors to its guests, although the term was not due to begin till September 7th.
>
> (School Magazine 1939-40, p. 8)

Hospitality was offered by families connected with the School, but the Ministry of Health did not permit this to be accepted until it had used all the billets required by the Government's official evacuation scheme for the children of Glasgow. Over five hundred evacuees had arrived in Kilmacolm on the day before war was declared. So for those first few weeks the School had only its own premises to offer the Park School pupils and staff. In fact the Park School, after adequate air-raid precautions had been made, opened in October 1939 and remained open. But seventy-six girls had come to Kilmacolm, of whom all but a few stayed for the first term, and by the third

*'Our guests': the Park School pupils at St Columba's, 1940*

term fifty-one were still resident. They were all made welcome and as comfortable as possible:

> The news of 'how very kind Miss McMurtrie was' was well spread round the west-end of Glasgow in those days.
>
> (School Magazine 1943-45, p. 15)

By the end of the summer term, 147 were still in Glasgow, and thirty-eight at Helensburgh.

During the first term Allanbank was vacated by its tenant to allow the older girls to move in under their English Mistress, Miss Roy, assisted by Miss McGlashan. Some stayed with family friends and some remained for varying periods at Shalott alongside St Columba's own boarders, but the majority went to Shieldhall (while the Preparatory School was moved to the main building) under Miss Sprunt, the Latin Mistress, and Miss Duncan. One of their charges, Elizabeth McCallum, could never look at these ladies in the same way again:

> . . . seeing, instead of the neat be-jumpered figures with hair in buns, motherly figures, hair in pigtails, wearing wrappers as they comforted a sad or sick school mate in the night . . . always kind and gentle to the frightened children, which we were in air raids.
>
> (Lightwood, *Park*, p. 99)

The following year only Shieldhall was needed for the Park School girls, and the preparatory department moved into Allanbank, relieving congestion in the main building. By the end of the session only twenty-two Park School girls remained at St Columba's and their parents were asked to enrol them as boarders if they were to stay. In September 1941 the Preparatory School moved back into Shieldhall, and Allanbank was used to accommodate staff.

The Park School girls settled in well at Kilmacolm, sharing lessons and all the school activities. They continued to wear their blue Park School uniforms with pride – until the gym tunics became embarrassingly short –

attaching St Columba's drill stripes when they won them. Morag Miller (Bruce), daughter of Winifred Bruce (Crawford), had been made Head Girl of Park and, forty years later, recalled how her natural disappointment at not being able to take up the duties at her school was allayed by the willingness of the St Columba's Head Girl, Muriel Gibb, to share everything pertaining to this office. All the girls of St Columba's top form shared every privilege and duty and 'were exceedingly gracious and welcoming about it'.

After lessons the boarders were kept busy knitting for the troops, and they all looked forward to Sunday evenings when they would congregate in the Mistresses' sitting room to listen to Mr Churchill's speeches on the wireless. It was a hard winter, but that was good news for the girls, especially those from Glasgow, who relished:

> . . . skating on the Knapps, sledging on Balrossie Hill and the beauty of a country town in winter
>
> (Morag Miller [Bruce], School Magazine 1979-81, p. 42)

An added excitement was:

> . . . the thrill of uniforms around – not school, but HM Forces! We had letters, boyfriends suddenly away into the Army, Navy or RAF, Valentines on the mantelpiece for all to share, and weekends at home with one's family, when it became evident that Glasgow was not for immediate destruction by the Luftwaffe.
>
> (Ibid.)

***Prefects 1939-40, including Park School guests***

Back row: Morag Allan, Margaret Thomson, Morag Bruce (Head Girl), Eileen MacGregor, Violet Denholm
Second row: Dorothy Howie, Margaret Galbreath, Muriel Gibb (Head Girl), Margaret Smith, Margaret Forrester
Front row: Mercedes Park, Phyllis Howie, Evelyn Herbert

*Hockey Team, 1940-41, with Park and St Columba's girls*

Back row: Beatrice MacGregor, Elspeth Bone, Beatrice Campbell, Edna Hart
Second row: Raonaild Allan, Mercedes Park, Pat Russell, Elspeth Kinnaird
Front row: Eileen Stewart, Margo Crawford (Elspeth Craig, absent)

Even playground games were influenced by the War. One game was called 'Britishers and Germans': the two groups would line up and charge each other, then push and shove, and try to push the opposing side against the wall. The wounded were taken into the sick room to have their grazes and bruises treated. 'It was really quite vicious,' recalls one former pupil.

Some Park School girls settled in so well that instead of returning in September 1941 they stayed on and became St Columbans. Two of those who stayed on, Janette Nicol (Wither) and Helen Laird, not only became top prizewinners and Head Girls, but continued their connection with St Columba's throughout their lives, one as a teacher, the other as Director and eventually as Chairman.

It was a time of much coming and going among pupils and staff. Some pupils whose parents were abroad, in the Far East or Canada, were taken away from the School to be with them, and others had come to Kilmacolm from schools in more dangerous places in England. Several of the staff were called up. It was also a time of great sadness, with regular news of fathers and brothers killed or missing in action. It must often have been with a heavy heart that Miss McMurtrie led morning prayers.

Miss Anne Collet, Head of music, remembered what the staff faced at the beginning of the 1939 autumn term:

> Besides a full teaching day, many of us were thrust into A R P and Red Cross work . . . practically every evening of the week, with full-team demonstrations and fire-watching at weekends.
>
> (School Magazine 1976-77, p. 61)

*The gardening club, drawn by Jenny Speirs, 1940*

Air-raid precautions at the main building took the form of sand-bags at the entrance and splinter-proof curtains across openings in the lower corridor, with wooden boarding to protect the windows and the glass door of the library. During the occasional air raid everyone came down to the ground floor and sat on the floor of the corridor and under the stairs. Sweets were handed out from a big jar. Fortunately the effectiveness of the precautions was never put to the test. Fire-fighting teams were organised and equipment installed (stirrup pumps for putting out incendiary bombs, and buckets of sand), and A R P demonstrations and practices were carried out. The Eredine garden was 'dug for victory' and vegetables were planted there and in other spare plots of ground by pupils who formed themselves into a gardening club.

In May 1941 an incendiary bomb landed in the grounds of Shalott, a stray from that night's bombing raid on Greenock and Port Glasgow, where many people were made homeless. Some of them were brought to the School and given temporary accommodation in the hall and gymnasium. The local Women's Voluntary Service, many of whom were Old Girls and parents of pupils, were kept very busy seeing to the needs of more than a thousand people that first day, and then to a diminishing number over two weeks. Dorothy Jackson (Jackson) and Margery Burnet (Taylor) were in charge of the rest centres and clothing depot.

## The School under Miss McMurtrie

Miss McMurtrie continued to uphold the School's tradition of sound academic teaching in all departments. Music was still the glory of St Columba's, and art teaching was also very strong. From early in the century all Mistresses of academic subjects had degrees in the relevant subject, some of them second degrees, and many also had teachers' certificates from St George's College, Edinburgh or Jordanhill College, Glasgow. Teachers of music, games and gymnastics, domestic science and art were all appropriately, and indeed often highly, qualified.

From 1931 every sixth form girl was given the opportunity to take a short course in cookery, for which the school kitchen was used. Miss Janet MacArthur, the sister of the future Headmistress, was appointed in 1936, the year in which the new domestic science room was opened, and the course was extended and developed so that girls taking the Leaving Certificate could include it in their group of subjects. The School continued to offer it as an option for girls in the sixth form not taking Leaving Certificates. Miss MacArthur left in 1942 to join the staff of the Edinburgh College of Domestic Science, and was replaced by Miss Jean Anderson.

*The domestic science room, 1936-37*
Miss Janet MacArthur is third from the right

St Columba's reputation in science was not as strong as that of its sister school in Glasgow. The Park School had been a pioneer in this subject for girls' schools in the West of Scotland, and its strong science and mathematics tradition continued. At St Columba's Miss Jarvis (MA, BSc, Edinburgh) was science Mistress from 1923 until 1932. From 1934 onwards science was taught by Miss Kathleen Millar, of whom more in Chapter Seven. Miss A F Mudie, a distinguished graduate of St Andrews University, taught mathematics from 1929 until 1940, and Miss Catherine Sherriff succeeded her.

Girls aiming for higher education worked for the Leaving Certificate, which was awarded for a group of passes in one diet of examinations. The minimum number of passes required after 1924 was two Highers and two Lowers, and from 1940 two Highers and three Lowers; one of the Highers had to be English. Girls aiming for university would take three Highers, or even, if they stayed on for a sixth year, four. In 1928, in the absence of a satisfactory national intermediate certificate, the three schools of the Girls' School Company introduced their own third year examinations and Certificate, the schools taking it in turns to set the papers; it was dispensed with only in 1960, when the Scottish Certificate of Education Examination Board introduced the new Ordinary Grade.

This was the era in which many of St Columba's special awards were instituted. The St Columba's School Society had presented in 1926 two medals, a gold for the best scholar in the Upper School and a silver for the best scholar in the Lower School. In 1928 Mr A M Adam instituted a bursary, worth £25, to be given annually to the best scholar of the year. Mr Adam was the owner of Windyhill, the Charles Rennie Mackintosh house in Kilmacolm (which had been commissioned by William Davidson, whose son Hamish had attended the Preparatory School), and, for twenty-five years, until his death at an advanced age in 1936, a familiar figure around the village:

***Mr A M Adam***

> . . . an elderly man . . . remarkable for his athletic figure, . . . he took long walks without an overcoat and often without a hat. . . .
>
> Mr Adam used to say he had known what it was to be in straitened circumstances and it was a great pleasure to him to give liberally when he had it in his power.
>
> (School Magazine 1936-37 p. 9)

The following year the Directors founded the Janet Waugh Scholarship, a prize, also worth £25, to commemorate Miss Waugh's headship, to be awarded for the attainment of a high standard of work in music plus four other subjects. Also in 1929-30 there was founded a prize for distinction in art, as high as that for the Silver Tablet for music. It was gifted by Mr D S Carson, whose name it bears, the value was £5, and the winner's name was inscribed on an illuminated scroll executed by Miss Lamb and displayed in the school hall. The Peden Fyfe prize for music was gifted in 1945 in memory of the late Chairman.

During the war years prize-givings were suspended and the prize money was given to various war funds. The gold and silver medals were simply not procurable, but in 1948 the St Columba's School Society had seven silver and six gold medals struck and made into the form of brooches, and they were presented to the girls who had won them during the years 1941-1946.

Some splendid characters taught at the School, some of them for the greater part of their careers. Such women were formative influences on generations of pupils.

## Miss Patton

Miss Alexandra Patton obtained her BA from the Royal University of Ireland, and Licence-ès-Lettres from the University of Rennes. She had been appointed Head of the modern languages department in 1912, and was Second Mistress from 1923 until her retiral in 1945.

'St Columba's has had few mistresses whose personality has counted for so much', said a tribute to her in the school magazine of 1943-45. This vivid personality and her long service make 'Biddy' Patton one of the best-remembered Mistresses of the School's first half-century. She brought a flavour all her own, laced with Irish charm, to everything she did. Her colleagues and pupils remembered her slim figure, dressed in moss-green tweed, skating gracefully on the Knapps when time and weather permitted. Her occasional French Evenings became something of a legend in the

*Miss Patton and Miss Hagart with the fifth form, 1928-29*

Back row: Moyra Clark, —, Margaret Watson, Margaret Walker, —, R MacKay, —, —
Second row: Jessie Cochrane, Isabel Coltart, Margaret Paterson, —, —, P Craig, Sheila Cannon, —, P Murray
Third row: —, —, Betty Smith, Miss Patton, Miss Hagart, Morag MacArthur, M MacKay, Joan Beavis
Front row: Mary MacLachlan, Isobel MacFarlane, —, Vida Hollick, Margot Hood

School. Her literary contributions to the school magazine show her to have been a distinctive prose stylist, and her French accent and intonation were superb, even to the ears of a native speaker. Impulsive in speech and actions, she often started her lessons far down the corridor long before she reached the classroom. Here she was often 'direct and disconcertingly honest' in her criticisms, and her presence also enlivened the staff room with her distinctive qualities:

> . . . original, interesting, forceful in character, sometimes delightfully impulsive and amusing, but never dull or pompous.
>
> (School Magazine 1943-45, p. 16)

**Mlle Duranton**

Native French speakers had been employed from Miss Waugh's day, but they stayed only for a year or so each. Mademoiselle Andrée Duranton was on the staff for seventeen years, from 1928 until 1945. She married a Glasgow dentist, Mr Scott, in 1938, and, in an exception to the general rule, carried on her work (still known as Mam'selle). She returned for a year in 1947-48 'to help us in our extremity'. She taught French by having her classes speak, sing and act in the language, and fostered an early love of it in very many of her girls. The benefits of having a native speaker on the staff were obvious, and she was given both the beginners and the senior pupils to teach, in order to 'start them off' and 'finish them off' correctly.

Mam'selle was very much loved. 'We felt that she was "on our side" and we loved her for it,' said one former pupil. 'Nobody ever misbehaved in Mam'selle's classes,' recalled another. The war years were especially difficult for her, and staff and pupils sympathised. One former pupil recalled her taking the class out to the Eredine garden in the very warm summer term of 1940, 'while we waited for Dunkirk to happen'. The girls were aware of the anguish of their French Mistress on that very tense day.

**Miss Lakeman**

Miss Ethel Lakeman, a former pupil of the Park School and an Honours graduate of St Andrews University, taught English from 1919 until her resignation for reasons of health in 1944, becoming Head of the English department when Miss Waugh retired. She was one of that band of long-serving Mistresses who put their life into the School. She was a believer in unremitting thoroughness in the teaching of spelling, punctuation, and grammar. When she encountered laziness in a pupil, her reaction was explosive:

> She'd raise the top of her desk and bring it down with a bang, we'd jump, all eyes on her, and she'd say clearly: 'If I were a man I'd say *damn*!'
>
> (Margaret Wolfram [Gillan])

Especial sharpness was reserved for those whom she recognised as being highly capable: 'I despair of you!' was a well-known remark.

She was a gifted teacher of oral and dramatic work, which by her day, and no doubt partly thanks to her influence, had become a notable feature of education at St Columba's:

> Her masterly but quiet control of great numbers on her famous Shakespeare evenings will long be remembered.
>
> (School Magazine 1945-46, p. 20)

Her knowledge and enthusiasm were wide ranging. A very junior pupil wrote:

> I recall being wafted in imagination to the ringing plains of windy Troy.
>
> (School Magazine 1984-85, p. 50)

All her youngest pupils received a grounding in the Biblical and Arthurian backgrounds too, and in the last year at school girls were taught Anglo-Saxon for one term.

Miss Lakeman took on the reorganisation of the school library in its new setting, and for nearly twenty years edited the school magazine, contributing, by her tireless correspondence with former pupils and staff, much of the 'family feeling' generated by the School. She kept up the editing of the former pupils' section of the magazine for five years after she left.

***Miss Lakeman with the third form, 1928-29***

Back row: Mary Mackintosh, —, —, Margaret MacKinnon, Margaret Turnbull, Miss Lakeman, —, Bella Young, Deborah Paton, Margaret Strang, M Biggart
Second row: Miss ?, Ellie Kennedy, —, E Milne, Isobel Mumme, —, —, —, —, Aileen Wylie, Miss ?
Third row: Aileen Russell, E Anderson, Elspeth Strathie, —, Olive Mumme, David Beavis, —, Isobel Cochrane, —, —
Fourth row: —, Janet Colquhoun, P Fletcher
Front row: Elinor Anderson, Joan MacRobert, D Millar?, —, JoanShanks?, —, Margaret McPherson, Muriel Storie

## Miss Hagart

Miss J R Hagart, an Honours graduate in history of Glasgow University, came to St Columba's in 1917 and was a fondly remembered and highly respected teacher. She started her work at the School as a temporary assistant to Miss Waugh teaching English and history. Her arrival coincided with the national

*Miss J R Hagart*

shortage of teachers of mathematics, and she not only 'knew the kings of England and could quote the fights historical', but 'was also very well acquainted with matters mathematical', as the tribute to her in the magazine of 1958 says. Miss Hagart taught mathematics when required, and also gave help with French. From 1945 until her retiral in 1958 she was Second Mistress. Her pupils recall her with admiration and fondness ('joke over, girls'), and from her history classes particularly remember her detailed digressions (so-called 'rough sketches'), from which she always returned to the point, and her sound, fact-based teaching.

***Miss Reid with the fourth form, 1928-29***

Back row: Landra Kerr, Vida McKelvie, Dorothy Bird, G McKillop, Frances MacRobert, Kathleen Macdonald, Miss Reid, —, Marjory Chalmers, Janet Murray, Margaret Kennedy, Betty Mories

Second row: Miss ?, —, Lilias Philip, —, Jean Lyle, Fiona Buchanan, —, Eileen Robertson, Eileen Martin, Nancy Harrison, —, Jean Murray, Miss Ford

Third row: O Stevenson, Winifred Bird, Kathleen McNeil, —, Miss ?, E Milne, Helen Greenlees, Nancy Biggart, Betty Lang

Fourth row: Annie Popplewell, —, —, Una Bremner, —, Maidie Bridge, —, —, —

Front row: Marjorie Popplewell, —, Sheena Wylie, Sheena Cochrane, Aline Arthur, Ruth Ledingham, Jean Little, Grizel Alexander

## Miss Reid

Miss Gladys Reid came as a somewhat unwilling recruit in 1918:

> Although I liked children and was keen on my subject, I had had in mind a career very different from teaching, and took rather a dim view of dealing with children and Geography concurrently.
>
> (School Magazine 1961-62, p. 8)

She soon found that she had a gift for that particular mixture, and she stayed so long that she earned the (private) appellation 'Granny' Reid. It was something of a coup for St Columba's to secure a geography specialist at a time when it had not long been offered as a subject for higher qualification in universities. Miss Reid had obtained the Diploma in Geography from the University of Cambridge, which still did not award degrees to women at the time. Since she did not have an academic gown, no one else on the staff, except the Headmistress, wore one either, which must have given the School a rather friendly and informal air. At Cambridge she had studied under some of the famous names of her day, and she had worked in the library of the Meteorological Office in South Kensington. She travelled extensively throughout her career. She taught in the big, bright classroom that is now the staffroom, where textbooks were *not* the main source of information:

> . . . rambles and expeditions, pictures and models, maps to make and to interpret, illustrations from lantern and epidiascope, lectures in town by great travellers and explorers.
>
> (School Magazine 1953-54, p. 25)

Without a long academic tradition behind it, the subject of geography could be approached in schools with a peculiar freedom and inventiveness, and Miss Reid was a great exponent of this method: her teaching, although unstructured and disorganised, 'constantly related to real things and real experiences'.

Everyone looked forward to reaching Form IVB (the equivalent of today's Transitus) which was the opportunity to make models, the results of which from time to time made their contribution to the School's fund-raising activities, pennies being charged for a 'Tour of the World' and suchlike. She retired in 1954, her interest in the School still active.

## The Preparatory School

The Preparatory School, after the addition of Form II in 1931, contained four year-groups instead of three, and was housed in Shieldhall. Miss Dorothy Bowie ('Bow-wow') came to be Head of the Preparatory School in 1926, which then had only forty-five pupils. By the time she left, in 1949, there were nearly one hundred, and it was usual for children to start in Kindergarten at the age of four. She was the typical Infant Mistress of her day – efficient, caring, and strict.

Assistants in the preparatory school came and went, but one former pupil who taught there for many years was Miss Quita Broadfoot. Unlike the other members of staff, she did not have the National Froebel Union qualification, but had trained as a children's nurse. She began as a 'trained assistant for supervision' in 1928, had a period of absence for VAD work during the War, and left in 1949 to marry. As Mrs Paterson she kept strong links with the School, being active for many years in the St Columba's School Society.

## Music

Music in Miss McMurtrie's day was a story of superb teaching from some colourful figures. Miss Renton's contribution is described in Chapter Three. She retired at the same time as Miss McMurtrie.

***Miss Bowie, Miss Broadfoot and Miss Stevens with the Preparatory School (Kindergarten, Transition and Form I), 1928-9***

Centre, back: Miss Bowie
Back row: Miss Broadfoot, E McKay, Margaret Burnet, —, Allan Paton, Margaret Greenlees, —, Betty Rowan, Olwen Buchanan, —, Miss Stevens
Second row: Waveney Bayly, Ann Franklin, Diana Cunningham, Jimmy Easson, Kenneth Walker, Flora MacDonald, Margaret Forrester, Morton Fyfe, George Marr, Naida White
Third row: Jean Strang, Constance Bridge, —, Charlie Arthur, Roy Paton, —, Mollie Simpson, Kitty Strathie, Clare Little, —
Front row: Marguerite Fenwick, Carol Fenwick, —, Mercedes Park, George Mundell, —, Joan Wylie

***The preparatory department in Shieldhall assembly room with Miss Broadfoot and Miss Bowie, 1931***

***A corner of the kindergarten, 1935-36***

***Miss Peterkin***

Miss R H Peterkin, LRAM, was Head of music and an outstanding teacher of piano from 1926 until her resignation in 1938 upon her marriage. 'Peter' inspired awe, bordering upon fear, in all the pianoforte pupils, each of whom had to go and play to her once a year. To her gifted pupils she was an inspiration, and to those who were merely talented she imparted an urge to work hard, for which many were grateful in later years. One, who attained the Silver Tablet in 1938 (as well as the gold medal and the Janet Waugh Scholarship), remembered:

> Peter's personal identification with each nervous player at Senior Concerts (this from the depths of the Prefects' Cloakroom!).
>
> (Margaret Shaw [Pollock] in School Magazine 1960-61, p. 12)

She was succeeded as Head of music by Miss Anne Collet, LRAM, ARCM, who taught for twenty-nine years; Miss Maneely taught music from 1935 until 1963 (see Chapter Seven).

Miss Anne Aitken, LRAM, taught piano from 1919 until she retired in 1949. She was an excellent teacher of piano and a keen supporter of all aspects of the music department:

> She and our old friend 'Miss Linford', were actively sympathetic towards the string department and both were sporting enough to have lessons . . . in order to become more intimate with the technique of string music.
>
> (School Magazine 1948-49, p. 33)

Some former pupils returned to teach music for a few years: Anna Bathgate (Whyte) and Phyllis Walker in the 1930s, and Una Morrison (Bremner) from 1938 until 1941. Phyllis Walker had her name inscribed on the Silver Tablet, won the gold medal and was the first winner of the Janet Waugh scholarship in 1930; she took her LRAM and degree of Mus Bac at Edinburgh, still aged only twenty. While teaching at St Columba's from 1934 until 1938 she added the ARCM. She later joined the staff of the Royal Scottish Academy of Music. Una Bremner took her LRAM six months after leaving school, studying under Miss Peterkin, and went on to study at the Royal Academy in London.

Several others distinguished themselves musically at school and later. Doris Tyrrell (Arthur), on violin, was one of the two successful Silver Tablet candidates in 1930. After taking her LRAM at the Royal Academy of Music in London, she taught at various schools, while becoming known as a singer, with performances with the Scottish National Academy of Music and for the BBC. By 1950 she was, with her husband, joint head of a prominent school in California. In 1981 the School received the endowment of a scholarship for music in her name.

Dorothy Jones triumphed in 1937 with the Silver Tablet, the gold medal, the A M Adam bursary and the Janet Waugh scholarship. Dorothy had passed her final grade Associated Board music examination with distinction, in violin,

***Prizegiving, 1937***
Left to right, standing: Isobel Cochrane, Iris Nicol (Carson award for art), Dorothy Jones (Head Girl, gold medallist, A M Adam bursary, Janet Waugh scholarship), Mrs McMurtrie, Mr Peden Fyfe, Miss McMurtrie, Mr Jack Kerr, Sir A T Taylor, Mrs Collins, Mercedes Park (silver medallist), Mr W Hill Jack, Sheila Cameron (athletic shield winner), Eleanor Barr (tennis champion; she also holds the sports picture, won by her form); seated, Dr Sara Annie Burstall, guest of honour, retired Head of Manchester High School for girls, and member of various advisory committees on education

***Betty Mories, Head Girl 1933***

when she was in Form VA, the equivalent of third year. She studied at the Royal Academy in London, gained the degree of Mus Bac from London University, and then went to the University of Wales, where she took Mus Bac with first-class Honours. From there she went to be Principal Teacher of violin at Cheltenham Ladies' College, and then assistant lecturer in music at Birmingham University. By 1945 she was known professionally as Hannah Jones, and was performing with major orchestras all over the country as well as on the air. She later performed under the name of Hannah Wishart.

Others who were both successful Silver Tablet candidates and winners of the Janet Waugh scholarship were Betty Cowan (Mories), Head Girl, in 1933, Dorothy Carmichael (Howie) in 1940, and Mercedes Campbell (Park) in 1941.

Diction and voice production were also offered as private classes. This department too produced some talented pupils, several of whom went on to take the LRAM in elocution or to study dramatic art. Some took teaching posts and one or two found acting work. Margaret Maclaurin returned to St Columba's to teach diction in 1947 and remained until 1961.

## Art: Helen A Lamb

> The spirit of ancient Celtic art comes to life in her again, with its delicate beauty of colour and form, its feeling for nature, its sympathy with the animal world and its deep religious perceptiveness.
>
> (School Magazine 1948-49, p. 25)

Helen A Lamb was awarded the Diploma from the Glasgow School of Art in 1913, and then studied for two further years at the Art School to train for teaching. Hers was another of Miss Waugh's inspired appointments, and she

*The art room in 1928 with Miss Lamb, far left*

taught at St Columba's on a part-time basis from 1920 until 1949.

Helen Lamb was an internationally renowned calligrapher and illuminator. She lived and worked in Dunblane for most of her life, and many examples of her exquisite illumination are on display in Dunblane Cathedral, including the Roll of Honour and the Cradle Roll, which has attained worldwide recognition through frequent reproduction. She was one of the foremost members of the Society of Friends of Dunblane Cathedral, for many years its President, and was Curator of the Cathedral's museum. She was instrumental in establishing Scottish Churches' House in Dunblane. In 1977 she received the Queen's Silver Jubilee Medal for her service to the community.

She was commissioned by the Church of Scotland to prepare illuminated addresses for the Sovereign on four occasions between 1935 and 1947. Her work is also to be seen in many churches around Scotland.

At St Columba's in 1931 Miss Lamb designed the St Columba panel, for the names of the winners of the D S Carson award for art, given in recognition of Miss Waugh's long service as Headmistress. She designed the new badge for the School in 1925: until then it had been a simple cross of St Columba (the form which can still be seen mounted above the door of the school hall).

'Purple circles' was a particularly resonant expression of hers, which stuck in the minds of the schoolgirls she taught and instantly evoked their art teacher. For girls who had artistic gifts she was a most inspiring teacher, and the art room was:

> . . . one of the most fascinating places in the School. At any period of the Session it well repaid a visit – most of the work was highly original, very individual and full of imagination and enterprise.
>
> (School Magazine 1948-49, p. 25)

Miss Lamb sent several girls to Glasgow School of Art. Nan McInnes (Anderson) was the first winner of the Carson award, in 1930, and took her Diploma in 1933. Jean Murray, who gained the Carson award in 1935, won the Newbery prize in 1939 for the most distinguished student at the Art School. Elizabeth Alston (Gray) (Carson award 1947) and her contemporary Elizabeth Wilson (Oldfield) were two of Miss Lamb's outstanding pupils, and both went on to have careers in this field, the former as a teacher and potter, the latter as a designer. Elizabeth Gray in 1946 painted a mural in the school dining room. Ann Sanders (Meade), another of Miss Lamb's pupils, who won the Carson award in 1948, became an artist of distinction, having painted and exhibited her work in two continents and taught at universities in the United States.

***Entrance to the school hall, by Daphne Vaughan Russell, c 1945 showing the pre-1925 form of the school crest***

***Mural in the school dining room***

*Netball, c 1928*

## Physical Education

Games under Miss McMurtrie were not compulsory, and she always said that the aim of physical education in the School was to encourage good physique for the many, rather than outstanding feats by the few. Lacrosse and tennis continued to be played, and in 1933 three netball courts were marked out at the Ashes.

> At present, netball in school is very rough and boisterous.
> (School Magazine 1934-35, p. 50)

The juniors had an enjoyable game against Kilmacolm Public School, and the next year were given coaching in the game. Swimming became ever more popular, practised from 1933 at the Paisley Baths (much more salubrious than Greenock's murky waters), where annual swimming sports were now held. White girdles were awarded for success and effort at lacrosse. House matches were played in lacrosse and tennis, and in 1932 a tennis cup was presented by Miss McMurtrie for the residents of Shalott. During the War outside fixtures were impossible to play, owing to transport difficulties, but in 1939-40 the St Columbans had the fun of playing hockey and lacrosse with their Park schoolmates.

Gymnastics, using equipment such as the vaulting horse, was quite different from drill, although everyone still called the stripes awarded for excellence 'drill stripes'. A display of gymnastics was put on each year for parents: it was an important event in the school calendar, as was the dancing display by the dance pupils (see Chapter Five).

Games and gymnastics flourished under a succession of enthusiastic and talented young teachers. Miss Siona Gunn arrived in 1933 and left in 1935:

> . . . after such a two years' record of energetic work as could hardly be equalled by anyone anywhere.
> (School Magazine 1935-36, p. 4)

She played for Scotland in the international hockey match against England in 1934. Miss Ella Vlandy, trained, like Siona Gunn, at Dartford, came to take her place, and played hockey for Scotland in the International against England in 1935, and the following year was selected for all three international matches, against England, Ireland and Wales, and for Scotland's match against South Africa. She left in 1937, to be succeeded by Miss Eileen Guthrie, who left in 1942.

Some of Miss McMurtrie's girls made a significant contribution to Scottish lacrosse in the 1940s. Several of them trained at Dartford and became teachers; one such was Doris Millar, joint winner of the Janet Waugh scholarship in 1939, who was selected to play for Scotland in the lacrosse International against Wales in 1947. In the same year Doreen Hairs, who had also trained at Dartford during the War, played lacrosse for Yorkshire where she was teaching. Margaret Brown (Burnet) and Joan MacRobert (cousins, descendants of Frank Burnet, Senior, the architect) both played for Scotland in the International against Ireland in 1948, with Doris Millar as referee, and in 1949 against England, when the referee was the new games Mistress, Christine Havelock. At this time Joan MacRobert was giving some of her time to coaching games at the School.

***Swimming sports, 1937***

***Lacrosse XII, 1929***

Back row: —, —, Betty Smith, Morag MacArthur, May Austin,
Second row: Isobel McGeachy, Rosie Kerr, Miss Splatt, Nan Little, Gladys Coltart,
Front row: Rona McKay, Landra Kerr

***Lacrosse team, 1938-39***

Back row: Mercedes Park, Margaret Smith, Lois Main, Pat Wilson, Xaveria Fyfe
Second row: Joan Hairs, Betty Watt, Janette Turnbull, Betty Broadfoot, Doris Millar
Front row: Carol Fenwick, Catherine Douglas

## Duchal, Kilallan, Craigmarloch and Strathgryffe

The house system was instituted in 1932 by Miss McMurtrie in order to stimulate more interest in games. Great excitement was generated in the School by this innovation:

> We had arrived at a great mile-stone in the history of the School,
> (School Magazine 1932, p. 6)

***opposite:***

***Tennis team, 1932***
Back row:
Margaret Watson,
Morag MacArthur,
Margaret Kennedy,
Front row:
Lilias Findlay,
Vida McKelvie,
Jean Lyle.
(Morag MacArthur later became a Director of the Girls' School Company)

and meetings of the staff and members of the Franchise Roll were called by the Headmistress, where:

> . . . proposals were made and rejected and details discussed with tremendous enthusiasm. Numerous and varied were the suggestions for the names of the Houses, and we finally selected the names of four places in the neighbourhood of Kilmacolm – Duchal, Kilallan, Craigmarloch and Strathgryffe. They were then given distinguishing colours – Red, Blue, White, and Yellow, respectively. The House System has already promoted much friendly rivalry. It has greatly encouraged the Junior and Middle School in Games, and has allowed many girls who are not members of the School team, to play for their House.
> (Ibid. pp. 6-7)

The following year there were four house trophies to compete for: a swimming trophy and tennis and lacrosse cups, and a fine model of the St Martin's cross in Iona, presented by Canon and Mrs Philip as an award of honour. House badges were introduced in 1934.

Enthusiasm for the house system ebbed and flowed. It was of course originally designed for boarding schools, and is always an artificial institution in day schools. In 1942 efforts were made to increase the team spirit:

> Careful records were kept, not only of marks lost through carelessness, but of creditable effort in gaining places in teams, gymnastic stripes, or high marks in verb-tests and spelling competitions.
> (School Magazine 1941-43, p. 20)

Those of the pupils who were boarders already had a strong and natural house spirit of their own, but this did not form part of the official scheme, and the boarders were split into four houses along with everyone else.

## Miss McMurtrie's legacy

The young teacher who had rescued a little educational opportunity from the ruins of war for the French children of the devastated villages had, in her maturity, steered a much larger School through a different War with the same calmness and quiet assurance.

She was gifted with understanding and humanity:

***opposite: House trophies***
Award of Honour,
Tennis Cup,
Swimming Trophy,
Lacrosse Cup

> Miss McMurtrie had a real respect for the individual, however unformed, and the patience and wisdom to let her grow at her own pace. She gave us precious time from her well-deserved leisure hours, patient encouragement from her certain knowledge that we would all grow up some time, and a very clear, uncompromising picture of those

values which she considered worth holding dear.
(Margaret Grant [Young], School Magazine 1961-62, pp. 66-67)

'She knew when to tighten the reins and when to slacken them,' said one of her pupils later, and it was this confidence and wisdom which marked her headship and made the School a happy place. Her educational vision went well beyond the production of good exam grades, and she was an admirer of Dame Louisa Lumsden's belief that:

. . . the whole aim of education was to learn how to learn and to teach oneself.
(School Magazine 1935-36, p. 7)

She believed strongly in the need to point the girls in an outward-looking direction, to make them aware of national events and to encourage an international outlook. She valued all kinds of contributions to school life, not just the academic. All these characteristics helped to shape the future development of St Columba's, and many of them can still be recognised in the present School.

***Miss McMurtrie and Miss Jarvis with the sixth form, 1929***

Back row: —, —, Isobel Hunter, Rosie Kerr, Margaret Parker, Joy Scott, Rona McKay
Second row: Nancy Laird, Rene McKeith, —, Isobel McGeachy, Mary Lakeman, —, Gladys Coltart
Third row: May Austin, Margaret Maclaurin, Betty Smith, Miss McMurtrie, Miss Jarvis, Sheena Hendry, —-
Front row: Nan Little, Nan Anderson, Anne MacArthur, —-

*Chapter Five*

# Highly Polished: School life in the first half-century

## Good housekeeping

Mrs Cameron was Housekeeper-Cook from the School's first day, assisted by her daughter Lizzie, who left when she married. Mrs Cameron presided over her household for seventeen years:

> What pride she took in keeping the School beautiful! How fresh and shining everything looked on Monday mornings, and with what vigour every corner was cleaned during the holidays!
>
> (School Magazine 1916, p.5)

She did not suffer gladly anything less than total dedication to the job in hand, and that was what she herself gave. Still, it was understood that her bark was worse than her bite. Mrs Cameron's cooking was greatly appreciated, and she rose grandly to special occasions:

> A school supper gave her scope for all kinds of artistic efforts; and she enjoyed preparing trifles and creams and jellies as much as we did eating them. What a triumph was her Charlotte Russe!
>
> (Ibid.)

***Lower corridor, 1948, by Ann Meade, showing the 1936 extension, looking north towards the domestic science room***

It seems to have been established that the Housekeeper-Cook should be a character, and the next to be appointed, Miss Catherine Gillies, who presided over the kitchens and the corridors until her retiral in 1930, did not disappoint in this, or indeed any other, respect. Excellent meals were served up every day: a main course of roast meat and two vegetables, followed by a superb fruit pudding with a fruit sauce, or her magnificent creamed rice. Miss Patton wrote an amusing tribute to her Highland qualities of reserve, dignity, loyalty and tact in the school magazine, illustrating the latter two qualities by recalling her habit of rescuing:

> . . . any girl marooned in the kitchen (out of bounds) by secreting her in the plate-lift, while the

> dangerous but unsuspecting visitor was held in parley on some quite alien topic but two yards away.
>
> (School Magazine 1931, p. 11)

Under Miss Gillies too, school parties were handsomely catered for:

> Leave the arrangements and the catering to her, and she would enter into the spirit and enjoyment of the thing with the fervour of a VIth Form girl, and an inventiveness all her own.

The housekeeper did the ordering, employed the staff and supervised their work. The maids worked from 8 am until 6 pm on weekdays and also on Saturday mornings, until Miss McMurtrie agreed with Miss Gillies's successor as Housekeeper, Miss Jenny Holmes, that they need not work on Saturdays. Jenny, as she was always known to pupils and staff, came in 1922 'just to help out for a couple of weeks'. She retired in 1968 after forty-six years' service. A tribute to her in the 1968 magazine recalled:

> . . . the special occasions when visitors have flocked into the dining-room after some pleasant function, to find Jenny and her helpers presiding smilingly behind immaculate, well-filled tables,

and also:

> . . . the days and months and years of ceaseless hard work to keep a growing school's domestic wheels turning smoothly – the unglamorous behind-the-scenes work necessary to maintain well-kept form-rooms and well-served meals.

***Domestic staff, 1968***

Back row: Rene Davidson, Agnes Hamilton, Angus McLeod (Janitor), Elizabeth Tanner, Agnes Gallacher
Front row: Lily McDermid, Annie Whittet, Jenny Holmes, Nan Stewart, Frances Crawford

*Dining room scene, by Mairi Crawford, Form VB (later Mairi Hedderwick), 1952*

One of those who served under Jenny and for many years afterwards was Annie Whittet. She worked for the School for about sixty years, having come originally, like Jenny, to fill in for two weeks in an emergency. Both women are remembered and loved by former pupils and staff alike.

Only the boarders and the girls who had travelled to school by train took meals in school. The others went home, many by bicycle. The original kitchen was in the basement and reached by a very steep and narrow stair, but there was a hoist for plates, occasionally put to illicit use, as Miss Patton recalled. The hoist transported the dishes to the upper kitchen, which is now the main office. A large trolley carried the dishes to the dining room, which was first in the present library, and then, after 1905, in the school hall. The tables were stored under the stage. When the new wing of 1936 was built, a new kitchen and servery were included, linking with a dining room created out of two classrooms (it was later divided again to become Rooms 1 and 2). The basement kitchen was no longer needed, and became a base for the janitor and groundsmen. With growing numbers of pupils staying for meals, the hall was again used as a dining room for the preparatory school children, who walked over from Shieldhall, and for the senior girls. The Mistresses had a table on the stage. Each girl supplied her own napkin ring and napkin, freshly laundered at home each weekend.

Meals at the School were always very good, which was fortunate as it was obligatory to finish everything on one's plate. During the Second World War it became impossible to buy food wholesale, and yet pupils from those years remember excellent and plentiful meals in the school dining room. They also remember the moment in 1944 when Miss Mowat, the secretary, came in one lunch-time to announce the news of the D-Day landings. A great cheer went up.

## Discipline

Discipline was strict but not harsh. According to one of her former pupils, such was Miss Waugh's commanding presence, that she only had to appear on any scene for silence to fall. A common punishment for transgressors was to stand in the corridor:

> . . . which was not a good place to be found standing by Miss Waugh, as she would want to hear in detail the reason for your being there. And she then reduced you to a smaller size.
>
> (Jean Service)

She would not have needed to say much to do so. Headmistresses of Miss Waugh's stamp maintained discipline by force of personality rather than by

punishment, and girls were generally very responsive to this. One former pupil, a boarder at Shieldhall before 1920, recalls a naughty escapade on a Brownie picnic:

> After our tea the leaders had wandered off for some peace and quiet and on returning had found us prancing about on the heather *au naturel* and probably practising our ballet steps!
>
> (Barbara Robson [Friend])

***The upper corridor, 1936 looking south***

Seventy-five years later she still remembers the awful words uttered by Miss Waugh:

'I did not expect this of you, Barbara.'

Also typical of girls' schools of the period was the silence rule. Talking on the stairs, in the corridors and cloakroom was forbidden, the cloakroom prohibition being particularly hard to adhere to. Miss Armit, the Latin Mistress, was in the habit of wearing crepe-soled shoes, making possible a silent ambush on cloakroom miscreants. An order mark would be dealt out on the spot. Talking in the dining room, on the other hand, was permitted, and there was a 'steady roar of talk' at meal-times.

When the bell sounded as the signal to change classrooms or proceed to the dining room, the whole School moved in single file like a giant mechanism, silent and well-oiled. Special indoor shoes kept the feet noiseless:

> Indoors we wore glacé kid dark brown strap shoes – the most comfortable shoes I have ever worn, quiet to walk in and ideal for sliding along the highly polished floors, kept in gleaming condition by Annie.
>
> (Elizabeth Gillies [Beaton])

Taking stairs two at a time was an offence that earned an order mark.

Outdoor rules of behaviour were just as strict as indoor. Groups of pupils walked two-by-two in crocodiles, of course; and if for any reason they were on their own on a school day in the village, behaviour and uniform had to be impeccable. Certain Mistresses were known to be particularly hard to satisfy on these counts. Girls were forbidden to go into the village shops on their way home from School, although some risked it. To be seen *wearing the school hat* eating ice-cream in the street was an affront to decency, and the perpetrator could expect a sound ticking off from the Headmistress.

In the early days forms were rewarded for good behaviour by a half-holiday. It was probably around 1916 that Miss Waugh introduced the Franchise Roll. This was a list of those deemed to have exhibited good conduct and willingness to participate in school activities, and the prefects were selected from among the senior girls on it. The first step was to appear on the list of those 'recommended for the Franchise Roll', and further efforts might then lead to possession of the actual distinction itself. Girls on the

Franchise Roll were rewarded with a half-holiday, and later with the privilege of using the Franchise Cloakroom, which was off the hall stage.

An order mark meant dismissal from the Franchise Roll, and, worse, the shame of hearing one's name read out from the hall platform by the Headmistress at order-mark readings. When the house system was adopted order marks were debited to one's house.

## Posture, propriety and panama hats

***Pupils in uniform, 1931***
Note the panama hats, the beige mackintosh hats, and the black velour hats with hatband

Early in Miss Waugh's headship gym tunics were adopted for wear on days when drill and games were done. The earliest tunic was dark green with a green velvet square yoke, and it was worn with a green-and-white striped square-necked blouse in winter, and a plain white blouse in the summer term. The gym tunic, square-rigged with its three box-pleats back and front, was intended to be exactly knee-length, but 'pie-frills' are remembered by at least one former pupil.

It was probably in the early 1920s that uniform became everyday wear. Besides the gym tunic, there was a uniform for special occasions, such as church services; it could also be worn, if desired, on ordinary days as an alternative to the gym tunic. It was a navy blue tunic and skirt (changed in the late 1930s to a smarter navy blue dress); the pocket of the tunic was embroidered with the new school badge in a green outline, and it had a green lace at the neck. Senior girls wore it with a detachable white collar. It did not outlast the start of the War, which ensured the demise of complicated or superfluous forms of dress, as well as some relaxation of the rules about uniform.

Black woollen tights were worn under gym tunics for gymnastics. Younger pupils wore regulation gymnasium knickers from the early 1920s. The games Mistress of 1920-24, Miss Ferguson, was responsible for the introduction of up-to-date costume for swimming and dancing:

***Summer uniform, c 1930, Mary Lakeman***

***Sixth Form 1931-32, in navy tunics and skirts***

Back row: Wieda Stevenson, Helen Greenlees
Second row: Lillias Philip, Margaret Hamilton, Vida McKelvie, Betty Mories, Margaret Kennedy, Kathleen Macdonald, Robina Bryson
Front row: Margaret Watson (Head Girl), Morag MacArthur, Marjorie Walker, Betty Davidson, Sheila Cannon

***Prefects and sub-prefects, 1936-37***

Back row: Iris Nicol, Margaret Findlay, Elisabeth Shanks, Margaret Horne, Maureen Graham
Second row: Katherine Broadfoot, Isobel Cochrane, Dorothy Jones (Head Girl), Margaret Young, Nancy McKinlay
Front row: Aileen Russell, Sheila McBride

> She was known . . . as 'The Bug' and she really made history in the school: the swimming costumes of that time were baggy, cotton, knee-length atrocities and these soon gave place to woollen swim-suits; dancing was done in gym slips but she managed to introduce mauve alpaca tunics, later changed to silk.
>
> (School Magazine 1963-64, p. 13)

The silk dance tunics were made in autumn colours; they made a pleasing aesthetic impression in the 'Grecian dances', performed barefoot with hoops and ribbons. The gym tunic was worn from 1930 with a white shirt-blouse and striped tie, or, on gym days, with a collarless, long-sleeved blouse.

For all major school events, such as concerts and prize-giving, white dresses were *de rigueur*. After the War the senior girls wrung permission to wear pastel coloured dresses instead of the hated white. And it was after the War that a new style of gym tunic began to be worn, without pleats, but with a plain bodice and a flared skirt.

Outdoor wear was a heavy navy blue coat and a dark velour hat with school hatband for dry days, and a beige mackintosh and hat for wet days. It was an offence to be seen outdoors without gloves. School hats were joyfully discarded on the last day by the leavers – some found a watery resting place in the Clyde at Greenock, others in the Gryffe at Bridge of Weir. Summer wear, a panama hat, with school hatband, and a blazer, which was optional, was not donned until the decree was issued each year by the School. A green-and-white checked dress for summer wear was introduced in the early 1920s.

But the wearers of the smart uniforms might spoil the effect by hunching their shoulders or slouching. Winifred McKenzie recalled early attempts to instil good posture by making the pupils walk around the hall with square wooden blocks on their heads. In 1926 good posture was encouraged by the introduction of Position Marks. The magazine explained:

> A possible total of ten marks is awarded to each Form every week throughout the year. Whenever a girl is seen holding herself badly, whether marching to, or from, prayers, or in the corridors, her Form loses a mark.
>
> (School Magazine 1927-28, p. 41)

It was usually the gymnastics Mistress who was given the job of watching for bad posture and deducting the marks, as the lines of girls walked down the corridors and into Prayers. At Prayers the staff sat on benches in a long line down the length of the hall, overseeing the classes drawn up in parallel banks at right angles to them. Position Marks were added to marks for the drill competition and so affected the awarding of the gymnastics cup. From around 1938 a special Posture Trophy was awarded each year to the best form; it continued to be awarded in the Senior School until 1973, when it was given to the Primary School, renamed the Deportment Cup, and presented as a House award.

## Helping others

From early days St Columba's associated itself with various charities, providing the girls with a window on a less fortunate world than theirs. In the winter term of 1907 the Secretary of the Glasgow Cripple Children's League visited the School. Soon afterwards a sewing afternoon was organised, and the girls set about sewing chemises, overalls, flannel petticoats and bodices. The girls sat at tables and on forms around the walls, and:

> Miss Waugh sat at a little table with her machine which sometimes would not go round.
>
> (School Magazine Easter 1908, p.13)

This was more fun than a normal sewing lesson:

> There was laughing and talking, and nobody scolded when the sewing had to be taken out and done again.
>
> (Ibid.)

There were happy plans for a series of sewing afternoons throughout the winter. Thus began a connection with the Cripple Children's League which lasted for many years. Miss McMurtrie was keen to make the contribution as personal as possible, and during the 1930s the pupils made several visits to this organisation's Christmas party for which they put on entertainments, and provided toys and knitted garments for children known to them by name.

Most of the School's other charitable interests up to 1945 were concerned with organisations run by women, of which the Queen Margaret Settlement, a charitable association founded by QM College, under the influence of Janet Galloway, was one. University settlements founded houses in poor areas of the city from which workers, in the case of QMS all of them women, attempted to alleviate some of the poverty around them. Many of the members of QMS were former pupils of the Park School, and a former Latin Mistress of St Columba's, Miss Joyner, left in 1914 to give her services to the Settlement. But the charity with which the school was most associated before the Second World War was another university settlement, the Missionary Settlement for University Women in Bombay, a place for girls attending that University to live. Miss Sorabji, a mission worker, visited the school on more than one occasion to talk about the Mission's work, and the MSUW sent regular newsletters. In 1940 Miss Margaret Ward, who had taught classics and English from 1935, went to Bombay to work for the MSUW.

Both Miss Waugh and perhaps especially Miss McMurtrie attached great importance to the widening of the girls' horizons beyond Kilmacolm, and by them the idea was firmly established in the minds of generations of girls that doing something worthwhile with your life counted for more than material rewards. Personal contact with workers for the School's adopted charities at home and abroad was carefully cultivated. No girl from Miss Waugh's day would have been ignorant of the work of the Charity Organisation Society, which had been founded to coordinate the efforts of various charitable bodies. It was a highly influential body which counted many women among its members, and another past Mistress, Miss Robertson, worked for it in Newcastle. During the First World War two of the School's university graduates, Margaret Renwick (Daisy Lang) and Anne (Nannie) Mowat, worked for the COS in Glasgow. This organisation, together with the

University Settlements, played an important role in training women for work in the field of social services.

In the Second World War much energy went into raising funds and making and collecting items for the troops. Many leisure activities had to be curtailed because of wartime restrictions, and time and effort went instead into school concerts and displays where collections were taken, and into:

> . . . individual efforts in the form of Exhibitions of Models, Boarders' Entertainments, Form Plays and Sales; and we must not fail to mention private enterprise in the way of a Gymkhana, Garden Fetes, and concerts given out of School.
>
> (School Magazine 1941-43, p. 14)

Money thus collected was given to the Red Cross and various war funds.

## By the School, for the School, about the School

Hail to our Magazine
So enterprising;
Long may it flourish green,
Ever surprising.

Big girls and little girls
Read it with wonder;
Past girls and present girls
Ne'er find a blunder.

Good poems, splendid prose,
Fine editorials;
All quite as good as those
Found in pictorials.

('Acta Floreat' by Anne Mowat, School Magazine 1907, p. 3)

*Form IVB 1904-05: the class which originated the School Magazine*

Back row: May Crawford, Mary Mann, E Bird, Phyllis Handley
Second row: Margery Graham Brown, Anne Mowat, Miss Taylor
Front row: Wilda Binnie, Dorothy Reid

In the Christmas term of 1903 Form IIIA felt the lack of decoration in their form room and decided to buy plants. The girls met on the heap of gravel which lay where the Lyle Road end of the hall now is, to discuss strategies for raising money. What emerged from that meeting was the Story Club:

> A large fat exercise book was purchased and in it every member of the Form had to write a story or a piece of verse every fortnight. For the privilege of reading what had been written, the outside public paid at the rate of one penny a night.
>
> (Anne Mowat, School Magazine 1926-27, p. 17)

The pennies rolled in and soon the classroom was a veritable bower of greenery. In the end the plants died and the Story Club did not long outlast them, but an idea had been sown on fertile ground, and two years later the same form produced something more like a magazine.

It was called 'The Scribbler', and it was hand-written by Margery Graham Brown and decorated by May Crawford (who went on to Glasgow School of Art in 1911). It was for private circulation only, but alongside the fashion columns and palmistry divinations it did 'chronicle the little events of the School'. The powers that be did not know of its existence, which was perhaps just as well, for some of the articles were 'of rather a revolutionary nature'. When the girls were in Form VA (the equivalent of Senior Three), in 1907, they aspired to a real magazine, and started to write contributions:

> One wet afternoon at the Crawfords' house, someone made the suggestion that, perhaps, we could have the Magazine printed. The idea was hailed with wild enthusiasm, and before we parted that night, plans were laid for a Super Cake and Candy Sale which should set the undertaking on a firm financial footing. The sale was held, and as a result the first number of the Magazine was published, the printer's bill was paid, and we had a small balance in the Bank, and an immense fund of self-gratification in our hearts. After all it was something of an achievement for a Fifth Form, with no experience to guide them, to have produced even a tiny magazine.
>
> (Ibid. p. 18)

***Janie Wood in 1906, who wrote (from Girton College, Cambridge) the Editorial for the first Magazine***

The original ambition, to produce an issue each term, proved to be unrealisable, but the magazine appeared each year with only a few gaps until the end of the Second World War, by which time it had been put on a well-established and more formal footing, and became an annual publication from then on.

The first few issues make especially delightful reading, giving a flavour of what it was like to be a schoolgirl at St Columba's in those days. The first editor was Anne Mowat, and the first issue was opened by Jane Marshall (Janie Wood), who wrote from Girton College a lively article on what a school magazine should be, coining what came to be its motto, 'By the School, for the School, about the School': this, by and large, is what the magazine was, salted with a little news from outside, generally letters from Old Girls, 'to keep us from being narrow-minded'. The wit and literary standard of most of the pieces would not have disgraced a professional publication, even if they were obtained only with much trouble:

> . . . for although the Staff and even some friends outside the Inner Circle of the School were always most helpful, . . . very little suitable matter of an original nature was forthcoming from the School. Prizes were offered, which sometimes brought in quite useful material. Looking back, I can see what a boon regular Games criticisms, such as now appear, would have been to the overwrought editors. With what delight we used to hail the Prize List, which was alwa ys good for at least two pages.
>
> (Ibid., p. 19)

The magazine was edited by pupils until 1922, no doubt with help from the staff, and then Miss Lakeman took over the responsibility from the next issue, which appeared in 1925, until her retiral in 1944. The plea for material was a constant theme of editorials, couched in ever more original and witty terms. New developments from the late 1920s onwards included photographs, showing games teams, prefects and some special school events, and artwork.

## From the hall platform . . .

> It is a festive scene, . . . two or three times a year. These nights are devoted to either concerts or plays. The school is quite glorified. Girls in white dresses and flowing scarfs and sashes, and gentlemen in conventional evening dress swarm in the passages. The girls have a certain air of superiority on these occasions, and a very distinct air of being at home.
>
> (School Magazine, Easter term 1908, p. 19)

***The Programme for the 1901 Christmas Entertainment (reproduced in the Jubilee Book)***

PART I

"THE ENCHANTED PALACE" *A. Somervell*

*King* . . . . . Elsie Marshall
*Queen* . . . . . . Edith Twist
*Princess Crystal* . . . . Edith Barr
*Prince Emerald* . . . . Elsie Linford
*The Chancellor* . . . . Janie Wood
*The Jester* . . . . Chrissie McCrone
*The Poet* . . . . . Jessie Burnet
*The Wise Man* . . . . Elsie Frew
*Fairy of the Palace* . . . Dorothy Reid
*Fairy of Light* . . . Wilda Binnie
*Fairy of Darkness* . . . Ada Ormond
*Fairies and Courtiers.*

Interval of half an hour

PART II

SCENES FROM "MIDSUMMER NIGHT'S DREAM" *Shakespeare*

*Quince* . . . . . . James Brown
*Bottom* . . . . . Henry Birkmyre
*Flute* . . . . . . Arthur Lang
*Snout* . . . . . . Frank Burnet
*Snug* . . . . . . Robert McCrone
*Starveling* . . . . . Jessie Burnet
*Puck* . . . . . . Nannie Mowat
*Hippolyta* . . . . . Edith Twist
*Theseus* . . . . . Elsie Marshall
*Philostrate* . . . . . Elsie Linford
*Lysander* . . . . . May McNab
*Demetrius* . . . . . Kate McNeill
*Hermia* . . . . . Edith Barr
*Helena* . . . . . . Mary Carmichael

CHRISTMAS CAROLS

*The First Nowell* . . . Traditional
*It was the Winter Wild*
Words, Milton; Music, Horrocks
*Good King Wenceslas* . . . Traditional

A very important part of school life was the performance of plays and concerts in front of parents and friends. The first such evening was at Christmas 1901. The entertainment was in two parts, *The Enchanted Palace* and scenes from *A Midsummer Night's Dream*, and was rounded off with Christmas carols. Miss Waugh delighted in school plays, often took on a large share of the work involved, and was an inspiration in rehearsals:

> She had a way of making the lines live so that a rather wooden little fairy or a bashful lover lost self-consciousness, and caught something of her dramatic power.
>
> (School Magazine 1927-28, pp. 10-11)

The School was not named St Columba's until April 1902.

***Junior pupils in a nursery rhyme play, c 1904***

Back row: Winnie Lang, Marion Sloan, Katherine Adams
Second row: Katherine G Wood, Doris Hunter, E Black, Jessie Thomson, R McCrone, Hester Twist, A Lang, J E Stewart, J M Crawford, L B Todd
Front row: Jack Mowat, Wilfred Graham, Dorothy Burnet, Winifred Crawford, Tom Twist (as the Mouse), Bryce Graham

**Hamlet, *1932, Form VIB***
Lillias Philip played Hamlet, and Margaret Kennedy played Ophelia. Miss MacArthur (centre, front row) directed.

***Miss Ford, Miss MacArthur and Miss Mudie, 1932***

**The Idea, *1906***

All the staff of course were involved in these events: the art Mistress in scenery and the sewing Mistress and others in costumes, the music department in teaching and rehearsing and accompanying the songs, and Miss Turnbull on the technical side:

> . . . when, mounted on a ladder, she threw coloured lights from the electric lantern on the scene.
>
> (School Magazine, 1927 -28, p.13)

The first play performed on the stage of the new hall in 1906 was *The Idea*. In 1908 a revue based on Lewis Carroll's *Alice* books was staged. The performance was a thundering success, and for the remainder of the session:

> . . . we all became so influenced by the story that we found ourselves saying things in a way which could only be described by coining a new word – 'Alicey!'
>
> (School Magazine, Summer 1908, p. 14)

Sketches and short plays by individual forms and the Preparatory School were occasionally put on, for the benefit of one of the war funds during both Wars, or of some other charity. The boarders put on plays in the boarding houses from time to time: some were deemed good enough to transfer to the school stage. More ambitious performances, involving most of the Upper School, continued to delight parents and friends. Milton's *Comus* was performed in the summer term of 1911. In 1913 a play by the contemporary writer W B Yeats, *The Countess Cathleen*, was staged.

Music and dancing featured strongly in most productions. A particularly talented generation inspired Miss Waugh in 1916 to organise the performance of an operetta, *The Princess Zara*, with some outstanding acting, dancing, singing and musical accompaniment, and exquisite costumes designed by the School's visiting art Mistress, Norah Neilson Gray. The creative energy expended in 1922 is particularly impressive. The production by Miss Ferguson, the games Mistress, of *The Search for a Happy Mortal* delighted its audiences:

> Artistic staging included skilful manipulation of lime-light to add charm to the picture of fairy-land, the scene of the play. Beautiful dancing was the outstanding feature.
>
> (School Magazine 1922, p. 15)

A month later Miss Linford's pupils achieved a *tour de force* in the production of a specially written operetta entitled *The Stolen Princess*, an enchanting fairy comedy. The main part of the libretto was composed by Miss Linford, while the music, and in many cases, the words of the songs were the work of her pupils. *Alice in Wonderland* was staged in June of that year.

The following year *The Merchant of Venice* was performed, Miss Knott the music teacher taking the part of Shylock, with musical arrangement by Miss Linford and Miss Aitken. In the summer term of 1924 the School produced the opera *Merrie England*.

By the time Miss Waugh retired she had established a real love of drama, and during the early 1930s Miss Katherine MacArthur found a community most receptive to her dramatic skills. With the support of Miss Ford and Miss Lakeman, there followed something of a four-year fiesta of drama, *The School for Scandal* being followed by *Hamlet*, *She Stoops to Conquer*, and entertainments based on Sir Walter Scott's novels and the life of Fanny Burney. With the departure in 1934 of Miss MacArthur and Miss Ford came a hiatus in the performance of full-length plays, which ended when Miss MacArthur was appointed Headmistress after the War.

The St Columba's School Society produced plays on the school stage about every three years (see Chapter Twelve). Staff appeared in some of these alongside former pupils.

Throughout the headships of Miss Waugh and Miss McMurtrie dancing displays were annual events. In some years they took the form of informal open afternoons, and in others they were evening performances with stage lighting. Under Miss Bisset, games Mistress from 1913 until 1917, this art form reached new heights of creativity:

> The classes have so increased in numbers and in proficiency that this festivity has come to be regarded as one of the events of the School year.
> (School Magazine 1917, p. 16)

With the collaboration of an extremely talented music department, troupes of elves, fairies, flowers and nursery characters year after year tripped their colourful way across the school stage. National dances in costume were a regular feature, as were ballets, some of them written by the pupils. One of the most talented of Miss Bisset's pupils was Daintry MacMorland (Johnson), remembered by her classmate Jean Graham (Jackson) as a bright, bubbly girl, tremendous fun, whose high spirits were on occasion the source of innocent trouble. In 1916 Daintry danced a solo entitled 'Invocation to Spring':

> Daintry was supported by eight children who were either flowers or trees. This was followed by a Grecian scarf dance by Phyllis Todd and Daintry Johnson in costume.
> (School Magazine 1916, p. 31)

Miss Bisset's successors lived up to the expectations she had created. Miss Diana Callard (1924-28) introduced more graceful movements into Swedish drill and was a particularly talented teacher of dancing. In the 1930s the dancers displayed 'natural movement exercises' and exercises in 'expression training', as well as choreographed dances.

***Inter-form trophies***
Senior Gymnastics, Sports, Junior Gymnastics, Tidiness of Form Room, Music (singing)

The School's Musical Association arranged several concerts each year, including the senior concert in June and the lower school concert at the end of the Easter term. The first concert of the season was always given by the music staff. In 1937 a chamber music concert was added to the list of regular features, Miss Renton having started a chamber music class. There was also the inter-form singing trophy competition, with the trophy, gifted by Betty Cowan (Mories), presented by an outside adjudicator. A new gramophone was acquired in 1932, and, with the gifts of gramophone records by former pupils and friends of the School, it proved a useful addition to the hall platform. Miss Peterkin gave talks to the Upper School, illustrated by recordings. From the mid-1930s onwards the Musical Association invited former pupils, some of whom had become professional musicians, such as Phyllis Walker, Doris Tyrrell (Arthur), Joyce Barr (Nicol), Amy Fryers and Una Morrison (Bremner), to the School to give recitals.

The School's diction pupils gave noted dramatic recitals, in which they could exercise their dramatic skills without having to mount a full-scale production. Miss Kathleen Morrison, visiting diction teacher from 1927 until 1935, rehearsed them and put on two performances a year, and in 1930 started annual diction competitions.

Miss Patton's *soirées françaises* were renowned for their polished character. The entire proceedings were conducted in French. Each form, from IIIB upwards, performed a sketch, recitations or songs; Form VIA in 1937 put on a three-act play. The object was to teach not merely correct pronunciation, but authentic intonation, something which Miss Patton likened to the 'tune' of the language.

School concerts were not the only occasions for the display of musical ability: on a daily basis the piano pupils also mounted the hall platform, taking it in turns to play the hymn for Prayers. In the magazine of Easter 1908, the statue of Helen of Troy, from her vantage point in the School's entrance hall, describes the daily scene:

> I observe a child of uncertain age lingering in the passage after second bell. Then she enters the office and returns shaking in her shoes. She has told the head-mistress the number of the hymn she has elected to play. She re-appears at the first interval covered either with glory or shame, generally the former.

Miss Waugh also introduced the practice of requiring every girl to address the School on a subject of her choice: the 'much dreaded speeches' bemoaned by the magazine of 1910. Maidie Hart (Bridge) recalled speaking from the platform, at the age of eight, on the (probably wholly appropriate) subject of 'Butterflies'.

On certain special occasions it was the pupils who had the pleasure of being entertained by the staff. Miss Waugh loved parties, and was in the habit of arranging them for pupils, especially at Christmas time. Typical was the Christmas party of 1924 for the Upper School:

> It was a very jolly party indeed. The hall was gaily decorated, and the programme with its artistic ornamentation was a thing of beauty. After a couple of dances, we enjoyed a delightful supper, a credit to the Domestic Science pupils who had helped in its preparation. Then came a great surprise: the Mistresses had prepared a variety entertainment for our benefit! . . . Songs and dances were encored one after the other, but the most popular items of all were a highly entertaining burlesque of Grand Opera and a Jazz Band!
>
> (School Magazine 1925-26, pp. 16-17)

What one would give to have been there on that occasion!

## Visitors to the hall platform

There was always an enthusiasm for drama in the School in Miss Waugh's day, but every few years there emerged an Upper School more than usually devoted to it. Perhaps some of the inspiration for the school productions of the 1921-22 session was derived from an event which drove the girls of that year almost wild with rapture, a visit by the famous Shakespearean actor Sir Johnston Forbes-Robertson:

> We shall never forget our feelings of mingled trepidation and delight, when the famous actor shook us by the hand, while remarking delightedly on the acoustic properties of the Hall!
>
> (School Magazine 1922, p.4)

Expectation was more than satisfied by his lecture-recital on 'Romance and Reality in Shakespeare's plays':

> The event, round which our whole existence had seemed to centre, was now a memory – but a memory which stirred up a deep pride that such a man should stand upon our school stage . . . and an overwhelming admiration.
>
> (School Magazine 1922, pp. 10-11)

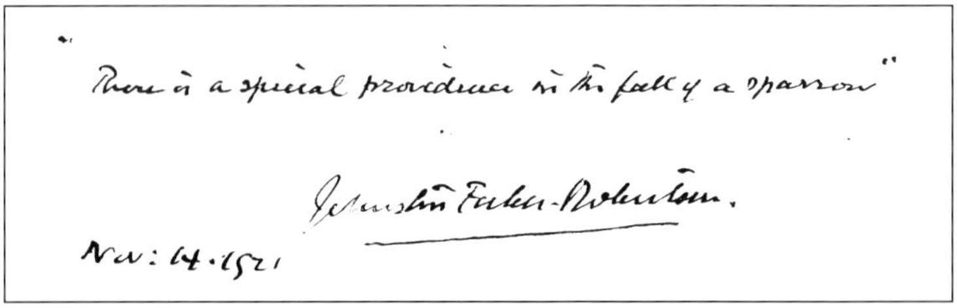


*From the Autograph Album*

He returned the following year to lecture on 'An Actor's View of Shakespeare': 'an unforgettable experience', in the words of the magazine.

Miss McMurtrie liked to invite guest speakers who reflected her great interest in current affairs, and during the 1930s her pupils heard lectures by Mr Donald Grant on subjects such as the League of Nations, the rise in power of Japan, and the Sino-Japanese conflict, and the threat to Europe of German nationalism. The girls often took the opportunity to ask questions and an intelligent summary of each lecture was written for the magazine.

The subscription concerts, which had flourished under Miss Waugh, continued for three years, bringing to the hall platform the London String Quartet, the Budapest String Quartet, Moiseiwitsch, Harriet Cohen, John Goss, Myra Hess, Jan Smeterlin and the Scottish National Players, among others.

## Venturing outwards

The First Kilmacolm Guide Company (the 'School Guides') was started in 1917 under Miss Bisset as Captain. It went on from strength to strength, under the leadership of Miss Reid and a succession of games Mistresses. Miss McIntyre helped to found the Second Kilmacolm Company in 1919. Miss Reid was District Commissioner for Kilmacolm from 1935 until 1943. The Guides enjoyed their first of many camps, at Toward Point, in 1922. Miss Mudie, the mathematics Mistress, took over as Captain in 1931 and remained until she left for VAD work in 1940. Miss Bowie, the Head of the Preparatory School, had a long association with Guiding in Kilmacolm: she was Brown Owl of the First Kilmacolm Brownie Pack from 1925 until 1943, and served terms as Guide Captain and District Commissioner. After the War another preparatory teacher and Old Girl, Doris Vaughan (Johnston) was District Commissioner for Kilmacolm for several years in the 1950s.

One former Kilmacolm Guide, Eleanor Murray (Morrison), who left school in 1923, became Chief Commissioner of the Girl Guides of South Africa from 1964 until 1969, and was made National President of the Girl Guides Association of South Africa for life. She also served as Treasurer of the World Association of Girl Guides and Girl Scouts. She was awarded the Silver Fish for her services to Guiding.

The first and only pre-War school trip abroad was in 1933. It was a highly successful visit, remarkable to modern eyes for the absence of any accompanying teacher from the School. The group was taken by train to London by the French Mistress, Mademoiselle Duranton, and thence with fifty other schoolgirls from English schools by their Parisian hostess, Mademoiselle Hamilius, to Paris. The group stayed at the Abbaye-aux-Bois, a convent run by nuns as a hostel for students, and were looked after by the nuns and the French teaching staff under Mademoiselle Hamilius, who also accompanied them back to London. There they were met by Mademoiselle Duranton, to be accompanied home.

Not everyone might be fortunate enough to go on a trip to Paris, but the whole school could join in the activities of the Venture Society, set up in 1933, to provide a variety of activities other than music and games. For the next six years the lives of pupils were enriched by excursions, nature rambles, debates, lectures, mock trials, dramatic entertainments, films and garden

*School group at Versailles, 1933. Maidie Bridge is at centre front*

*opposite, upper: Guide Camp at Dunure, 1930. Miss Stephens, Captain, centre of middle row*

*opposite, left: Miss Mudie, Captain, Camp at Kildonan, 1933*

*opposite, right: Miss MacArthur, Camp at King's Cross, Arran, 1932*

*Form picnic at Blairmore, c 1926*

There were many outings and picnics in the environs of Kilmacolm, and others to places such as Loch Lomond and Blairmore on Loch Long.

parties. There were many visits to Glasgow, to the theatre, the Empire Exhibition, the offices of *The Glasgow Herald*, and Templeton's carpet factory. The War, blackout and travel difficulties put an end to the Venture Society.

## Blue and Scarlet

> Had any stranger happened to stroll into School last January, and walked through the class-rooms, he would possibly have been surprised to see them decked with gigantic posters and notices, while the 'young ladies' of the establishment stalked about decked in bright blue or scarlet ribbons.
>
> (School Magazine 1910, p. 2)

A political crisis in 1909 led Prime Minister Asquith to call a general election in January 1910:

> From Land's End to John O'Groats the country was ringing with talk of Free Trade, Finance Bills, and foreign invasion.
>
> (Ibid., p. 21)

The School was infected with the mood of fervent political debate; there was also a determination to show that 'St Columba's is not a select seminary for young ladies', in the words of the magazine. To the delight of her pupils, Miss Waugh gave permission for a mock election in the School. The candidates were 'Sir N Mowat' for the Liberals, proposed by 'Mr K Adams', and 'the Right Honourable M G Brown' for the Unionists, introduced by 'Mr D Hunter', alias sixth formers Anne (Nannie) Mowat, Kitty Adams, Margery Graham Brown and Doris Hunter. Electioneering was enthusiastic, and the chiefs had, 'marshalled their forces on both sides and primed them well with facts and figures'.

***'Sir N Mowat'***

***'Mr K Adams'***

On the day of the mock election the candidates addressed the meeting and sat down 'amidst cheers and hisses', and the debate was then thrown open to the floor. After a lively session of questions, answers and heckling, the voting took place:

> In a short time it was declared that The Right Honourable M G Brown, the Unionist Candidate, was elected by a considerable majority. The cheers and hisses were loud and prolonged.

Margaret Holmes, whose father was to become MP for Govan in the election of December 1911, was a fervent supporter of the Liberal party. Her lifelong interest in politics had already begun, inspired by her parents, but it was at St Columba's, and probably at this mock election, that she had her first taste of political activity:

> I used to go to school with my pockets full of Liberal pamphlets . . . 'Down with the House of

*'The Rt Hon M G Brown'*

*'Mr D Hunter'*

> Lords' and all that kind of thing, . . . and all my little school friends were waving Union Jacks to show that they were members of the Conservative Party.
>
> (Interview recorded by Mrs Maureen Lochrie for Paisley Museum, 1981)

At the end of 1911 Margaret Holmes left St Columba's to go to Westminster with her family; she sent back an account of the House of Commons for the 1913 magazine. After her marriage to William Wedgwood Benn, Liberal MP for Leith, who later became Viscount Stansgate, she was politically active on his behalf; her most important political legacy, though, was her son, the Right Honourable Tony Benn, MP. Although in a minority, she was not the only Liberal in the School. There were in Kilmacolm two congregations of the Free Church, which was traditionally inclined to support the Liberal cause, and one Old Kirk, which might have been expected to favour the Conservative and Unionist side: perhaps the result of the mock election was not an entirely foregone conclusion.

## The spirit of the School

What kind of school had the Company and the Headmistresses created at Kilmacolm? It was not like the public schools of England with their robust insistence on team spirit, their multiplicity of rules, their denial of femininity and their social exclusivity: nor did it conform to the rigorously academic, work-hard-play-hard, fast-paced style of the Girls' Public Day School Trust schools and St Leonards. The regime at St Columba's was gentler, catering for the needs of artistic and sensitive girls as well as the highly energetic.

Standards of music lessons and performance were very high indeed. Art teaching was inspirational, and some wonderfully creative work was done on the school stage. In some areas of the curriculum higher standards were undoubtedly reached in the Park School, with its tradition of science, its high academic profile and its university families. At St Columba's the standard of teaching was high and many girls were prepared for higher education, but there was a serene acceptance that not every girl would leave school with qualifications:

> Perhaps she might never gain a Leaving Certificate, but she could be interested, she could be kind and wise, and she could be a centre of happiness.
>
> (Resumé of Miss McMurtrie's speech at Prizegiving 1933, School Magazine 1933, p. 6)

Diversity of talents was respected and enrichment of the personality was the goal. Friendly cooperation was encouraged, and the reception which the Park School girls and Mistresses were given in 1939 shows that it had become a communal habit of mind.

Until the Second World War began many of the pupils left St Columba's around the age of thirteen or fourteen and were sent to boarding school in England, so that until 1938 the number of girls taking the leaving certificate at the School was always in single figures. From then on it was in double figures, including those who, from 1942 onwards, took the examination of the Oxford and Cambridge Joint Board and the Oxford School Certificate. It may partly have been the desire for their daughters to sit these exams that motivated parents to send them to boarding school, but it was also a wish to let them broaden their horizons and meet new friends. The boarding-school finish was considered desirable in families that could afford it.

A feature of St Columba's dating from its beginnings and persisting today is its family spirit, shown in the number of former pupils sending their children there, wherever in the world they found themselves after marriage. The village site fostered strong local connections. Some girls even acquired husbands, met in the Preparatory School, as well as an education at St Columba's.

Despite the rural surroundings, the School was not a cultural backwater. The Headmistresses fostered aspects of school life which made the School look outside itself, such as the subscription concerts with their cosmopolitan mix of players, the charitable work, and the lectures by invited speakers. Old Girls were encouraged to write for the magazine about their new lives and to come back to report. The news from this front was most encouraging, proving beyond question that 'St Columba's was not a select seminary for young ladies'.

*Chapter Six*

# Learning to Fly: Miss Waugh's and Miss McMurtrie's girls

> With mixed feelings of joy and sorrow, I cast a lingering look at the School buildings as the car rounded the corner. School days left behind! It seemed almost too much to grasp – but at last the chance had come to learn to fly.
>
> (Winifred Drinkwater, School Magazine 1930-31, p. 13)

The educational aims stated in the prospectus for 1926-27 are as follows:

> . . . to prepare girls for the duties and responsibilities of social life, and to enable those who desire it to proceed to the wider training of the Universities, Colleges of Music, Schools of Art, etc.

Throughout Miss McMurtrie's headship, too, the school prospectus proclaimed these aims in similar terms. In fact, to judge from the record of

***Miss Waugh with the sixth form, 1904-05***

Back row: Mabel Brydie, Chica MacNab, Cara Leask, May MacNab
Front row: Janie Wood (Head Girl), Christina McCrone, Miss Waugh, Anne Fullarton, Edith Grieve

***Mlle Lacaille with the fifth form, 1904-05***
Back row:
Lulu Clarke,
Cicely Twist,
Greta Fleming,
Daisy Lang
Front row:
J (Daisy) Burnet,
Mlle Lacaille,
M Ward,
Marjorie Martin

achievement of Miss Waugh's and Miss McMurtrie's girls, the School succeeded in preparing very many of them for an active and independent role in life. The prominence given to social preparation perhaps reflects parental concerns and anxieties about education for girls which still existed. In practice the girls left school equipped to make a creditable appearance in a world not bounded by tennis courts and drawing rooms. And the two world wars tested the abilities and characters of the young women of this time in ways that they could never have dreamed of when they started school.

Both Headmistresses sent many girls on to the Colleges of Music and Schools of Art, as Chapters Three and Four have shown. University beckoned many others. The first girl to go to university from St Columba's School was Jane Marshall (Janie Wood), Head Girl in 1904-05, who had attended the School from the first day. She matriculated at Glasgow University in 1905, and after one year there went up to Girton College, Cambridge in 1906, emerging in 1909 with a pass in the Modern and Medieval Languages Tripos – but with no degree, for women were still not permitted to graduate from Cambridge or Oxford.

The Scottish universities did award degrees to women, and Margaret Renwick (Daisy Lang), Head Girl for two years, 1906-08, graduated with the degree of MA from Glasgow University in 1911. Lulu Clarke, who had passed the University Preliminary Examination in the same year, 1907, died before finishing her examinations for the degree of BSc. Anne (Nannie) Mowat gained a pass in the Economics Tripos from Newnham College, Cambridge in 1915 and the same year Katherine Tancock (Kitty Adams), joint Head Girl with Nannie Mowat in 1911-12, passed with second class honours in modern history at Somerville College, Oxford. Katherine G Ludlow (Wood) also went to Somerville College and passed the final exams, about which she wrote rather ruefully, in 1918:

***Margaret (Daisy) Lang, Head Girl 1906-07 and 1907-08***

> I feel a little bitter at the moment on the subject of degrees, since I am sitting for the exam myself in a fortnight, though I get no degree as a result, even supposing I do get through!
>
> (School Magazine 1918, p. 6)

The Old Girls were encouraged to write about their university experiences for the magazine, and several accounts of the joys of college life were produced to enthral and enthuse the schoolgirls back at St Columba's. Dorothy Whyte, at Newnham in 1920, described a classroom setting very different from that of Miss Waugh's establishment:

> A mind accustomed to the discipline of St Columba's received several shocks. Not a class arises when its lecturer arrives, though it may stamp and clap if it feels inclined. . . . Not a class sits in solemn silence through the lecture, unless perchance it is dull (and not always then), but every argument proved receives its applause, every piece of apparatus is cheered, and every witty point is recognised appreciatively.
>
> (School Magazine 1920, p. 6)

Dorothy Whyte came down in 1923 having passed the Geography Tripos, and went on to have an interesting and varied career. She taught at Craigholme School, and was acting curator of Paisley Museum and Art Galleries during the Second World War, drawing on her expertise gained there on Paisley shawls to write several monographs on the subject. She spent three years on the editorial staff of R & W Chambers, and then continued her career as a museum consultant and specialist on costume (and shawls in particular) and was appointed Vice-Chairman of the Costume Society of Scotland in 1963.

Janie Wood went from Girton to an Oxford teacher training college, and taught until her marriage a few years later. There followed at first a steady trickle, and then a stream, of girls from St Columba's into university and teaching. Most of them had to look to English schools for jobs, for the public and endowed schools in Scotland, even for girls, still mostly employed male teachers. Women might get jobs in the independent schools, such as St Columba's, but there were few of these north of the Border. During the First World War there was a sudden opening up of the teaching profession to women, as many women were asked to take the place of a schoolmaster who had joined the forces.

Katherine Tancock (Adams) and her sister Meta were thrown in at the deep end in their first posts in village schools in Hampshire, to replace teachers who had joined the army. Katherine went on to obtain her teaching diploma from St George's, Edinburgh, with distinction, and was in later years appointed history Mistress at King Edward High School for Girls, Birmingham; after her marriage she and her husband set up their own school. Margery Graham Brown, Head Girl in 1909-10 and 1910-11, having studied at the Sorbonne and having gained her Teachers' Certificate from Cambridge Training College in 1915, also taught in place of a man during the War. She went on later to Lady Margaret Hall, Oxford, and graduated with a second class honours degree in modern history in 1926, and then continued her teaching career. Anne Mowat, after distinguished war work at the Admiralty, for which she was awarded the MBE in 1918 (when she was only twenty-four), became Headmistress of St Cuthbert's School, Bournemouth in 1932. A few years later she moved her school to Lillesden in Kent, from which she retired in 1962, still Chairman of the Association of Headmistresses of Independent Schools.

Outside teaching the range of options for pre-First World War leavers was very limited. Within the teaching profession there was a demand for kindergarten specialists and 'physical culture' teachers, both of them respectable and attractive fields for educated young women from the beginning of the century. St Columba's sent many girls to Bedford and Dartford to train (see Chapter Three). Margaret Cork (Harrower) studied at the Froebel Educational Institute in London, and taught in preparatory schools. Her sister Winifred Gentleman, after taking her Diploma at Glasgow School of Art, went to work at an experimental school where self-development and expression were encouraged. Later she too qualified under the National Froebel Union.

When the medical schools of the universities were opened to women in the 1890s, they did not tarry on the doorstep. The School's first medical graduate was Winifred Bruce (Crawford) who, in 1916, before she took her finals at Glasgow University, was appointed acting house surgeon at the Royal Alexandra Infirmary, Paisley. She was followed by Helen Lochhead (Wingate) in 1920, who went to work at the Royal Infirmary before setting up in general practice, and was elected a Fellow of the Royal Faculty of Physicians and Surgeons in Glasgow in 1938. Katherine Garrett (Kitty Shankland), Head Girl in 1916-17, took her MB, ChB at Glasgow in 1923.

*Katherine (Kitty) Shankland, Head Girl 1916-17*

Elinor Rutherford (Jackson), Head Girl in 1917-18, went up to Newnham College, Cambridge in 1918 and was, for her two years there, among the most distinguished of the University's medical undergraduates. She wrote in her letter to the school magazine that, the previous October, women had outnumbered men by ten to one. (Despite this, the dons had not yet shed their habit of addressing the students in lectures as 'Gentlemen'!). Elinor voiced the expectations of very many people when she wrote:

*Elinor Jackson, Head Girl 1917-18*

> Gradually the men began to filter back, and now men and women are in the proportion of 100 to 1. You will understand then that there were bound to be changes, and we are not quite such insignificant worms as we were before the war. We are doing our best now to be accepted by the university, and perhaps before I go down, the women will be seen, too, in cap and gown.
>
> (School Magazine 1919, p. 12)

But, while Oxford did concede degrees to women in 1920, it was not until after the second World War, in 1948, that women from Newnham were permitted to graduate. In 1920 Elinor transferred to Glasgow University, where she graduated MB, ChB in 1924, having been awarded the West of Scotland R A M C prize for the highest aggregate marks in the final examinations for that year; after practising gynaecology, she was elected a Fellow of the Royal College of Surgeons of Edinburgh in 1929 and went into private practice with fellow St Columban Helen Wingate in 1930. After marriage and children she continued to practise, and was a GP in Kirkcudbright for many years.

However reluctant the Cambridge establishment may have been to accept the fact, the War had changed things irrevocably for women. From 1915 onwards the girls who had left school threw themselves into all kinds of war work. The Government encouraged women who had begun their degree courses to continue their studies as part of the national war effort, and some did. Many other St Columbans trained for VAD work and were posted to hospitals at home and in France. Others did voluntary work at canteens in stations and clubs. Wilda Sadler (Binnie) wrote a fascinating account of her work in charge of catering at the Girls' Munition Colony at Covington:

> I came here last October to help in the Club and fell into the open arms of the kitchen, where I have reigned ever since as caterer for eight hundred souls. I spend hot strenuous days guiding cooks and scullions to bright efforts of economy and cleanliness. The economy is doubtful, also the cleanliness.
>
> (School Magazine 1917, p. 9)

One girl did forestry work, another part-time work in a munitions factory, others farm work, gardening, Red Cross supply work, and cleaning sphagnum moss for surgical dressings. May Crawford, having taken her Diploma in Art, worked as a draughtsman in Weir's engineering works. Several did clerical work that had been done by men before the War, some of them in their fathers' offices.

A war story of a different kind is told by the pages of the school magazine listing the Old Boys of St Columba's serving with His Majesty's Forces. Most moving of all is the Roll of Honour with which these war-time issues end, listing the names of the nine Old Boys who gave their lives.

After the War ended Miss Waugh continued to send her girls out into the world well prepared for further training, whether professional, vocational or commercial. Many distinguished themselves in their fields. Teaching attracted very many of the graduates. Euphemia (Effie) Russell was one of Miss Waugh's outstanding pupils: the School's first gold medallist in 1926, and Head Girl in 1926-27, she won an exhibition to Lady Margaret Hall, Oxford, to read Greats, and graduated in 1932. Her promising teaching career was cruelly cut short in 1941, when she was killed in an air raid over Paisley. Others went on from university into social services, one into translation work and one into journalism. Elizabeth Handasyde, Head Girl in 1922-23, took a first in English from Edinburgh in 1928, and a B Litt from Lady Margaret Hall, Oxford, in 1931. She published her book on George Granville, Lord

***Kilmacolm Red Cross Volunteers, 1915, including four Old Girls***

Back row: third from right, Frances Hendry; far right, Nancy Hendry

Front row: far left, Agnes McCrone; far right, Greta Fleming

***Euphemia (Effie) Russell, Head Girl 1926-27***

**Roll of honour**

JAMES W. BROWN, MC., Lieut. 11th Batt. Royal Scots, missing, believed killed.

WILFRED GRAHAM, Lieut. 3rd Batt. H.L.I., att. Ist Batt. Cameronians, wounded and missing Dec. 1914.

HENRY S. DAVIDSON, Lieut. 3rd Batt. att. Ist Batt. H.L.I. killed May 1915.

JAMES MACLAY, 2nd Lieut. 7th Batt. Scottish Rifles, missing, reported killed, June 1915.

ARTHUR LANG, Lieut. 6th Batt. Argyll and Sutherland Highlanders, killed.

GORDON SCOTT, Lieut. 3th Batt. att. 2nd Batt. Argyll and Sutherland Highlanders, killed.

JOHN M. MOWAT, Lieut. 3rd Batt. North Staffords, att. R.F.C., accidentally killed while flying.

OSWALD FARQUHAR, Lieut. Q.O. Glasgow Yeomanry, killed March 1918.

ALEC. MACNAB, 2nd Lieut. R.F.A., died of wounds.

***Roll of Honour, 1914-18***

***Elizabeth Handasyde, Head Girl 1922-23***

***Agnes (Nancy) Macdonald, Head Girl 1918-19***

Landsdowne, in 1933, and embarked on a career in adult education and university settlement work, which eventually led her into a responsible post in welfare work with the Ministry of Health. Dorothy Courtney was awarded the Diploma in Social Organisation and Public Service by the University of Leeds in 1922 and, by 1946, as Principal Boarding-out Officer for the London County Council, she was helping to rehabilitate girls from approved schools. Nancy Macdonald, Head Girl in 1918-19, graduated BA Hons from St Hilda's, Oxford, in 1927, and became Assistant Editor with McDougall's Publishing in Edinburgh. She then went to R & W Chambers for whom she edited, in 1950, Chambers's Shorter English Dictionary. She was one of the chief compilers of the revised edition of Chambers's Twentieth Century Dictionary, published in 1959, and for her revised edition of 1972 she was awarded the OBE. Jean Laurie and Janet Macdonald became doctors in the late 1920s; Janet was killed in a road accident three years after graduating. Betty Beaver (Irvine), emerged as the most distinguished dental graduate of her year at Leeds University in 1930, and went on to work in the public health field. Margaret Kerr (Fullarton) graduated with first class Honours in zoology from Glasgow University in 1930, and lectured first at Queen's University, Belfast, and then at Leeds University.

***Margery Reid, Head Girl 1919-20***

The young women who left school from 1920 onwards found that the world was at their feet. Jean Findlay (Parker), who left in 1927, trained at Dartford, and in the 1930s while teaching in Montreal was on the committee set up to develop physical training in Canada. Later, after involvement with the League of Health and Beauty, she had a similar post in South Africa. Margery Reid, Head Girl in 1919-20, worked for the education department of the London County Council, who gave her leave of absence on a number of occasions in the 1950s and 1960s to work for the Kenyan Government in the rehabilitation of the Mau-Mau held in detention camps, for which purpose she learned Kikuyu, and to go Thessalonica with a Quaker team to do educational work, this time learning the local Greek dialect. Mary Cognasso (Marshall), LRAM, BA Hons, (in French, Spanish and Italian) was evacuated during the Second World War in charge of fifty girls from Roedean to a school in Canada; she became the Head of the Canadian school, and after her marriage took her MA in Spanish literature from the Ohio State University, followed by a Ph D in Spanish while teaching at the University and writing textbooks. Muriel Barnett (Robertson) took her MA Honours in geography from Edinburgh University in 1930 and went on to have a career that included meteorological observation for the British Glaciological Survey, university lecturing and freelance journalism, in which she was still active in 1998.

***Winifred Drinkwater***

In a class of her own was Winifred Drinkwater, who in 1930 at the age of seventeen became the youngest woman to qualify as an aircraft pilot, after only a month's training. She wrote about her training for the school magazine, remarking on the most difficult feat to master before the first solo flight: landing, mental preparation for which continued even in her sleep:

> . . . I found myself, in my dreams, trying to make the butter-knife do a three-point landing on the butter, or I lay awake mentally landing the bed.
>
> (School Magazine 1930-31, p. 14)

By the age of twenty-one she was the youngest commercial pilot in Britain and was qualified as a ground engineer. It was while she was dismantling an engine that Francis Short, the director of Short Brothers, the Belfast aircraft manufacturers, visited Renfrew Aerodrome, asked to be introduced to the young celebrity, and within four hours was engaged to her. They were married two weeks later.

During the 1930s and 1940s many more avenues were opened to women, to the benefit of Miss McMurtrie's girls. Once again the unlooked-for occurrence of war opened up new opportunities and challenges.

Secretarial training had long been open to women. With St Columbans the Glasgow and West of Scotland Commercial College was popular, and some of the girls were, by the late 1930s, taking a training course after gaining a university degree. A new path taken by several St Columbans from the late 1930s onwards was that of medical secretary.

Domestic Science courses continued to attract very many girls, the overwhelming number of them choosing the Glasgow and West of Scotland College of Domestic Science for their training. This course of study might now lead to a career: at least six St Columbans went on to teach at the College during the 1930s and 1940s. One such was Moyra Gourlay (Clark), who trained there from 1931 until 1933 and won the prize for the best student. She was probably taught by a fellow former pupil, Alice Jackson, who in 1940 became Head of the College's institutional catering department. Margaret Little, who qualified in the early 1930s, became Principal Lecturer in haute cuisine twenty years later. Joan Hairs won the prize for the best cookery student of her year, and by 1949 was lecturing at Natal Technical College, Durban. As well as teaching, a domestic science diploma could lead to a career in catering, and, for Elsie Lilburn (Cook) in 1934, dietetics in an Edinburgh hospital.

*Margaret Little, front row, 3rd from right, c 1920*

*Doris Johnston, Head Girl 1940-41*

*Jean Anderson, Head Girl 1942-43*

*Betty Peden Fyfe in Labrador for the Grenfell Mission, 1936*

Froebel training continued to be popular. It could lead to posts in kindergartens like that of St Columba's and in nursery schools at the opposite end of the social spectrum. Doris Vaughan (Johnston) left school in 1941, took her NFU certificate at Bedford where she won the award for most distinguished student, and in 1948 came back to St Columba's to teach in the Preparatory School for four years. She retired in 1985 after twenty-five years' teaching at Glasgow Academy (and brought her classes of little boys to Kilmacolm on many picnics). One or two other girls trained at the Rachel MacMillan College in London and went to teach in nursery schools. Isabel McNeil (McGeachy) worked at the open-air nursery school in Niddrie.

Women who became teachers might now hope to obtain secondary school posts outside the private sector, and from the mid-1930s a few St Columbans taught in Local Education Authority schools. But until the 1940s, most of the women who qualified as teachers took up posts in independent schools, many in England, some further afield. Janet Scobie (Jenny Speirs), who in 1941 won the gold medal and A M Adam bursary and was joint winner of the Carson award, had a long career in education in Nigeria, finally becoming Headmistress of a girls' school. Another of Miss McMurtrie's girls, Martha Steedman (Hamilton), after serving in Bhutan as a missionary, became Principal of Paljor Namgyal High School in Sikkim, and later Headmistress of St Leonards School.

Some came back to teach at St Columba's. Mona Laird returned to her old school to teach from 1944 until 1949, when she became Headmistress of Craigmount School at Scone, which she later transferred to the Hawick area. Jean Paterson (Anderson) came back to teach from 1958 until 1966, taking classes in the Junior School and teaching English in the Senior School; she later became Headmistress of the Beacon School in Bridge of Allan. Betty Peden Fyfe, the daughter of the Chairman, went to the Royal College of Art in London in 1927; before establishing herself in her teaching career, she made several trips to Labrador to work for the Grenfell Mission looking after the children of trappers and fishermen. A gifted teacher and craftswoman, she combined her part-time teaching job and service to the St Columba's School Society with continuing work for the Mission, becoming Secretary of its Scottish Association. Another former-pupil-turned-teacher, from Miss McMurtrie's time, Kathleen Weir, spent a short time at Perth Theatre before returning to St Columba's to teach in 1949, later becoming Head of the Junior School and then Deputy Head.

Several others achieved notable success in various fields. Margaret Sykes-Wright (Kennedy), who left school in 1933, became a freelance feature-writer and a scriptwriter and broadcaster for the BBC; an interesting career was cut short by her early death. Her slightly younger contemporary Janet Shearer (Murray) made a career in politics for which she was awarded the OBE in 1958, although her campaign as a Conservative candidate in the general election of 1954 was unsuccessful. She later became Lady Avonside. Margaret Sheila Hewitson (Cannon), who also left in the 1930s, was a teacher for many years before becoming the Chairman of Scottish Conservative Women, and being awarded the MBE for political services in 1986. Kathleen Macdonald, gold medallist and Head Girl in 1933-34, after a career in teaching became Principal Educational Psychologist for Stirlingshire. Maidie Hart (Bridge), gold medallist and Head Girl in 1934-35, took a First in English from St Andrews University in 1939, and went on to play a major role in ecumenical affairs in the church. She made an important contribution to the promotion and advancement of women's role in church and society. She was National President of the Church of Scotland's Women's Guild, and as a member of the executive of the Women's National Commission she coordinated the events in the UK to mark International Women's Year, 1975. She founded the Scottish Convention of Women and was a founder member of the Ecumenical Forum of European Christian Women. Nancy Spells (Harrison) worked for ICI before 1944, and in later years was Co-ordinator of International Relations for the British Federation of University Women; she also served on the finance committee of the International Federation of University Women.

***Maidie Bridge, Head Girl 1934-35***

The School's first architecture student, Esmée Bodgener (Cousin), joint winner of the Carson award in 1941, was one of the most distinguished students of her year at the Royal College of Science and Technology, Glasgow, winning the bronze medal in 1943 and the prize of the Royal Incorporation of Architects in 1944. In 1947 she was awarded the Tite Prize by the RIBA. A year later Edith Hawley (Forrester) went to the Royal College of Science and Technology to study engineering, the first St Columban to do so. Beatrice Cahalan (Beta Campbell), gold medallist and joint winner of the Janet Waugh scholarship in 1943, took her BSc Honours from Edinburgh University and worked for the London Scientific Research Section of London University as an atomic scientist. Industry and the law were slow to utilise the skills of women. But from the 1940s even these areas were being colonised by St Columbans.

Only a couple of girls entered medical courses in the 1930s, one of whom was Morag MacArthur, gold medallist in 1932. She became a public health physician, and as County Medical Officer for Renfrewshire in the 1960s found herself in contact with her old school in a professional capacity. She had kept up a lively interest in all the School's affairs, and was a Director from 1963 until 1985. There was a change in the trend in the 1940s, when fourteen girls from the School graduated in medicine.

One or two girls went into dentistry, and the 1930s saw the emergence of nursing as a career suitable for middle-class girls. It became a popular choice. In the 1940s various other paramedical outlets presented themselves, and girls went into orthoptics, pharmacy, radiography, radiotherapy, speech therapy and occupational therapy.

Phyllis Howie, who left school in 1940 and began her career as a kindergarten teacher, retrained ten years later in occupational therapy. She came top in all England in her final exams, and after practising for a few years and helping to pioneer the country's first functional assessment unit, she took a higher qualification and went into research. In 1968 she was appointed Principal of the College of Occupational Therapy in Liverpool. In 1983 the College of Occupational Therapists accorded her its highest honour, making her an Honorary Fellow of the College.

Another new career presented itself in the late 1930s:

> You want to be a Hospital Almoner? Very well, you must train here at the University Settlement for two years. After that, you will spend one year in London.
>
> (School Magazine 1937-38, p. 20)

So wrote Anna Keys in an article describing her training. The London year would be spent with the Charity Organisation Society and in one of the big hospitals. All the girls would have been familiar with the work of the University Settlements and the COS, thanks to the School's active interest in charities (see Chapter Five). Margaret Moodie (Andrew) became a hospital almoner, and later made an important contribution to the National Deaf Children's Society and other charitable bodies. Some of Miss McMurtrie's girls also did post-graduate courses in social service, and took up social work or welfare work in large companies.

A career in massage and physiotherapy, was, for girls who left school from the late 1920s onwards, a chance to train in exciting new techniques for therapy. Doris Thomson (McCrone) and Martha Pool (Laird) were two of the first to take this path. Doris taught medical electricity in the early 1930s at the Swedish Institute in London and was an examiner in the subject for the Chartered Society of Massage and Medical Gymnastics. Martha was the most distinguished Scottish candidate in the final examination of the Chartered Society of Massage and Medical Gymnastics in 1930, and went on to train in medical electricity and artificial sunlight. After qualifying as a nurse, she completed her training in massage, medical electricity and bio-physics. By 1940 she was working in a mission station in Northern India as a Matron-Inspector in the Indian Army. Back in the more humdrum world of the Edinburgh Orthopaedic Clinic, Betty King was providing massage, medical gymnastics, medical electricity and sun-lamp treatment to the poor of Edinburgh for minimal fees. Ten years later she was Superintendent Physiotherapist at the Western General Hospital in Edinburgh.

Many girls from the School went to train in massage at Glasgow's Western Infirmary, and some of them went on to use their skills in the service of their country. Doris French (Craig) was a masseuse with the VAD from the end of 1941, helping to set up a physiotherapy department in a military hospital, where she and her colleagues:

> . . . massaged, pummelled and exercised hapless Tommies of all shapes and sizes, learned all manner of terms military, and soon were more 'army' than the army.
>
> (School Magazine 1941-43, p. 33)

They also taught exercises to French, Italian and German prisoners of war – of her attempts to train the Vichy prisoners she lamented:

> If only I had been more attentive to Miss Patton and to Mademoiselle!
>
> (Ibid. p. 34)

***A cross-section of 1940s careers***
Lacrosse XII, 1940-41
Back row: Nellie Archibald, Beatrice Campbell, Frances Snodgrass
Second row: Margaret Craig, Joan Craig, Mercedes Park, Esmée Cousin, Edith Forrester
Front row: Hilary Clarke, Enid Miller, Doreen Hairs,
E Cousin, E Forrester and B Campbell were pioneering St Columbans in architecture, engineering and atomic science respectively. Nellie Archibald took her B Sc at St Andrews; Frances Snodgrass (MA, St Andrews) made a career in social service; Mercedes Park (MA, Glasgow) became a teacher of modern languages; Enid Miller went into nursing, and Doreen Hairs trained in physical education.

Once again a War was providing a new challenge for women, and for middle-class, educated women the Second World War proved more of a revolutionary force than the First. During the Second World War the civilian population of Britain was mobilised as in no other country, with the possible exception of Russia. Women volunteered or were called up for a great variety of jobs, some of them highly responsible. Whether she was managing her brother's coffee shamba in Kenya while he was in the Air Force (Cicely Twist), training as an aircraft engineer and becoming an instructress with the Aeronautical Inspection Department of the Ministry of Aircraft production (Betty Fairman [Buchanan]), working on Radar stations for the WAAF (Muriel Gibb), running a play centre for children of war workers in London (Margery Reid), driving tractors and working with farm horses (Waveney Bayly), or felling trees for the Forestry Commission (Elspeth Speirs), the St Columba's girl, like others fortunate enough to have had a serious and sound education, found that she had acquired the discipline, know-how and capacity for hard work necessary to rise to the challenge.

Many found themselves dealing for the first time with situations which they would never have encountered in peace time. For example, the artist Alison McKenzie as an officer in the ATS had to deal with fights among the girls under her charge, and her sister Winifred organised print-making classes for Polish soldiers in St Andrews. Others found opportunities which would not have come in peace time to women recently graduated or newly out of training. Margaret Brown (Burnet) was assistant principal in the Raw Materials department in the Ministry of Supply, a responsible and demanding civil service post, while her sister Mary Rose Arntzenius was working as a programmes engineer with the BBC. Fiona Buchanan was made Head of occupational therapy at the Royal Crichton Hospital, Dumfries, and Jean Walker (Shannon) was Head Physiotherapist at Arbroath Infirmary.

There were representatives from St Columba's in the WAAF, the WRNS, the ATS, the Indian Army, the VAD, the Royal Army Medical Corps, the FANY (First Aid Nursing Yeomanry), Queen Alexandra's Nursing Service, the Mechanised Transport Corps, the Red Cross Transport Service, the Women's Land Army, the National Fire Service, the Women's Auxiliary Police Corps and the YWCA. The school magazine kept Old Girls in touch with each other, a service more vital than ever. Doris Dempster (Richardson) went as a WRNS officer in 1943 to the Quebec Conference, at which Churchill and Roosevelt announced progress in curbing German submarine activity. Isobel Hayward (Cochrane), having become a doctor, achieved the rank of Captain in the Army. Siona Hanscomb, formerly Miss Gunn the games Mistress, was sent to Sicily and Italy to set up and run YWCA clubs for women members of the Forces. She was mentioned in despatches, as was Doreen Paton, WAAF, and perhaps others, of whom the School did not hear. Many Old Boys of course served with His Majesty's Forces, and the magazines for the War years listed those whose service was known to the School.

Those who were at home with family responsibilities joined the WVS and helped with evacuees – of the five hundred who came to Kilmacolm on the first day of the War, many stayed on – as well as canteen and first aid work.

The Kilmacolm canteen fed about eighty evacuees a day for the first two years of war:

> Mrs Cuthbertson (Elsie Hislop) and Mrs Graham (Jean Jackson) are helping as cooks, and other Old Girls as potato peelers and washers-up. A flourishing Forces Canteen . . . now serves on an average seventy suppers and a hundred and fifty teas every evening. Mrs Alan Jackson (Dorothy Jackson) Deputy Leader of the Kilmacolm WVS, is the Secretary, and copes most successfully with numerous official forms, food points and the NAAFI. Mrs Graham, the Emergency Food Officer, is to be the Convener of the WVS Canteen for the Forces, soon to be opened.
>
> (School Magazine 1941-43, p. 37)

After the Clydebank blitz in March 1941 mobile canteens went from Kilmacolm with a large party of volunteers under another Old Girl, Jean Semple (Birkmyre) to feed the homeless.

Letters to the school magazine are a reminder of yet another sphere in which many Old Girls did useful, though often unsung, work: as wives of members of His Majesty's Forces and civil servants overseas they assisted at medical stations and participated in various kinds of voluntary work which but for them would have been left undone.

Both Miss Waugh and Miss McMurtrie realised the importance of careers for women in an uncertain and ever-changing world. They gave personal encouragement to each girl to aim for a worthwhile occupation, and during their headships articles appeared in almost every magazine by former pupils about their training and jobs. The first half of the century had seen progress from the position at which teaching was virtually the only option for women who wished to make their own way in the world, to the point where they could take wing into almost any profession or vocation.

*Chapter Seven*

# Katherine C MacArthur 1945-1966

A year before her retiral at the age of sixty Miss Katherine MacArthur broke the news of her coming departure to her staff. Soon afterwards Miss Croft, the Head of the Preparatory School, heard the mother of one of her new pupils say of the Headmistress:

> Isn't she full of zest and enthusiasm for her work? But, of course, she's young, and it makes all the difference having a young headmistress, doesn't it?
>
> (School Magazine 1965-66, p. 21)

Back in 1934, when Miss MacArthur had been even younger, she had left the School after four years teaching in the Junior School and as English teacher to some of the senior classes. Maidie Hart (Bridge) was in Form IVA when Miss MacArthur first came to St Columba's to teach, and she remembered:

***Miss MacArthur, 1946***

> . . . her arrival in our Form room. She was young, bright and pretty. I'm sure she must have been a little apprehensive as our Form had quite a reputation for being an unruly lot! The question was, of course, how far the 'baddies' could 'take a loan' of her. It did not take them long to find out that they couldn't. For all her quiet demeanour, she had . . . an indisputable air of personal authority and – additionally, that twinkle in the eye and the ready, deep, throaty chuckle that she maintained to the end; and that disarmed even fourteen year olds!
>
> (School Magazine 1987-88, p. 53)

Her English lessons were a joy to all: she 'had us acting our Shakespeare, who suddenly came alive', and 'we twisted her arm to act out a light-hearted poem about St George and the Dragon every Friday afternoon.' She knew how to fan the spark that she found in a pupil such as Maidie, and:

> . . . English became exciting and enthralling as she opened up for me the world of poetry and literature.
>
> (Ibid.)

**Treasure Hunt,**
***SCSS play, 1957***

Left to right: Harry Lester, Katherine MacArthur, R D Linton, Sarah Marr, Seona Anderson, Jim Lester, Joan MacRobert

Katherine MacArthur was educated at Perth Academy and Edinburgh University where she graduated with honours in English in 1929. She went on to teach at Edinburgh Ladies' College and at the Nottingham High School for Girls, a Girls' Public Day School Trust school.

Miss MacArthur's scholarship and wide reading were in evidence nowhere more than in her speeches, especially those at prizegivings, which were literary gems, her wide-ranging and apt allusions and clever humour contributing a lightness of touch which never detracted from their seriousness of purpose. Her thoughtfulness and insight on the subject of teaching ensured frequent invitations to address educational conferences, especially the Association of Headmistresses (to whom she once described her place of work as 'a small but complicated school'). For her other great talent, acting, she had fewer outlets during her headship (although she was a memorable Aunt Anna Rose in the SCSS's *Treasure Hunt* of 1957).

'Miss Mac', as she was known among the girls, was utterly charming in appearance as well as in manner, always beautifully dressed. Her graciousness in dealing with everyone with whom she came into contact pervaded the School and was an influence the pupils carried away with them. Her understanding of her pupils was far-seeing and unblinkered, and they responded, especially those who shared a home with her as boarders, with trust and love.

The baton had been passed to one who understood and valued the best traditions of the School, and who was to continue them, remarkably little changed, into an era quite different from the first half-century.

## Stretching in all directions

Miss MacArthur inherited a school of 249 pupils, which, after twenty-one years of careful husbandry, she passed to her successor as an establishment of 420. The increased demand for places brought several changes. The Preparatory School was outgrowing Shieldhall, and in 1951 the house next door, Westmarch, was bought for £5000 and altered at a cost of £3500, in order that the Preparatory School might reside if not under one roof, at least side by side. The garden of Westmarch at that time extended down as far

*Westmarch from the garden, 1952*

*A corner of the kindergarten, Westmarch, 1952*

as Duchal Road, not far from the main school building, which made a convenient route between the two parts of the School.

Continuing increase in numbers brought the need for a more radical reorganisation. The Preparatory School was relocated to Shalott in September 1958, to share this large house with a decreased number of boarders. The Junior School, Forms IIIB, IIIA and IVB, equivalent to Primary Five, Six and Seven, was also reorganised, by the introduction, in the 1957-58 and the 1958-59 sessions of a double stream into each form. The six classes were transferred from Duchal Road to Shieldhall and Westmarch, vacated by the Preparatory School. Form IVC, which had been the year between Primary Six and Primary Seven, was discontinued.

The top six forms, IVA to Ex-VIth, equivalent of Senior One to Six, had for several years been known as the Senior School, rather than the Upper School, and for the first time they had the main school building to themselves. As the double stream came through from the Junior School, the Senior School grew steadily bigger.

By 1962 the numbers had risen to 420, a total higher than had been envisaged in 1958 when the new system had been put in place. The ratio was 2: 1: 1 between Senior, Junior and Preparatory departments. Over 360 lunches were served by the School each day, and a double shift system for meals had been started in 1959. The final act of stretching in this period was the extension of the school day by twenty minutes in 1963, in order to give more flexibility in the timetable.

## 'A small but complicated School'

With the acquisition of Westmarch, St Columba's now had five buildings, on four sites. The boarding house, Shalott, was converted for use by the Preparatory School at a cost of £10,000 in 1958, with the boarding accommodation now confined to the top floor. Ingenuity was needed to satisfy fire regulations, as it has been in every major alteration the School has undertaken since. Alterations were made to Allanbank in 1954, which was converted into two flats, the top one for rental by Dr Macdonald the modern languages Mistress, and the lower one for the accommodation of the janitor

*The new doors and entrance, 1959, drawn by Morvyn Hood, Form VIA*

*The science block, October 1965*

***The opening of the science block:***
Miss MacArthur,
Sir David Anderson,
Sir Eric Yarrow,
Mr John Tindal

***Sir Eric Yarrow addressing the gathering on the opening of the science block***

and his wife. (Mr and Mrs MacDonald worked for the School as Janitor and Cook from 1948 until 1960. The excellence of Mrs MacDonald's cooking, in particular her speciality of apple dumplings, is well remembered.)

At the main building the entrance hall was panelled in light oak and given a decorative arch and new lighting, all made possible by the gift of the St Columba's School Society, with some help from the Company. A handsome new set of double entrance doors was given by Mrs Graham as a symbol of the life-long interest which her late husband, W Bryce Graham, had taken in the School. There were improvements to the kitchen and servery, and the long cloakroom was made between the hall and the original building in 1961-62. A new set of stacking chairs for the school hall may seem a modest improvement in comparison to these, but they were perhaps just as warmly appreciated by the audience at prizegiving, as they heard Miss MacArthur express her gratitude to the SCSS and other benefactors for this gift, which, to the staff and pupils:

> . . . who have formed the conveyor belt which keeps the chairs in constant motion round the School, . . . will mean nothing short of a technological revolution.
>
> (School Magazine 1959-60, p. 16)

The largest and most troublesome building project of Miss MacArthur's headship was the construction of a new science block, which was built in response to the need created by the Scottish Education Department's introduction of a new science syllabus. It was formally opened in October 1965 by Sir Eric Yarrow. The two-storey building was designed by Frank Burnet and Boston and constructed on part of the Eredine garden at a cost of nearly £30,000, three times the sum the Directors had originally planned to spend on a single-storey prefabricated building. It contained three laboratories, newly equipped and fitted out, which replaced the old and inadequate science rooms in the main building. The original attic science room was given over to art, a purpose which it still serves, and the other, larger, science room became a staffroom and is now a geography room.

## Direct Grant and the problems of finance

The Girls' School Company had to struggle to finance new projects at Kilmacolm, Glasgow and Helensburgh. The schools had for some years depended on the grant-in-aid given by government via the local authority, but grant was not available for capital expenditure or repayment of loans, merely for everyday running costs. Until the late 1950s the Directors acted to expand accommodation whenever it was needed in response to increasing demand for school places and the requirements of the changing curriculum. All three schools were highly successful and were full to capacity, but the financing of capital projects was done on an unsatisfactory hand-to-mouth basis. In 1955 the Directors began to set aside a portion of the revenue from fees as a capital reserve. The application for grant could be made on the difference between the balance of fee revenue and the running costs. There were strict regulations distinguishing expenses which were claimable from those which were not. There were regulations governing the maximum amount that could be set aside and the minimum level for fees.

In 1958 new legislation abolished the Education (Scotland) Fund from which the grants-in-aid were drawn, and the independent schools were invited to apply for Direct Grants. The Company's schools were accepted for the new scheme in the financial year beginning in 1959, with very little change to the regulations imposed by the previous system; the chief difference was that the Local Education Authorities no longer sent representatives to sit on the Board. Over the next few years the Scottish Education Department approved several increases in the sum allowed for capital reserve, and by 1963 it had increased almost sevenfold from the original 1955 allowance.

In 1962 the Company was granted remission of rates by fifty per cent on all its properties by virtue of its charitable status. But during the late 1950s and early 1960s all the other running costs, especially salaries, rose. Equal pay for women teachers came in 1955. Running costs for grant claim had to be estimated accurately in advance. But despite great care in these estimates, and strict economy in the running of the schools, it proved to be impossible to build up any sizeable capital reserve. There were certain costs which were neither claimable as grant nor capital projects, and the capital reserve drained away into the sand almost as fast as it was gathered in.

The Girls' School Company schools were by 1964 three of the twenty-nine Scottish schools receiving Direct Grants, at a cost to the Government of a million and a quarter pounds a year. In 1965 the Scottish Education Department issued Circular 600, declaring that the Scottish education system would henceforth become comprehensive. For the direct-grant schools the signs looked ominous:

> Those authorities in whose areas there are grant-aided schools will no doubt wish also to consult the governing bodies of these schools as to the part they can play in a comprehensive system.
>
> (Circular 600, Section 19)

The seeds of uncertainty about the future of these schools had been sown; the real struggle for survival was still to come.

## The Directors

> The tiniest nut, bolt or screw of equipment is not too trivial for their consideration; the broadest concepts of education are not too extravagant for their sympathy and support.
>
> (Miss MacArthur, Prizegiving 1947, School Magazine 1946-47, p. 16)

There were two chairmen in this period, and they did valiant service for the Girls' School Company in these years. Mr Norman Millar resigned at the end of 1954, after twenty-three years' service, ten of them as Chairman, and Mr John Tindal, on the Board since 1946, took his place. Mr Sutherland the Secretary retired in 1958, and his place was taken by Mr Gordon Wilson. Much credit for the Company's survival in the difficult economic terrain must go to two accountants who became Directors, Mr W Maxwell Simmers in 1952 and Mr G N Ferguson two years later. Maxwell Simmers also served Glasgow Academy as Chairman of the Governors. He had joined the Board in place of Mr William Hill Jack, that old soldier of the Girls' School Company who died in 1950 after forty-two years' active service. G N Ferguson was appointed along with another local man, a former distinguished member of HM Inspectorate of schools, Mr D D Anderson, CBE, after the deaths of two local Directors: Mr James Cuthbertson, a former pupil of St Columba's whose sudden death in 1954 had ended a too-short term of two-and-a-half years as Director, and Sir A T Taylor, a central character in the School's development from the beginning (see Chapter One). D D Anderson retired in 1959, having given much assistance in the Company's dealings with the Scottish Education Department.

***James H Cuthbertson, Director 1952-54 and a stalwart of many S C S S plays:*** His first appearance on the school stage was as 'a very small Tweedledum'. Much later 'he was Lord Richard in *The Pantry*, the father in *The Grand Cham's Diamond*, the Colonel in *Alice-Sit-by-the-Fire*, George Radfern in *Laburnum Grove*, and, best of all, Mr Bennet in *Pride and Prejudice*.'

The other representatives of St Columba's on the Board were Mr John G Kerr and Mr W Bryce Graham. The Board was to lose them in the mid-1950s. The untimely death in 1955 of Mr Graham caused much sorrow. He had been a pupil in the preparatory department, he married a former pupil, Jean Jackson, and he remained deeply interested in this 'community of individuals' as he saw it, quietly doing much valuable work, and bringing:

> . . . an almost boyish gaiety to many school functions, especially when the children were involved.
>
> (School Magazine 1955-56, p. 10)

'Uncle Jack' Kerr retired from the Board in 1957, having been a Director for twenty-seven years, and having served both as a representative of Kilmacolm and on the executive committee. He took it upon himself to know the name of every girl in the School, and he was especially devoted to the boarders and to the sporting side of school life. When he retired Miss MacArthur asked 'Uncle Jack' to continue to watch:

***W Bryce Graham, Director 1944-55.***

***Uncle Jack Kerr at the Preparatory School Sports, 1957***

> . . . with a sympathetic eye, the game of life as it is played in St Columba's – from the touch-line if you wish, in the melée at the centre if you will.
>
> (School Magazine 1956-57, p.8)

And so he did. He earned the undying gratitude of pupils by his regular gift of ice-cream for all at sports days and prizegivings, and no prizegiving was complete without his leading of the School in 'three cheers for the holidays'.

To take the places of these two gentlemen the Directors appointed Mrs W Bryce Graham and Mr John Bingham. Mrs Graham has never broken her connection with the School, and rejoices just as much in her title of longest-standing associate of St Columba's, having first hung up her coat in the cloakroom in 1909, as she does in her position as Honorary Vice-Chairman, conferred upon her in 1984, on her retiral from an active role on the Board. Mr Bingham put in five energetic years on the Board, until he moved South in 1962. In his place the Directors invited another former pupil of St Columba's, Dr J Morag MacArthur (no relation of the Headmistress) to be a Director. Morag MacArthur, who had left school in 1932, was by this time County Medical Officer for Renfrewshire, in which capacity she had dealt with the School. She remained a Director until 1985.

In order to help the Company across the minefield of direct grant claims, capital reserve and curriculum changes, the Directors in 1959 invited onto the Board Sir David Stirling Anderson, Director of the Royal College of Science and Technology, later to become Strathclyde University. He was a local Director for St Bride's, but more significant was his role in liaising with the Scottish Education Department and advising on matters to do with curriculum and finance. When he stepped down in 1964, having been asked to chair the new Scottish Certificate of Education Examination Board, he allowed his name to remain on the list of Directors and made himself available for consultation on the many matters in which he was expert.

With the invitation on to the Board of some distinguished Old Girls of St Bride's and the Park School, the Board was by 1964 for the first time evenly divided between men and women. Sir Cecil Weir, K C M G, who was the originator and organiser of the Empire Exhibition of 1938, the co-ordinator of Scotland's civil defence operation, and the holder of several important posts in Anglo-European trade after the War, was, from 1946 until 1960, the first Honorary President of the Girls' School Company. The next Honorary President, from 1965, was Lord Muirshiel, resident of Kilmacolm at Knapps, who, as John S Maclay, was a former Secretary of State for Scotland (and former pupil of the Park School kindergarten).

Miss MacArthur enjoyed a personal friendship with the Headmistresses of the other two schools, Miss Rachel Drever Smith of St Bride's and Miss Janie Robertson and her successor Miss Joan Lightwood of the Park School. The Heads worked closely with the local Directors, who gave them considerable discretion in the running of their schools and were happy to take their advice on many matters. Miss MacArthur had a knack, which she exercised sparingly, of getting what she wanted in the way of staff management and benefits for pupils, and on more than one

***Prefects 1947-48***

Back row: Heather Wilson, Isabel Hendry, Sheena Clarkson, Moira Baird, Jean Nicol
Second row: Edith Rolland, Elizabeth Duncan, Ann Ross, Winifred Reid, Irene Stevenson, Agnes Gallacher, Myrtle Emslie
Front row: Clayre Paton, Sheila McAuslan, Helen Laird (Head Prefect), Marion Baird, Ruth Andrew, Margaret Paton (absent)

occasion the Directors gracefully rescinded a previous Minute in the face of a *fait accompli.*

## Variety without disorder

> The staff are well qualified for the work they undertake, and they successfully set good standards of behaviour as well as of educational attainment. English subjects, handwriting and nature study, in particular, were favourably commented on. The performance of the pupils in public examinations is very creditable. In all subjects teaching [is] lively and on modern lines, and the general attitude and response of the pupils [is] very good. The cheerful, friendly spirit of the school and the good manners of the girls were also frequently mentioned.

If this report on St Columba's School by Her Majesty's Inspector were found floating in the Gryffe, it would be impossible to assign it to its date, for it might have applied to any year since the School's foundation. In fact it was made in 1964. Miss MacArthur's stewardship left the School greatly increased in numbers and remarkably little changed in educational terms and in style. The abhorrence of cramming in any form persisted, the Headmistress being just as scornful as Pope of:

> Bookful blockheads, ignorantly read
> With loads of learned lumber in their heads.
> (Prizegiving 1949, School Magazine 1948-9, p. 15)

Universities demanded three Highers and two Lowers for entrance, and, as in most schools at the time, that is what the girls were usually limited to, unless they stayed on for a sixth year and converted the Lowers into Highers. The old fears of over-straining the mental capacities lived on, as did the laudable desire to encourage the development of the diversity of gifts which, at St Columba's, were in no danger of going unrecognised. When Miss MacArthur, referring to the definition of democracy in Plato's *Republic*, stated her philosophy for the School:

> *Our* endeavour must be to achieve variety without disorder, and the sort of equality that gives everyone an opportunity, but not necessarily the *same* opportunity,
>
> (Prizegiving 1949, School Magazine, 1948-49, p. 13)

she might having been speaking for any of her three predecessors.

The prefect system still underpinned the approach to discipline, and the Mistresses through whose hands a particularly high-spirited fourth form had just passed could console themselves that there was something to be gained from turning into gamekeepers those with 'a preternaturally acute insight into the malefactions of a younger generation', as Miss MacArthur once said. Thanks to the prefects many girls left school with minds well stocked with poetry, memorisation of which was often dealt out as a punishment.

There was one institution which persisted from an earlier era that is remembered with loathing by everyone. Mark-readings in the school hall were the climax of each diet of exams in school. It was a solemn occasion. Everyone sat on the floor, grouped in classes. Each class in turn stood, while the Headmistress read out, from the platform, the marks of each girl in each subject in order from top to bottom, down to the pass mark, and each girl sat down only when her mark had been read. Looking back, the subjects of this practice are baffled as to its purpose in a school in which, as they were frequently reminded, many types of contribution were valued and a wide academic range of pupils was welcomed.

## Schoolmistresses

It was still the era of the dedicated unmarried schoolmistress, for whom teaching was a vocation and not merely a career choice. Several of this species stayed for decades rather than years at the School. Married women now began to appear on the staff list, but men were unusual, the occasional fleeting bird of passage visiting for a few weeks to cover for absent staff in an emergency.

The Preparatory School was headed by the formidable Miss Cowper from 1949 until 1956; when she left for health reasons, Miss Hutchison took over until 1959. The new Head was Miss Margaret Croft, Old Girl, who had been on the staff since 1948. Her reign was kindly and long: when the Preparatory and Junior Schools were merged in 1973 she became Head of the new Primary, and continued until her retiral in 1981. A frequently remembered feature of her dispensation is that in keeping perfect order she never raised her voice. A mainstay of the Preparatory, and later Primary, School was Miss Elizabeth Conacher, who taught Form I from 1953:

> . . . she had the ability to pass on her knowledge and enthusiasm to her pupils and to arouse an interest in Nature which many have maintained into adulthood.
>
> (Miss Margaret Croft)

***Staff 1946-47***
Back row: Mrs Scott (Mlle Duranton), Miss Millar, Miss Broadfoot, Miss Jean Anderson (domestic science)
Second row: Miss Havelock, Miss McKenzie, Miss R Hetherington, Miss Laird, Miss Wyllie, Miss E J Hetherington, Miss Williamson, Miss Burrows
Third row: Miss Cheyne, Miss Collet, Miss Maneely, Miss Aitken, Dr Macdonald, Miss Sutton, Miss Mina T Walker, Miss Mathieson, Mrs Jones
Front row: Miss Mowat, Miss Lamb, Miss Hagart, Miss MacArthur, Miss Reid, Miss Sherriff, Miss Bowie

Miss Conacher, herself an Old Girl, was a Fellow of the Botanical Society of Edinburgh and a member of the committee for the study of Scottish flora. She retired in 1990. In the spring and summer tadpoles, frogs, minnows, snails and crabs joined the collection of tropical fish in the classrooms, and:

> . . . we have a newt in school too. It is in the sink and nobody can get a drink or wash their hands.
>
> (School Magazine 1963-64, p. 37)

How pleasant it was to be very young and at 'St Clumbers'! The children in the Preparatory School from 1958 onwards were especially fortunate to be housed in Shalott:

> The ample and wooded grounds made every break-time an adventure. We had the boarders' see-saw, swings suspended from strong old tree branches, wonderful places for dens and hide-outs and a kindly stone lion to guard his out-of-bounds lawn. On summer days, some classes could be taken outside, under the trees. Class gardens also flourished in these early days at Shalott.
>
> (Miss Margaret Croft)

Miss Kathleen Millar came as Head of the science department in 1934, and departed in 1968, having been Deputy Headmistress for her last ten

***Channel Crossing*, by Mairi Crawford (later Hedderwick), Form VIB, 1955**

***Holland, Easter 1956***

***Rome, Easter 1959***
Left to right: Miss Margaret Walker,
Miss Clare Morrison (later Mrs Robertson), Miss Croft,
Miss Millar

***At the Villa d'Este, Rome, 1959***

*Miss Millar, second from the right, at the opening of the science block, 1965*

***Staff, 1961-62***

Back row: Miss Bancroft, Miss Weir, Miss Campbell, Miss Kellagher, Mrs Notman, Miss E Anderson
Second row: Miss Margaret Walker, Miss Wyllie, Miss Peden Fyfe, Miss Jean Anderson (Junior and English), Miss McDiarmid, Miss Tytler, Mrs Robertson
Third row: Mrs Martyn, Miss Allison, Mrs Scott, Miss MacRobert, Mrs Hunter, Miss Hutton, Mrs Couper
Front row: Mrs Jones, Miss Collet, Miss Millar, Miss MacArthur, Dr Macdonald, Miss Maneely, Miss Milne

years, and having ushered in the new science syllabus in the School and inaugurated teaching in the new science block, which she helped to plan. Miss Millar's kind and generous nature was sometimes taken advantage of by pupils: some of them remember the occasion when the National Anthem was being played on the piano in the music practice room next door to the old top-floor science laboratory. The class rose to its feet as one, and continued to do so each time the pianist started the anthem anew. Miss Millar and Miss Margaret Walker took school trips abroad, to France, Belgium, Holland and Rome, in the Easter holidays from 1955 until 1959. Miss Millar could be depended upon even when travel arrangements were put into disarray by fog in the Channel, as an observer testified:

> There she was responsible for all these children, missing all the carefully planned connections for a long journey to Rome and yet, outwardly, appearing calm and composed. I never even heard her raise her voice.
>
> (School Magazine 1967-68, p. 20)

Miss Catherine Sherriff was Head of mathematics from 1940 until 1957, and was careers Mistress from 1945. Pupils remember her as a brilliant mathematician, who perhaps lacked the guile necessary to keep one step ahead of her mischievous pupils. They recall her delighted and absorbed attention in solving for their benefit some difficult mathematical problem while having her hairpins delicately removed by magnet from behind. Miss J M Hutton succeeded her and retired in 1965, and Mrs Anne Couper, who taught from 1956 until 1970 is remembered with an especial fondness completely understandable for one of whom so many could say, 'She got me through my O-grade Maths'. Few things went on in the School with which she did not have something to do, whether cheering on the teams on the playing field, playing in Staff v Girls matches, arranging flowers or helping with expeditions and the debating society.

Dr Sheila Macdonald was appointed as Head of modern languages in 1945 and retired in 1971, having spent her last three years in school as Deputy Head. She was a brilliant linguist and highly effective teacher of French. She knew how to motivate her pupils:

> I was failing in French, and when she first arrived she assessed each one of us and promptly placed me in the top division. To this I objected, and told her she must have been mistaken. No, was the reply, and so I went from a D level to A. Because she had found something in me that no other teacher had found, I *tried* to learn, and it worked.
>
> (Margaret Wolfram [Gillan],
> in letter to St Columba's F P Association)

Memorable French Evenings were held, with girls acting short plays, some written by the girls themselves, and singing French and German songs. But the best remembered events staged by the modern languages department were performances, in 1949 and 1958, of Racine's *Esther*, with the contemporary music of Moreau, play and music having been originally commissioned by Madame de Maintenon for a seventeenth-century girls' school, and given 'a rare

*Performance of* Esther, *1949*

***The cast of* Athalie, *a play put on by senior girls, March 1952***
Ruth Richardson, Jean Laird, Phyllida Blackater, Shirley Denholm, —, Jean Thomson, Hilda Garvie, Fiona McAdam

and impressive performance' by their twentieth-century Scottish successors. Dr Macdonald was assisted by Miss Barbara D Holl from 1949 until 1962, by Miss M Little from 1947 until 1959, and by Old Girl Mrs Nancy Scott (McKinlay) in 1947-48, again from 1959 until 1970, and part-time from 1982 until 1985. Mrs Scott had an especial gift for understanding girls, put to good use as Form Mistress and careers Mistress, and a colleague paid tribute to her 'verve and wisdom, humour and enthusiasm, sympathy and a steely-true critical faculty untouched by fear or favour.'

Miss Margaret Walker presided over the stoves and sinks of the domestic science department from 1947 until her retirement in 1971. Behind the scenes, too, she was a tireless worker and organiser of the multifarious tasks generated by a growing school, and her practical skills were in evidence everywhere. Geography was taught by Miss Christine Campbell from 1957 until she left in 1967 to take up the headship first of a school in Belfast and then, in 1972, of St Bride's, and later of Albyn School in Aberdeen. She started field study courses for geography students in 1958, and organised the School's first involvement with the Duke of Edinburgh's Award Scheme in 1961. Miss Elspeth McDiarmid was Miss Hagart's successor in the history department from 1958 until 1968. Vibrant with her love of her subject, she would already have the lesson under way as she walked through the classroom door.

***June 1957, VIA geography***
Lizzie Angus, Irene Gibson, Patricia Holmes, Alison Cameron, Miss Campbell, Anne Young

Miss Jane Milne, 'scholar, authoress and teacher – a gentle spirit', taught Latin from 1947 until 1962. She wrote children's books, and as a treat used to read her class a chapter or two on the last day of term. She was assisted by Miss Mina T Walker from 1946 until 1958, who was fondly remembered and much missed, for her unstinting effort in all departments of school life, and in work for school charities in particular. She lived until the age of 103, still clear of mind. Another fondly remembered Latin teacher was Old Girl Clare Robertson (Morrison), who taught from 1958 until 1962 and again from 1983 until 1987. Miss Milne's successor as Head of classics was Mrs Jean Kerr. When she left in 1968 to go to Marr College, the School lost a teacher as

**Twelfth Night,** ***June 1956***
***The Musicians' Gallery***

**The Winter's Tale,** ***1961***

**Where Do We Go From Here?**
***A musical play presented by the Junior School, 1960.***
'From Spain to where?' Dirk reads the next clue.

**One Came From Erin,** ***1963***
***A pageant about the life of St Columba, put on by the Junior School, directed by Miss Weir***
'Saints of today, as he of yore'

**The Little Shepherd**
***presented by the Junior School, 1951***

**A Midsummer Night's Dream,** ***June 1950***
Back row, standing: Judy Wilkinson, Jean Wallace, Kirsteen Taylor, Jane Wilkinson
Left-hand group, from back: Sally Cook, Leslie Blackater, Patricia Holmes, Margaret McLaren, Rosemary Davidson
Right-hand group, from back: Mairi Crawford, Maureen Webster, Elizabeth Holmes, Pat Speirs

effective in teaching her pupils to think for themselves, as in conveying the beauty of Latin poetry.

Mrs N M (Rita) Jones arrived in 1946 to head the English department and to usher in a new era of school plays, starting with *Everyman* in 1948. The dramatic performances were characterised by her 'unique combination of imagination, insight and artistry':

> Among these were *A Midsummer Night's Dream*, in 1950, of which one critic wrote: 'This production was so deeply imbued with a sense of faery that it is difficult to describe it in prosaic terms.' In 1953 *The Queen's Grace* – one of the 'most beautiful and memorable performances ever staged in school'; in 1955 *Twelfth Night*, which provided 'an enchantment of illusion'; in 1961 *The Winter's Tale* – 'a performance to be pondered over and long remembered with pleasure'; in 1964 *The Tempest* – 'the performance surpasses the highest expectations'; in 1967 *Romeo and Juliet* – still so excitingly fresh in all our minds. Mrs Jones was always ready to help with other productions for which she was not directly responsible – *The Little Shepherd – Esther* (in French) and Old Girls' plays – *Milestones, Bonaventure, Treasure Hunt*, and *Isle of Sirens*.
>
> (School Magazine 1966-67, pp. 22-23)

A former student of the great Sir Arthur Quiller-Couch, Rita Jones was a well-known producer of polished amateur drama in West Renfrewshire. At school she would survey each new class with a casting director's eye, silently marking down certain individuals for future roles, which then determined her choice of play. In addition to her dramatic work Mrs Jones edited the school magazine from 1947 until her retiral in 1967, a *magnum opus* in this era when it nearly doubled in size. Above all she is remembered by every one of her pupils as an outstanding teacher:

> Mrs Jones's lessons were always illuminated by wit and understanding. All her lessons were in a sense 'productions', presented with a similar colour, charm and perception.
>
> (School Magazine 1989-90, p. 53)

Rita Jones's long-serving colleague in the English department was Mrs Freda Martyn, who taught from 1957 until 1971. Scholarly and enthusiastic, and an accomplished amateur actress, she devoted much time and thought to nurturing the individual abilities of her pupils.

Miss Sophie Tytler came to teach art in 1955. To her young charges, mesmerised by a style of dress they had never before seen on a teacher, she was like a creature from another world, with her glamorous interests and exotic tastes, including frequent travel to California and the South of France. To everyone who knew her:

> Miss Tytler's speed and energy were amazing: driving through from St Andrews in her big Jaguar at the start of a long day's teaching, or hanging a show of pictures with a sureness and skill that left one gasping.
>
> (School Magazine 1968-69, p. 25)

She often arrived with arms full of flowers and foliage to make beautiful arrangements for the entrance hall and elsewhere. Her retiral from the School in 1969 was regretted, and she left behind many friends. Her assistant was Miss Betty Peden Fyfe, Old Girl (see Chapter Six) and visiting teacher, specialising in craft, from 1946 until 1964. The properties cupboard had, in 1949, inherited a windfall in the form of costumes from the family of former pupil Lettice Glen-Coats, 'relics of the splendour of Paisley Fancy-Dress Balls', and the efforts of Miss Tytler and, especially, Betty Peden Fyfe augmented this collection and added scenery and props far above the usual school standard.

## Games and physical education

On her arrival in 1945 Miss MacArthur lost no time in making games compulsory for every girl in the School. Miss Christine Havelock, appointed as games Mistress in the same year, set about improving the standard of play with energy and determination. The lack of opportunity to play against other schools in the war years had resulted in the inability to win any outside fixture in 1945-46, but by the time she left, to marry Old Boy George Mundell in 1950, the first lacrosse team was a force to be reckoned with. She was succeeded by Miss Sarah Howse, a former pupil, who also married an Old Boy (William Marr) two years later. Miss MacArthur lamented:

> It seems that our Physical Training mistresses have a fatal attraction for the young men of Kilmacolm,
>
> (Prizegiving 1952, School Magazine 1951-52, p. 16)

and her words proved to be prophetic for the next appointee, another former pupil, Ann McGarva (Ross), who married and left in 1954. This was also the

***Lacrosse team, 1959-60***
Back row: Ann Ferrier, Morvyn Hood, Sheila Carter
Second row: Rosalind Essery, Margaret McGregor, Elspeth Reid, Elizabeth Cumming
Front row: Lynne Gardner, Ruth Baker, Norah Brown (Captain), Margaret Clark, Helen Anderson

fate of several of the young and enthusiastic games Mistresses who succeeded them, notable among whom were Miss E Haydock (1955-59) and Miss R Guthrie (1962-1964). Throughout these years much valuable help in coaching was given by Old Girl and Scotland player Joan MacRobert.

These were good years for lacrosse:

> John Knox speaks of women as 'tender creatures, soft and pitiful'! I wish he could have seen the 1960 variety giving an account of themselves in the finals of the Schools' Lacrosse Tournament where, once more, they were narrowly defeated by St George's, Edinburgh.
>
> (Miss MacArthur, Prizegiving 1960,
> School Magazine 1959-60, pp. 18-19)

Playing against other schools usually entailed a long journey, but there was much enthusiasm among the talented pupils, and great competition for admission to the First XII. The game, technically difficult and physically tough, did not suit everyone, and one Old Girl recalled that her position of choice in a school practice match was 'first attack on the losing side' which gave her as little as possible to do. Another remembers matches against St Leonards School, who appeared on the lacrosse pitch 'as if they were going into battle, with face-guards and body-armour.' By 1958 senior girls were allowed to opt for netball instead.

Swimming was taken up with enthusiasm by an increasing number of girls, some of whom trained for Royal Life-Saving Society awards. From 1960 the School sent representatives to the residential sports course at Inverclyde. Also in 1960 a crew of three girls competed in the Schools' and Universities' Yacht Races on the Gare Loch, and were joint runners-up in the girls' section of the week-long competition; in 1962 the St Columba's team won the Christie Cup for the most successful girls' crew. Later that year the School provided the first girls' team for the Curling League of Britain, making a creditable showing against the male competitors.

***Schools' Yacht Races, 1960***
The St Columba's crew: Elspeth Reid, Ann Ferrier, Heather Cockburn

***Gymnastic and dancing display, 1957***

***Tennis team, 1965***
Back row: Maureen Williamson, Fiona Keyden, Anne Duff, June Hay
Second row: Anne Storrie, Marjory Love, Anne Forrester
Front row: Elizabeth Cockburn, Susan Farrow
This was the year in which Marjory Love reached the quarter-final in the Junior Championships of Great Britain at Wimbledon.

***Prefects, 1945-46, showing some of the pioneers of the Current Affairs Club***

Back row: Rona Plumpton, Joyce Mudie, Pat Baxter, Rona Houston, Joan Morrison, Sinclair Russell
Second row: Winifred Brown, Nan Houston, Margaret Pratt (Head Prefect), Sheila Arnott, Janette Wither
Front row: Janette Dick, Dorothy Donald

Gymnastic and dancing displays continued to be held each year. Many and varied were the dances performed, and all in appropriate costume. But when, in 1957, the senior pupils danced the Royal Empress Tango:

> . . . amusingly incongruous were the tango rhythm and the fresh, pretty, but decidedly un-Latin summer dresses worn by the performers.
>
> (School Magazine 1956-57, p. 39)

All the seniors learned ballroom dancing, essential preparation for school leavers, although those who had to take the part of men (the taller girls) found themselves at a disadvantage in later life.

Athletics was developed throughout the period – but not hurdling, as Miss MacArthur held that it was an activity completely unsuited to the physiology of girls, and could never be persuaded otherwise. By 1962 the School was in a position to compete in inter-school athletics. Various other sports were taken up around this time, including golf. Tennis was always a favourite, even though the short Scottish summer term did not favour the game. Marjory Love had many successes: while at Edinburgh University, where she took her LL B, she was British University Champion three times; she appeared in the Scottish Senior Ranking Lists for many years, and was ranked Number One in 1976, 1977, 1978 and 1979; she won the Scottish Championships in 1969 and 1974, and the Scottish Hardcourts Championships on five occasions. She represented Britain in Australia in 1994, and was Captain of the Great Britain Ladies over-45 team in the Margaret Court Cup in Australia in 1996.

**Extra-curricular**

Like her immediate predecessor, Miss MacArthur was concerned to encourage her charges to look beyond Kilmacolm to the outside world. In 1947 the whole School, wearing poppies and bringing their sewing, assembled in the hall to listen to the Royal Wedding broadcast on the wireless. Miss MacArthur continued Miss McMurtrie's practice of inviting Mr Donald Grant to give occasional lectures on world affairs. At these and other occasions it fell to one of the senior girls to propose the vote of thanks, a daunting task but useful experience for later life.

In her first year as Head she encouraged the girls to form a Current Affairs Club to replace the Venture Society. It started off very well:

> Miss Robinson [English Mistress], who taught in Palestine for several years, gave an interesting talk on the conflicting claims of the Arabs and Jews. The following Friday there was a debate led by Rona Houston and Margaret Pratt on Nationalisation. Janette Wither gave a talk on UNO and . . . Joan Morrison played three gramophone records which were very much enjoyed. Miss Snodgrass gave a talk on Indirect Rule in Nigeria. There was a talk on Food and Famine, given by Janette Wither. Nan Houston gave a gramophone recital. Miscellaneous postcards were shown on the epidiascope, . . . and Sinclair Russell gave a talk on Private Flying in the USA.
>
> (School Magazine 1945-46, p. 24)

The club continued to meet in the library on Fridays at lunch time, and the programme varied from year to year depending on the tastes of those responsible for organising it. Lighthearted topics and a humorous approach were tried in some years, and at other times there were attempts to steer the membership onto more serious subjects. Election years provoked the School to go to the polls, for the first time since the mock election of 1910 (see Chapter Five), with predictable results, although, in 1959:

> . . . it is encouraging to note that there are ten Socialists!
> (School Magazine 1959-60, p. 49)

The School's first debating society had been started in 1920, with Margery Reid as President and Dorothy Whyte as Secretary, but after an enthusiastic beginning, with a debate on 'Should Women Smoke?' (it was answered in the negative, by 19 votes to 8), little more was heard of it. Nearly thirty years later formal debates were held under the auspices of the Current Affairs Club, but it took several years for girls used to musical and dramatic performances to feel quite comfortable addressing their fellow pupils in this way, and sometimes staff led the way as main speakers. In 1960 Diana Bingham and Irene MacKenzie (Hogarth) reached the Final of the Inter-Schools' Debating Competition in the West of Scotland for the English Speaking Union. In the Friday lunch-time meetings in the library, subjects close to home were guaranteed to draw the crowds, although they could prove more difficult of solution than the knottiest of international problems, and it is recorded that in 1957 when there was debate on 'School Franchise, Order Marks and the Prefect System':

> . . . even after two meetings we arrived at no satisfactory conclusion, and many very interesting points could well have been discussed further.
> (School Magazine 1957-58, p. 44)

The Public Speaking Society was formed in 1963, initiated by Miss Jean Anderson, former Head Girl, a Junior School Mistress who contributed some English teaching in the senior school, and carried on by Mrs Kerr. Debating was then put on a more organised footing, and girls were entered regularly for the English Speaking Union debates. The experience of lively and noisy meetings hosted by other Renfrewshire schools did not deter them, for debating had now become a serious pursuit.

***Visit to Dundonald House, June 1950, for the opening ceremony*** The guest of honour was the Countess of Minto, far left.

The charitable work started so long ago continued just as energetically. In 1949 there was formed for three of the junior classes (Forms III A, IV C and IV B) a Circle of the Scottish Children's League, the junior branch of the Royal Scottish Society for the Prevention of Cruelty to Children.

This became the juniors' own special charity, and they made regular visits to Dundonald House, taking gifts for the children. Jean Graham (Jackson) was Kilmacolm Secretary of the Scottish Children's League, and she was very active in the Circle on behalf of the School. The senior girls organised their own fund-raising activities form by form for a charity of their choice, and much energy, thought and creativity were put into them.

## Modest changes

When Miss MacArthur became Headmistress gym tunics were still worn, both in the school and on the field. But around 1947 the lacrosse players abandoned stockings – bane of the game – and played in socks. Never again would the cry of 'Smiles!' from the games Mistress bring a lacrosse match to a grinding halt. This was something of a mystery to the Old Boys at their annual match against pupils, until it was noticed that there was a correlation between 'Smiles!' and the discreet adjustment of stockings to eradicate the band of flesh that had appeared between the top of the inconvenient hosiery and the hem of the tunic. The temptation to issue the warning cry themselves at odd intervals during games became irresistibly strong to some ungallant youths.

***Lacrosse team, 1945-46, still playing in stockings!***
Back row: Margaret Sugden, Nan Houston, Elspeth Johnston, Ann Meade
Second row: Doreen Chapman, Pat Baxter, Joan Morrison, Mary Main, Sheena Grant
Front row: Ann Ross, Moira Williamson

It is remarkable how few changes were made to the general style of things in Miss MacArthur's reign. She stuck fast to the uniform rules, explaining at one prizegiving speech that:

> . . . a feeling of inferiority where natural endowments are concerned may sometimes be inevitable, but it is a pity to add unduly to the embarrassments of the young in the matter of twin-sets, wedge-heeled shoes and variegated bobby-socks.
>
> (School Magazine 1950-51, p. 15)

But by 1955 she had conceded a little change:

> Humbly, and with a certain Scottish reserve, we in St Columba's have introduced such changes as seemed to meet with majority approval. The pudding-basins will become more stream-lined, the 'monstrous tunic' will be replaced on most occasions by reasonably elegant skirts and kilts, and of that cruellest of all impositions, that fierce battleground of maternal solicitude – the white frock for Prize-Givings – soon nothing will remain but a faint antiquarian memory.
>
> (Prizegiving 1955, School Magazine 1954-55, pp. 15-16)

Helen Anderson of Form IV A accepted the concessions on behalf of the School with suitably dignified gratitude:

***Prizegiving, 1955***

Back row: Elizabeth Holmes, Mairi Crawford, Elspeth Stirling, Sheila Hill, Fionna MacGregor (Head Prefect), Irene Hogarth (silver medal) (E Holmes, S Hill and M Crawford shared the Peden Fyfe award; S Hill and E Stirling shared the Janet Waugh scholarship)
Front row: Mr Bingham (Guest of honour), Joan Sharp (gold medal, A M Adam bursary), Miss MacArthur

***Prizegiving, 1960: 'in the summer, poplin shirts'***

Guest of honour was the Rt Hon John S Maclay, Secretary of State for Scotland (later Lord Muirshiel).
Left to right: Norah Brown, Lynne Gardner (joint athletics champions), Elisabeth Shearer (Peden Fyfe award), Miss MacArthur, J S Maclay, Helen Anderson (Head Prefect), Elspeth Reid (gold medal, A M Adam bursary), Irene Hogarth (Janet Waugh scholarship)

School uniform has changed at last,
A great improvement on the past;
Instead of tunics, smart, green skirts
And in the summer, poplin shirts.

In winter, when the skies are grey,
Our black velours we'll put away,
And wear a hat of gaberdine
To match our coats of bottle green.

In Summer – this is best of all—
When we assemble in the Hall,
We'll be no longer 'saints' in white
But wear checked ginghams crisp and bright!

(Ibid. p. 21)

Contact with the opposite sex was confined to the occasional lacrosse match (against Old Boys, and holiday matches against the boys of Glenalmond School) and, latterly, debates against Paisley Grammar and other Renfrewshire schools. But when, in 1963, Miss MacArthur gave permission for senior girls attending the school dance to bring boyfriends, St Columbans knew that they had entered the modern age.

### Music

St Columba's reputation for serious musical study was continued under Miss Anne Collet, who, from 1938 until 1967, headed a music department that saw remarkably few staff changes. Miss Collet had studied at the Matthay School of Music, and she brought with her a tradition of fine music scholarship. For Mrs Jones's school production of *The Tempest* in 1964, she was responsible for:

> . . . exquisite music drifting in at appropriate moments to suit the mood of the verse and . . . carefully selected for the most part from the songs and instrumental works of the period and played on recorders, harpsichord and muted violins.
>
> (School Magazine 1963-64, p. 31)

Miss Collet's programme notes for this production show the results of her research into the original settings for some of Shakespeare's songs, her choice of sixteenth and seventeenth century music for others, and her own compositions for yet others. This is merely one example of the results achieved again and again in performances from the School's hall stage, from the Ensemble ('part of the training necessary for concert work') at which girls performed works ranging from baroque to modern in front of pupils and parents, through the annual junior and senior concerts, always highly praised, to the Silver Tablet performances, rare on account of the exacting standard demanded, by Moira von Elzenbaum (Baird), Moira Moodie (Williamson), Violet Ross (Shearer), Clare Robertson (Morrison) and Mairi Hedderwick (Crawford). Miss Collet was more than a fine musician and scholar: she knew how to communicate her enthusiasm to her pupils, however young. Faced with a reluctant small beginner, David Laird, she removed the back of the piano, and starting thus from the basis of fascination, proceeded to teach him to play.

One of the pupils in whom Miss Collet took most pride was Archie Shearer, who after graduating from St Columba's Preparatory School stayed with his teacher, and obtained his performer's LRAM certificate at the age of seventeen, while studying a full school curriculum. Archie was brought back to the platform several times:

> How nice it is to see Archie's smiling face as he walks on to the platform in the Hall! And how happy he makes all of his audience right from the start!
>
> (School Magazine 1953-54, p. 51)

He and others of Miss Collet's pupils from St Columba's played for BBC Radio's *Children's Hour* on more than one occasion. Several of her pupils made careers in teaching music: Belinda Gooch held many prestigious teaching posts and became Chairman of the National Association of Youth Orchestras. The School produced so many talented musicians that several prizes were taken each year from the Glasgow and Renfrewshire Music Festivals, especially the latter, with many firsts and honours certificates.

Professional musicians invited to perform for the School included the oboeist Leon Goossens (again) and the pianist Dwight Henderson.

From 1935 Miss Marjorie Maneely taught piano and solo singing, with conspicuous success, but it was as a teacher of class singing that she was best known and loved:

> We knew more about breathing correctly and voice production by the age of eight than most other students knew when I joined the Royal Scottish Academy of Music.
>
> (Joan Davis [Morrison] in St Columba's F P Association newsletter)

A colourful figure who dressed dramatically and conducted brilliantly, she formed a voluntary choir, rehearsed it in lunch hours, and entered it, in its first year, for the John C E Chapman Challenge Trophy at the Glasgow Music Festival, 'just for the experience':

> Much to the surprise of the *cognoscenti* in such matters, we won.
>
> (Ibid.)

***Voluntary Choir, 1945-46***
Miss Maneely and Miss Collet, centre, front row

Another former pupil, Margaret Wolfram (Gillan), recalled that:

> . . . her classroom exercise was 'The tip of the tongue, the teeth and the lips', and we sang it up and down the scale, dropping our jaws as far as we could when we sang 'tongue'.

She left, much regretted, to continue her career in Hong Kong in 1963.

Miss Nancy Wyllie taught piano from 1946 until her retiral in 1981, and then part-time for many more years. She too was a gifted and exacting, yet sympathetic, teacher, who gave unstinting time and effort to bring out the best in hundreds of pupils.

Christmas carol services reached new heights, with some really ambitious programmes undertaken, including the performance of Cedric Thorpe Davie's sequence 'Rejoice and Be Merry' in 1961, and, for Miss MacArthur's last Christmas at the School in 1965, 'Words and Music for Christmas', a feast of literature and song in St Columba Church, of richness and range (Shakespeare to T S Eliot, ancient traditional melodies to Thiman, songs and readings in English, French and German) that surely can have been equalled by few schools in the country. It was a fitting climax to Miss MacArthur's reign, embodying as it did so much of what she aspired to for her girls:

> . . . its difficulties had evoked an amazingly mature response; throughout, there was a depth of understanding, a delicacy of expression, an inflection of tone and voice in both verse-speaking and singing which conveyed a true appreciation of a most demanding programme.
>
> (School Magazine 1964-65, p. 21)

## Miss MacArthur's girls

To write of the achievements and exploits of even half of the girls whom Miss MacArthur thought of as 'hers' would make a book in itself. The blossoming of careers for women that had started in the 1930s and 40s had now reached full and glorious flower. Miss MacArthur sent girls out into, *inter alia,* industry and civil service; art and illustration; town planning and architecture (one girl worked for Basil Spence, the designer of Coventry Cathedral); broadcasting, journalism and publishing; the stage, television and music; commerce and secretarial work (one of the girls became T S Eliot's private secretary); law and medicine, nursing, occupational therapy, pharmacy, cancer research, the diplomatic service, school and university teaching, social work and veterinary medicine. In each of these fields there was at least one St Columban who achieved notable success.

Patricia (Tricia) Scott, daughter of Nancy Scott (McKinlay), was forever associated in the minds of those who saw Mrs Jones's production of *The Tempest* with Ariel, having given a hauntingly ethereal interpretation of the character on the school stage. After she left school in 1964 her acting career took wing, and she performed with theatre companies all over the country and made many television appearances. After her untimely death in a car accident in 1985 she was commemorated at the School by the Tricia Scott garden at Cargen Lodge.

***'All hail, great master!' Tricia Scott as Ariel,* The Tempest, *1964***
Jacqueline Fraser-Campbell as Prospero, Patricia Gillies as Miranda

Several of the former pupils of this time have achieved high public recognition. Among those known to the School, three of the present six female Deputy Lieutenants of Renfrewshire are St Columbans: Helen Laird, OBE, Margery Tough (Baird) and Patricia Thomson (Holmes). Allison (Sally) Cook, who left school in 1955, was awarded the MBE for services to politics in 1997. Jinty Blackenhagen (Janette Laird) became Director of the Breast Care and Mastectomy Asociation, and received the MBE before her death in 1992. Myra Winter, winner of the gold medal in 1956 and the Janet Waugh scholarship in 1957, took a first-class Honours BSc in pure mathematics from St Andrews University, and after working as a research scientist in industry and taking an MSc in statistics, was, by 1987, an administrator in the cabinet office. Myrtle Simpson (Emslie) has made her name as an explorer and writer, and is a Deputy Lieutenant of the City of Glasgow (see Chapter Eight). Mairi Hedderwick (Crawford), who won the Janet Waugh scholarship in 1956 and attained the Silver Tablet in 1957, became a highly successful author and illustrator of well-loved books for children and adults with a Highland setting.

Miss MacArthur sent leavers to university every year, and there were some notable academic successes. What perhaps stands out more than anything else is the fullness of the lives that were formed by St Columba's. Much voluntary and supportive work is unpaid and unsung, and most of it is done by women. The value of this kind of service was so deeply rooted in St Columbans that most of them would, by the time they left school, take its performance as a matter of course, whether, like the Saint, 'in clachans where the seagulls cry' or in more urban surroundings.

It had been a remarkable two decades, presided over by a remarkable woman. The aura of modesty, emanating from the Headmistress and characterising the products of her reign, ought not to obscure the rarity of the St Columba's experience:

> I remember that some time during my time at School there really was a Blue Moon. Does anyone else remember that?
>
> (Elizabeth Gillies [Beaton])

*Chapter Eight*

# The Boarders and the Train Girls

> At 6.55 there is profound peace. The owners of the four little beds are all asleep and the only sound to be heard is that of their gentle breathing, with now and then a faint snore from the occupant of the corner bed, who has just shot the only goal in a very thrilling hockey match, and who dreams on with a blissful smile on her face. Her neighbour is dreaming that her concert piece has just been encored five times. She is just acknowledging the furious applause of her audience with a deep curtsey, and refusing gracefully to play a sixth time, when a voice breaks through her dream (oh, hated voice!) announcing cheerfully, 'It is seven o'clock, girls, and time you were up!'
>
> 'Oh, how cold it is!'
>
> ('Seven a.m. on a January Morning', School Magazine 1920, p. 16)

From the beginning, the Company's schools at Helensburgh and Kilmacolm required boarding accommodation if they were to attract enough pupils. In 1896 Miss Paterson of Kilmacolm informed the Directors that she intended to open a private boarding house at Newhall, and the Directors put the information in the school brochure. Some girls boarded with her from the time of the School's opening until 1909, when Miss Paterson gave up the work because of ill-health. The Company installed a new Matron, Miss Routley, and kept on the lease of Newhall for another year.

***Craigrowan, c 1926***

***The entrance hall of Craigrowan, c 1926***

***Shieldhall, c 1926***

***A bedroom at Shieldhall, c 1926***
This was the West Room, which had four or five beds. The other dormitory, with ten beds, was known as the Peter Pan Room.

In 1910 the Company took the lease of Craigrowan, a large house on the corner of Rowantreehill Road and Glencairn Road (now called Corby Knowe), for the boarding house of the school, and Miss Waugh made it her home. Miss Routley continued as Matron. Three years later Miss Waugh herself took over the lease and assumed responsibility for the house, relieving the Company of the liability. By 1917 the number of boarders had increased and more accommodation was needed. It must have been around this time that Parkhill was taken as a temporary additional boarding house, as was Oakdene on the Bridge of Weir Road in 1920:

> It is a very comfortable, friendly sort of house, and is already full. During the first fortnight, Miss Reid was in charge, and under her guidance the girls grappled with the domestic problems raised by a shortage of help. They all seem to have enjoyed it!
>
> (School Magazine 1920, p. 4)

Miss Helen Hislop, Old Girl and domestic science Mistress, arranged a domestic science course at Oakdene, which became the home of senior boarders who wished to study this subject. Other temporary boarding accommodation was found around this period at two other houses, High Tor and Southpark. Permanent accommodation was acquired in 1918 with the purchase of Shieldhall from A T Taylor for around £2000, and this became the boarding house for the younger pupils.

By 1928 the time had come to relieve Miss Waugh of the liability for Craigrowan, and the Company purchased the lease from her for £3000. Miss Waugh offered to waive the payment for a period of ten years, in the form of a loan to the Company, and this was gratefully accepted.

## Boarding house life in the 1920s and 30s

> One by one they arise, and while they proceed with their dressing, such remarks might be heard as, 'Now, if I were at home today, I wouldn't rise at this unearthly hour.'
>
> Unanimous chorus of, 'Neither would I! Rather not!'
>
> 'Hockey today', says some bright spirit.
>
> 'Stupid, can't you see it is snowing?'
>
> 'Well', said the optimist, 'there are only thirty-three days to the holidays.'
>
> 'So there are. Perhaps we shall manage to exist till then.'
>
> A head appears round the corner of the door. 'Say, you people, you have only five minutes.'
>
> Consternation ensues, but when the breakfast bell does ring, all the Craigrowanites appear, looking remarkably well, and yes, it is a fact, looking cheerful too, and pleased with life, in spite of its various hardships, and their own real and imaginary grievances.
>
> ('Seven a.m. on a January Morning', School Magazine 1920, p. 16)

*Miss Routley*

***Halt at Craigrowan***

***At Loch Lomond***

***On an island in the Gryffe, Kilmacolm***

All from the Boarding Prospectus, 1926

Miss Waugh was assisted as Housemistress at Craigrowan first by Miss Routley and then, from 1920, by Miss Esther Stewart. Miss Routley, a country woman from Somerset, who had worked as a nursing sister in Hull, came to Craigrowan in 1910, and then took charge of Shieldhall in 1920 until her retiral in 1930. She was a fair-minded and beneficent ruler of the household of children, Mistresses and maids. She also had a sense of fun:

> With what zest used she to enter into the 'Ploys' at Shieldhall, the entertainments got up with so much enthusiasm and wrapped in such mystery until the night of the performance came, and the Craigrowanites and some favoured friends were received with form and ceremony and seated in state in front of an improvised stage.
>
> (School Magazine 1930, pp. 9-10)

The Craigrowanites themselves were in the habit of getting up plays and entertainments, and if a production was judged to be good enough they were allowed to re-enact it in the school hall for the amusement of all the pupils and staff. Miss Waugh used to invite the boarders to literary evenings in her room at Craigrowan, and in the winter of 1912-1913 these included readings from Kipling, Goldsmith and Walter Pater, ballads and ghost stories:

> But it was not at all easy to feel eerie in a fire-lit room full of people.
>
> (School Magazine 1913, p. 5)

The younger boarders of Shieldhall were often invited up to Craigrowan on Sunday evenings to join in an evening of fireside games, and they all foregathered at Craigrowan to set out to church on Sunday mornings.

Boarding was a useful adjunct to what was primarily a day school. Parents from Renfrewshire and the neighbouring counties sent their daughters to board because they wanted the education offered by St Columba's but did not live within easy reach of rail transport. These girls could board on a weekly basis. (St Bride's at Helensburgh had a larger boarding element, serving as it did an area with many rather remote towns and villages.) Others lived further afield and chose the school because of some personal connection, especially that of being a former pupil. A number of girls had parents abroad in various parts of the Empire. Even Kilmacolm families might avail themselves of the boarding option occasionally, when, for example, there was a sick brother or sister to be nursed at home.

In 1927 Mr Peden Fyfe persuaded the Directors to institute a scholarship at St Columba's for the benefit of boarders. It was worth £60 a year, which at that time covered around half of the boarding fee, and was granted at the discretion of the Headmistress to a girl of about thirteen or fourteen years of age, to last for three or four years.

Miss Waugh, Miss McMurtrie and Miss MacArthur lived with the boarders throughout their headships. This arrangement ensured that the boarders had a special relationship with the Headmistresses and were in no danger of feeling themselves to be at the margins of school life. A highly cultural atmosphere was the air those ladies breathed, and this literary and artistic quality to the boarding house life was a happy and important influence on girls deprived of home life with their families.

## SCHOOL OUTFIT LIST

### UNDERGARMENTS, &c.—Continued

4 pairs Cotton or Thread Stockings (Black).
2 pairs Evening Stockings.
24 Handkerchiefs.
2 Overalls for wear in Laboratory, Studio, &c. (Green).
1 Warm Shawl.
1 Warm Dressing Gown.
1 Dressing Cape or Jacket.
1 Umbrella.
1 Napkin Ring.
1 Writing Case.
1 Work Bag, provided with everything for Sewing and Mending.
3 Shoe Bags (green)
Music Case.

*EVERYTHING must be marked with the owner's name in Cash's woven names and a complete list of clothing and belongings must be fastened inside the lid of each girl's box.*

*WARDROBE accommodation is limited, and girls should not bring more garments than are necessary. No Valuable Jewellery should be brought. Underclothing should be very simply and strongly made.*

## SAINT COLUMBA'S SCHOOL
## KILMACOLM

# *OUTFIT LIST*

## SCHOOL OUTFIT LIST

2 pairs Sheets.
4 Pillow Cases.
4 Bedroom Towels.
2 Bath Towels.
4 Table Napkins.
2 Linen Bags.
2 Nightdress Cases (washing).
2 Brush and Comb Bags (washing).
1 Small Down Quilt.

### TO BE OBTAINED FROM SPECIAL FIRMS TO SECURE UNIFORMITY

Gymnasium Tunic, green serge, supplied by Mr. Watson, Tailor, Kilmacolm.

Gymnasium Blouses (2 for winter, 2 for summer), Gymnasium Knickers, green; Regulation School Frock; Rainproof Coat, with Hat to match: supplied by Messrs. Copland & Lye, Sauchiehall Street, Glasgow.

Hat Bands, Blazer (optional), Tie and Scarf in School Colours, supplied by Messrs. R. W. Forsyth, Glasgow.

### Other Articles Required
### HATS AND GLOVES

Two White Panama Hats for summer, one for school wear, one for special occasions.

Two Black Velour Hats for winter, one for school wear, one for special occasions.

Two pairs of Gloves, one pair to be tan gauntlets.

*Girls, who join in September, should bring to school only the Rainproof Hat and the Black Velour Hats referred to above.*

## SCHOOL OUTFIT LIST

### COATS AND FROCKS

A Warm Dark Navy Blue Coat.

A Best Coat and Skirt, Navy Blue, or, in the case of little girls, a Best Frock, Navy Blue.

Two White Silk Shirts for wear with Coat and Skirt.

A Frock for ordinary evening wear (warm for winter).

A White Frock for special occasions.

### BOOTS AND SHOES

2 pairs Walking Boots or Shoes (Black).
2 pairs Slippers, one for house wear, one for school (Black).
1 pair Evening Shoes.
1 pair Snow Boots or Wellingtons.
1 pair Gymnasium Shoes (Black).
1 pair Bedroom Slippers.

*All Boots and Shoes must be marked and should have low heels.*

### UNDERGARMENTS, &c.

3 Nightdresses or 3 pairs Pyjamas (woollen).
3 pairs Woven Combinations.
2 Over Petticoats or 2 pairs Knickers to match Frocks, with linings to change.
1 Warm Petticoat or Knickers (White) to wear with White Frock.
4 Camisoles.
4 pairs Woollen Stockings (Black).

## From the Boarding prospectus, 1926-27

*opposite: Outfit list, from the 1926 Boarding Prospectus*

The food is good, abundant and varied, and the needs of individual children are considered. Presents of cakes and sweets, except on the occasion of birthdays, are considered undesirable, and anything of the kind sent will be looked upon as meant for general consumption.

Girls are expected to take a sponge bath, hot or cold, every day.

Girls are not allowed to visit their school companions without express consent from home, but this having been obtained, they are occasionally allowed to accept an invitation for Saturday afternoon. No visiting is allowed on Sunday.

There is an excellent School Library which affords a wide choice of Books. Girls are not allowed to read other books without previously obtaining permission from the Head Mistress.

Great care is taken to guard against infection. Every pupil on coming to School must bring with her a note signed by a responsible person to the effect that she is, so far as can be known, free from infection.

## Shalott

Early in 1930 the Directors tackled the problem of boarding accommodation, which, they acknowledged:

> . . . had for years been an unsatisfactory factor in the School life, and . . . the standard of comfort provided was not in accordance with the Fees charged or equal to that existing in Boarding Schools of a similar character.
>
> (Minutes Book, 26 February 1930)

It was decided to purchase Shalott, a large house set in five acres of ground, for use as the sole boarding house for both the junior and senior boarders. The house had been built in 1884 and the Park laid out by Alan Birkmyre, the uncle of John Birkmyre, by whom it was sold to the School. It was a

*Shalott, 1931*

*Dining room, Shalott, 1931*

far-sighted decision to purchase such a property, and it was to make possible expansion of the School on more than one occasion in the future. The School named it St Columba's House, but in popular thought it was always Shalott, and this was the name that stuck. By September 1930, after a few minor alterations, it was occupied by all eighteen boarders, along with Miss McMurtrie, the Housemistress Miss Stewart (who had masterminded the 'flitting' from Craigrowan) and various resident Mistresses, and declared to be 'proving a most comfortable House'. Shieldhall became home to the preparatory department, and Craigrowan was put on the market (see Chapter Three). When Miss Stewart retired in 1934 she was replaced as Housemistress by Mrs Cameron White who resigned in 1942.

The number of boarders in the 1930s reached a gentle peak in the middle of the decade at twenty-four. At the outbreak of War the number, having dropped to sixteen, immediately doubled. During the War there were never more than thirty-six St Columba's girls at Shalott, but the number rose to forty-five in the 1945-46 session with the admission of a new group of girls, and it remained fairly constant for the next ten years.

## The boarding life

The boarders felt themselves, and were felt by the others, to be distinct from the rest of the School. 'They tended to go around together,' observed one of the day girls, 'and they always seemed a cheerful set.' They were not an exclusive clique, however, and certainly not at break time, when many of them had their meagre 'break' supplemented by day girls. It was especially during the War years that the boarders had a reputation for being a hungry lot. Jenny, who cooked very good and plentiful lunches at Duchal Road, was understanding and always kind to them.

The boarders were a 'set' even at weekends, when they wore uniform, except for Saturday evenings. Every Sunday they could be seen walking to and from morning service, afternoon Bible class and evening service at the Old Kirk, or one of the other churches, in their regulation green Harris tweed

*'The Babes' on Miss McMurtie's terrace on a warm Sunday evening, c 1935*

suits and black velour hats, and in their navy napp coats in winter. The tweed suit was also worn on the last day of term. The boarders felt it gave them an enviable air of distinction.

Some of the boarders, especially those who had come from India and other parts of the Empire during and after the War, felt themselves to be very different in outlook from the local girls. Others had come from the South of England, from schools which had been dispersed by the War, and from homes bombed or otherwise disrupted. Many had parents serving abroad, some of them stranded in the Far East for the duration of the War, some of them in prison camps. Some had no parents. The lives of these girls had been thrown into turmoil, and it was Miss McMurtrie's aim to settle them into a calm and secure environment both at school and in the boarding house. In the unsettled years immediately following the end of the War, too, Miss MacArthur took in girls for whom boarding school was the latest episode in lives of startling contrast and dislocation.

It made an extraordinary mix of individuals, with the potential for much unhappiness. One boarder from those years attributes the avoidance of this outcome to the insight of the two Headmistresses. Myrtle Simpson (Emslie) was sent to St Columba's after many years in India, her father having been killed in the War in the East. Miss McMurtrie had arranged for the cost of her schooling to be met by the Girls' School Company. She had seen the potential in this extraordinary girl, who had had practically no formal education, and Miss MacArthur, too, saw that for once the normal boundaries were not applicable: it must have taken a certain nerve to turn a blind eye to her disappearance for long rides over the moors, and even for camping out overnight.

Myrtle repaid the far-sightedness of her two Headmistresses after leaving school by astonishing them regularly with news of her exploits. In the 1960s she went with her husband Dr Hugh Simpson on several scientific expeditions, taking their young family with them to Spitzbergen and the South American jungle and the Canadian Arctic (from where the Simpsons

***Boarders on the steps of Shalott, on a summer evening, c 1940***
Back row: far left, Catriona Dempster
Middle row: Elspeth Bone, Joan Craig, Christian Boyd, —, Shiela MacFarlane, Joan Morrison, Mary McKerrow
Front row: far right, Beatrice Campbell

***Tennis court, Shalott, 1931***
A Shalott Cup for tennis was awarded each year.

attempted to walk to the North Pole). In 1965 Myrtle was the first woman to cross the 400-mile ice-cap of Greenland, part of a team which, on skis and without dogs, made the fastest crossing since Nansen's in 1888. She was awarded the Mungo Park medal for Arctic exploration in 1970. She produced several books about their adventures, and went on to write many others, notably *Simpson the Obstetrician*, about the great humanitarian doctor who discovered the use of chloroform as anaesthetic. She has served as Chairman of the Scottish National Ski Council, and has become a prominent figure in the promotion of outdoor sports and activities in Scotland.

The School privately encouraged all the families of day girls to be kind to the new boarders, and many opened their doors to them and offered friendship. Many a boarder, overcome by homesickness, found a member of staff at hand to dry her tears. Several of the Mistresses used to invite boarders to tea. Miss Reid invited them all, in twos and threes, to Sunday tea, and let them make scones. Uncle Jack Kerr took them to the theatre in Glasgow, and generally made a fuss of them. And of course, great friendships were established among the girls themselves, in many cases lasting throughout their lives.

**I remember . . .**

The solemn church parade on Sundays, . . . and Sunday lunch when we had to take it in turn to sit beside Miss McMurtrie and 'make conversation'. Never for a moment did she betray boredom, but listened gravely and attentively to our fumbling opinions. I remember the 'Newspaper Class' for the seniors on Wednesday evenings, where we learned to be not wholly uncritical of the printed word. One of my very favourite memories is of Sunday evenings, when we took our sewing to the study and were read to. Through her skilful 'skipping', we were steered adroitly through many a classic we might otherwise have shirked, and, through being allowed to borrow freely from her shelves, many of us came to have a lasting love of reading and some of her sense of the beauty of language.

(Margaret Grant [Young], School Magazine 1961-62, p. 66)

Walking through the corridors of Shalott in the evenings . . . hearing the sound of three or four pianos, the girls all practising in various rooms throughout the first floor. I love the sound of scales, they always bring back those school years.

(Margaret Wolfram [Gillan]
in letter to St Columba's F P Association)

We were all kept off school one day in the Autumn term. I can't remember why – it may have been a scarlet fever scare. We were sent up to Misty Law for a picnic. We made a bonfire in the wood and roasted potatoes in it.

(Moira Moodie [Williamson])

One of the trials all new girls had to go through was to climb out of the window of Dorm Three, onto the balcony, and get across the gap to the balcony outside the bathroom and come in that window. This was only discovered in 1957, when Miss Murray, the assistant housemistress, was sitting in the staff garden, and saw somebody doing this. Next day the window would only open sufficiently to allow the passage of air, not bodies!

(*The Story of Shalott*, p.7)

Being wakened in the night to go to the cellars for safety; mince every Saturday lunch and roast potatoes with the meat on Sundays; prayers at 7 pm after supervised prep; everyone going down with German measles in the summer term of 1944; being read to as a junior by Miss Ross and Miss Hetherington; Belle and Alice cleaning the dorms endlessly singing 'You are my sunshine'; washing up the tea dishes in teams on Sunday evenings; 'Hut Sut' handing out our pocket money on Saturdays and scrutinising every darn with eagle eyes; drying our hair round the common room fire on Friday night and Saturday morning; Mam'selle knitting endlessly for her beloved Free French soldiers when she supervised us on Wednesday evenings; dancing to the gramophone on Saturday evenings; the fancy dress Christmas party which the Directors came to and we danced Eightsome Reels and Dashing White Sergeants till we were exhausted; writing letters home on Sunday mornings before Church; being allowed the wireless from 8 pm till 9 pm for Paul Temple and Steve; midnight feasts at the end of term and regretting it by morning; buying Bourneville chocolate and Ovaltine tablets to supplement the quarter pound sweet ration we could have a week; cycling for miles in the summer with our picnics on good Saturdays.

(Ann McGarva [Ross])

***The common room, c 1945-55***
This was the original drawing room of the house, used only on special occasions, such as the wedding of the eldest Miss Birkmyre. It was the common room from 1930 onwards. Prep and Prayers were also held here. When the Preparatory School moved in in 1958 it was used as an assembly hall.

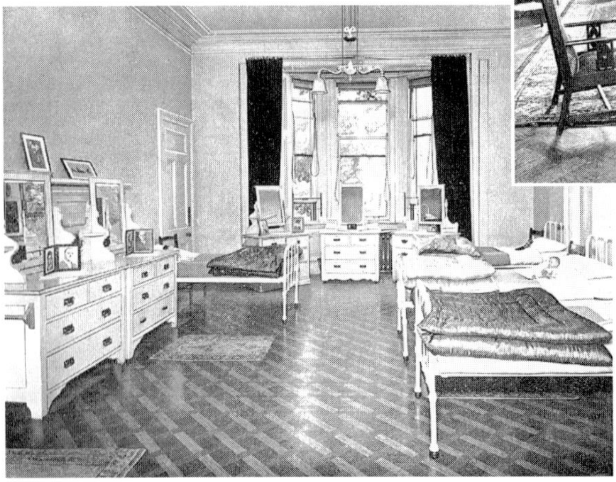

***Dormitory 7, 'the Babes' dorm', Shalott, c 1945-55***
When Shalott was a private house this was the Blue Spare Room. It was renamed 'The Babes' Dorm', and this name stuck, even when, after 1958, it accommodated eight girls from IVA. For a period before this it had been the junior playroom.

## War-time at Shalott

The immediate effect of the War was to bring in the Park School girls whose parents wished to send them to Kilmacolm. They were mainly housed in Shieldhall and Allanbank, but some were accommodated in Shalott, which became rather crowded, particularly since the difficulties in travelling caused by wartime restrictions doubled the number of St Columbans who required to board, some of them on a weekly basis. After the first two years of the War almost all the Park girls returned to Glasgow, and those who stayed on became St Columbans.

Air-raid precautions meant an emergency dormitory of close-packed iron bedsteads in the cellars. Down they scurried in air raids, with their siren suits and gas masks, looking forward to a ginger snap biscuit out of the big tin. The smell of anthracite from the furnace always evokes those air-raid nights for wartime boarders:

> I was a fire-watcher and my place of duty was the top floor of the tower. I remember when Tate and Lyle's sugar factory was bombed – the sky was quite spectacular.
>
> On Sunday afternoons we would walk across the fields to a point above Langbank. One day from that point we watched the liner *Queen Elizabeth* in battleship grey leaving the Clyde to act as a troop ship.
>
> (Jean Herbert [Newton])

> I have a vivid memory of being on fire duty at Shalott on the night of the Greenock blitz, when Miss McMurtrie spent the night shuttling between the cellars and the tower making sure all was well and that the girls up top had hot cocoa. Somewhere I still have a piece of incendiary bomb which we were each given by Miss McMurtrie a few days later – a memento of the night we were on duty when the Germans dared to drop a bomb in the grounds of Shalott.
>
> (Sheila Ross [MacFarlane], School Magazine 1961-62, p. 67)

***May 1941: the choir setting off for afternoon service from Shalott***

During the War, kilts with white shirts and school ties were Sunday uniform. Note the gas masks.
Back row: Elspeth Craig, Catriona Dempster, Elspeth Bone, Alice Ritchie, Joan Craig, Christian Boyd
Front row: Catherine ?, Margaret Sugden, Mary Main, Margaret Williamson, Sheila MacFarlane, Mary McKerrow, Joan Morrison

*The entrance hall as it was in the 1940s and early 1950s*

*The boarders and boarding staff, 1947*

Back row: Miss Burrows (Prep School staff), Jeanette Beattie, Elora Morrison, Kirsteen Taylor, Moira Baird, Sheena Grant, Agnes Gallacher, Agnes Balfour, Ann Ross, Moira Sinclair, Miss Mathieson (Prep School staff)
Second row: Marjory Harrison, Isobel Hunter, Jean Dalgleish, June Close, Mary Chisholm, Jean Hamilton, Anne Drysdale, Margaret Paton
Third row: Ruth Richardson, Marion Alexander, Ann Ewing, Miss Hetherington (Prep School staff), Jean Wallace, Miss MacArthur, Sheena Faichney, Miss K M Sutton (Housemistress), Margaret Gillan, Edith Harrison, Rosemary Long-Price, Nan Rae
Second row: Elizabeth Gallacher, Beth Duncan, Isobel Speed, Elizabeth Gray, Miss Haworth (Nurse), Dorothy Donald, Jean Alexander, Myrtle Emslie, Patricia Willaimson
Front row: June Kemp, Fiona MacAdam, Anne Hibbs, Eleanor Ewing, Margaret Napier, Fiona Morrison, Elspeth Buist, Maire Campbell, Mary McTaggart

## Boarding in the 1940s and 50s

Shalott was governed, from 1943 until 1954, by Miss Kathleen Sutton, a Housemistress of wide experience. 'Hut Sut', as she was known, after the popular song, was strict but fair, and was never known to deviate from her high standards. She must have turned a blind eye – and a deaf ear – to some things, though, for some former boarders have admitted to practising vaulting in the dorms after lights out, and leaping from the mantelpiece onto beds. 'She did handle us with great understanding,' remembers one former boarder:

> . . . even when she opened the dorm door to a face full of feathers from a wayward, airborne pillow.
>
> (Margaret Wolfram [Gillan])

She had trained in 'physical culture' and would willingly join the girls in dancing, games and other outdoor activities. A believer in the bracing effect of fresh air on health, she is remembered by her former charges as having them out of doors at the first possible opportunity during their recovery from German measles, for long walks or bicycle rides. She herself was a familiar figure around the village on her 'iron steed'. On Sunday afternoons all were sent out for a walk, whatever the weather. Her remedy for spots – whatever their cause – was a glass of cabbage water three times a week. Colds were warded off with quinine. Her remedy for untidiness, on the Saturday morning tour of inspection, was to tip the contents of the offending drawers out onto the floor, which is where their owners found them on their return.

She was assisted by two of the preparatory Mistresses, Miss Margaret Ross, from 1941 until 1944, and Miss Rita Hetherington, from 1941 until 1955. Both lived in Shalott, and are remembered as kindly guardians of the junior girls, some as young as seven. Nurse Jackson, a cheery, motherly person, arrived to take up the post of Matron in the mid-1940s. Mlle Duranton came every Wednesday evening and stayed the night, on Miss Sutton's evening off; she and the girls conversed in French.

***Boarding prefects at Shalott, summer 1951***

Back row: June Close, Marslaidh Howie
Second row: Isobel Hunter, Elora Morrison, Elizabeth Pinkerton
Front row: Sheana Faichney, Ruth Richardson, Joan Kemp

Shalott was quite a little conservatory of cultural life. In the Christmas term of 1941 the boarders formed the 'Shalott Musical, Operatic and Ballet Society' under the leadership of Margaret Ross (Williamson) and Hilary Loudon (Baxter). Hilary, who later joined Ballet Rambert, had the girls practising at the 'barre' on the top landing each morning before breakfast. They performed before their fellow boarders and the house staff, and Miss McMurtrie, surprised and delighted, deemed it good enough to take to a wider audience in the school hall. *The Firebird, Bouquet, Schubert, Felicity Dances* and *The Mikado* (they had seen the D'Oyly Carte performance in Glasgow with Uncle Jack) were some of the productions which they were allowed to stage before the School.

***Saturday afternoon picnic, June 1949***
Margaret Adam, Ruth Richardson, Joan Kemp

Miss MacArthur encouraged the performances, and all her boarders also remember the weekly literary evenings in her room, when she read to them, or they read plays. Her sitting room was the large Red Room, always warmer in colour than in actual temperature.

There were few if any luxuries, and life in the large, rambling house was somewhat austere, for staff and girls alike. There were more pianos than bathrooms, and the large rooms were difficult to heat. It took a stoical character to adapt to boarding, and those who did not have that acquired it before their time was through.

## The last decade of boarding

In 1958 the requirements of the increased number of pupils made it necessary to transfer the preparatory department to Shalott, and to confine the boarders' accommodation to the top floor. It had been decided in the previous year to admit no more boarders for the next two years, and, while letting those already boarding finish their education, to let the boarding side of St Columba's come to a gradual end. Since 1945 the number of boarders had averaged forty-five, but in the 1957-58 session the number was down to twenty-five. Despite the original intention, the number was maintained at this level for the next ten years. There was still a considerable demand for boarding, and Miss MacArthur was personally committed to it. It was generally to far-flung places that the boarders dispersed at the end of each session: Singapore, Malaya, Tanganyika, Iraq, and Kenya, for example. Other girls came from the Western Isles and other parts of Scotland.

Miss Brenda Galloway was Housemistress from 1957 until 1968. Her background was Army and Cheltenham Ladies' College, and she ran the boarding house with unwavering efficiency and untiring attention to detail:

***The boarders with Miss Galloway, 1958***

*The dining room after 1958 with smaller tables for a reduced number of boarders*

> Miss Galloway spent many hours organising functions of various kinds for the boarders and her flair for thinking up new and unusual forms of decoration and entertainment will long be remembered by all those concerned. Her varied 'productions' included a Midsummer Night Staff Party, nativity tableaux, judo and dancing displays, handicraft exhibitions and numerous Christmas and other parties at which both the young (from the Bridge of Weir homes) and the old (from Auchenbothie) were entertained.
>
> (School Magazine 1967-68, p. 21)

Among the Matrons of the time were Miss Ann Ewing (an Old Girl) and Mrs Janet Henderson. Their morning and evening surgeries were very popular, as tender loving care was freely dispensed even if medicine was not needed.

Under the regime of 'Brenda' boarding house life still reflected the manners of pre-War society. There was a certain graciousness about day-to-day life in the House, with its fine public rooms adorned by Miss Galloway's beautiful flower arrangements. The dress code was still strictly enforced. A dress had to be worn on Sundays, and green Harris tweed or gaberdine coats, according to the season and the weather, had to be worn outdoors, always with the regulation hat. Trousers were permitted on Saturday mornings only, and girls changed into skirts and jumpers for lunch. When they went out in the afternoon, school uniform had to be worn, except by the senior girls. They had to change into their own clothes again for tea.

Punctuality and correct appearance at meals continued to be of the highest importance. A list was put up each term of the seating arrangements at table. Everyone advanced one place at table each day, except for the member of staff and the prefect, one of whom sat at each end of the table. A rota of table duties was attached to the seating plan. It was obligatory to make suitable conversation, and it was not permitted to ask for anything to be passed. One had to wait for salt and sugar and suchlike to be offered.

It was forbidden to go out on one's own. Each girl was allowed to go out on a visit once a fortnight, but never on a casual basis. Invitations were issued,

***Boarders practising judo, 1968***

***Tea in the garden, Shalott, 1964***
Foreground, left to right: Susan Middleton, Sandra Jack, Barbara Penrose, Tina Berry, Valerie Ferguson, Valerie Gordon

***Boarders in uniform, 1964***
Left to right:
Louise Vilvandré, Tina Berry, Margaret Kitchen, Barbara Penrose, Robin Genge

***The hoop dancers, from the boarders' entertainment performed before the whole School, 1962***
Back: Ann Hazel; Front: Marnie Kesson, Janet Warnock, Irene Malloy
The K stood for Kilmacolm Kapers, another of the acts. 'No one would have guessed that Miss Galloway had skilfully adapted school tennis dresses.'
(School Magazine, 1961-62, p. 34)

written permission had to be sought from parents – even if this meant sending to Singapore for permission to visit a friend whom one saw every day and who lived a minute's walk away – and Miss MacArthur read out a formal list at Prayers each week of these social engagements and arrangements for travel. The telephone was strictly out-of-bounds to the girls. A television set was donated in 1960, and the boarders were permitted to walk over to the main school building to watch Perry Mason on Saturday evenings. (It was kept in the reception room which is now the Rector's room.) The days of freedom to roam on bicycles at weekends were gone: there were now few places considered safe enough from traffic, and although some girls had bicycles in the summer term there was not much that could be done with them except ride to school.

Boarders' time was as highly structured as ever. Pianos and practice times were assigned by rota. There were Prayers after tea each evening, and Silent Prep at seven o'clock. Everyone lined up for Sweetie Cupboard at eight o'clock and a prefect unlocked it and distributed one item to each girl out of her own hoard. Pocket money to buy those sweeties was handed out after lunch on Saturday, and accounts had to be done on Sunday detailing how it had been spent: this sometimes called for creative accounting. Even the 'midnight feasts' on the last day of term were organised. They started at 8.30 pm.

There was a little tradition after the last-night feast of the Christmas term, preserved, along with many other memories, in a book compiled by the boarders of 1966 for Miss MacArthur:

> At the end of the Christmas term, the house staff, prefects and leaving girls tour the dorms by candlelight, singing by request carols in each room, when the dorm feast is over.
>
> (*The Story of Shalott*, p. 17)

The boarders' outings, picnics and parties were eagerly looked forward to and assiduously prepared for. In 1962 the twenty-five boarders produced a variety show in the school hall for the entertainment of the entire school, keeping their large audience enthralled for two hours with a short, light-hearted play, dances, comic songs and piano pieces. The boarders enjoyed great companionship and fellowship, and there was a house spirit which arose naturally among them.

***Dormitory 7, 1968***

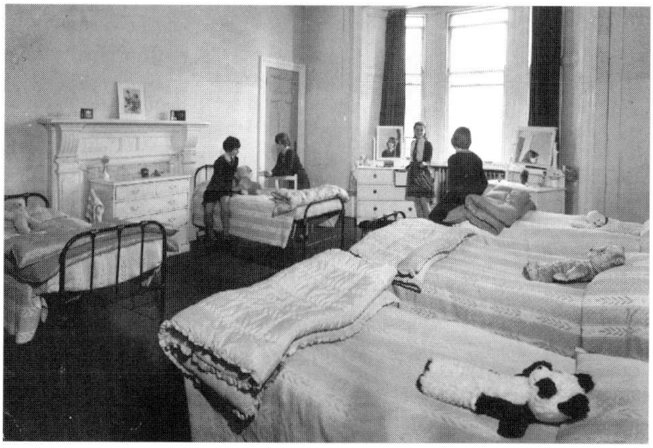

In 1956 Miss Margaret Birkmyre, who had lived in the house as a girl, presented to the boarding house the eighteenth-century Flemish tapestries which had originally hung in the entrance hall or 'tapestry room'. They were re-hung, and the room, which had been used as a library and quiet reading room, became a common room for all the boarders except the juniors; later it was used as a sixth

*The tapestry room, 1964*

form common room and often resounded to the songs of The Beatles from the wireless, record player and guitars kept there.

With the retiral of Miss MacArthur in 1966 the residence of the Headmistress in the boarding house ended. When Miss Galloway left in 1968, the post of full-time resident Housemistress was not filled. Some of her duties were undertaken by Miss Anne Kellagher, who taught science at the School from 1957 (and after her marriage, as Mrs MacInnes) until 1976. A housekeeper, Mrs Morrison, was appointed to carry out domestic duties. By the opening of the 1969-70 session the number of boarders had halved to eleven, and the House was no longer economically viable. At the end of the session the nine boarders who were not leaving school were offered places at St Bride's, and the St Columba's boarding chapter was closed. From 1970 onwards the Directors and Miss Clark devoted their energies to developing Shalott to accommodate the whole of the preparatory and junior school.

## The train girls

It was the railway that brought to Kilmacolm the families who provided the subscriptions – and the daughters – necessary to start St Columba's. The trains of course brought pupils too, from Bridge of Weir and beyond as far as Paisley, and from Greenock and Port Glasgow. 'Train girls' were important to the School, as without them, and the boarders, it would have been too small to survive. Travel by train, like boarding, was a little subculture of school life, necessitating special arrangements and rules and defining one's place in the system. 'I was a train girl,' is how many a former pupil begins the description of her time at St Columba's.

From early days the School made arrangements for the safety of girls travelling in. A first-class carriage was reserved for the pupils. (By the late 1930s three first-class carriages were reserved on the Greenock train.) In 1904 Mlle Lacaille was asked by the Directors to reside in Bridge of Weir and take responsibility for the pupils on the train journey. She was paid £10 a year in addition to her salary and given a season ticket.

*Kilmcolm from the station, 1901*

At some point Mistresses were relieved of this job and supervision of the girls travelling to School became the responsibility of prefects. Special train prefects were appointed, each with a deputy and a substitute, and they had to report to the Headmistress on the behaviour of the girls. The walk to the station had to be decorous: it was on no account permitted to run to catch the train. Each prefect was assigned a group of around eight pupils, and in these groups the pupils lined up on the platform to await the train. Miss Mary Mowat, who had been a pupil under Miss Waugh and Housemistress of one of the School's temporary boarding houses during the First World War, went on to become Secretary to Miss Waugh and the two successive Headmistresses, and then Bursar from 1951 until her retiral in 1957. She travelled for many years on the 'school trains', and organised this aspect of school life. She also made it her business to patrol the platform at Kilmacolm, and, after her retiral:

> . . . even now she laughs to see a surreptitious pulling on of gloves when she appears on the station road.
>
> (School Magazine 1956-57, p. 9)

Despite the attendance of Miss Mowat and prefects, behaviour, like so much of school life in those days, was a curious mixture of decorum and high jinks. When the train stopped at Lynedoch Street, halfway between Greenock and Port Glasgow, the girls had to put their gloves on. But less ladylike behaviour might precede and follow. Two Greenock pupils, Frances Graham and Ida McCallum (Diack), have memories of some of the things that went on:

> . . . carriage 'tig' with us up on the seats and racks above whilst one girl was blindfolded and searching for us; dancing in whatever form we could manage; somersaulting from the luggage rack – hanging from the rail edge and somersaulting onto the seat below.
>
> Someone once threw her lacrosse stick into the carriage one day before getting in herself – the stick continued its flight through the door window and landed on the other line.
>
> While we waited at Kilmacolm one afternoon a special trainload of US Navy sailors on liberty from the NATO fleet caused a lot of fun when they took several Polaroid photographs of us – in the 50s we'd never seen instant colour photos.
>
> The last day of term was celebrated by the very popular carriage feasts. Lots of food and sweets were consumed and the leftovers were kept for the ever-hungry boarders.

The interruptions to normal service that were a feature of the War meant that for some pupils it was simpler to board. For the Greenock girls travel was often made chaotic by troop movements to and from this key port. Many of them remember during the build-up to D-Day seeing the *Queen Mary* and the *Queen Elizabeth* arriving on alternate weeks at Princes Pier and Greenock Pier, offloading hundreds of American troops, through whom they struggled onto the trains. When they arrived at school after an exhausting journey an hour or more late, Miss McMurtrie saw to it that they were taken into the reception room and given a cup

***'Train Girls' by Mairi Crawford (later Hedderwick), Form VIB, 1953-54***

of Bovril and a biscuit by Jenny. The War could also make travel more interesting, and many pupils remember the American soldiers throwing Hershey Bars and chewing-gum onto the platform, exciting and yet tantalising for young ladies forbidden to move from their lines in order to pick them up. It was useful to have friends among the boys from Dardenne Preparatory School, as they were under no such restriction.

By 1954 more than two hundred girls (out of a total of 333 pupils) travelled to school by train, and the train strike in the summer of 1955 meant that transport by bus had to be arranged for most of them. When the Greenock line was closed for good at the end of January 1959, bus travel became a permanent arrangement. Beeching threatened to axe the Kilmacolm-Paisley service in 1964, but to the relief of the School and the many parents who had protested, the village was reprieved. The station was eventually closed in 1983, and bus transport took over from the Paisley direction too.

There was one important feature of train travel that everyone missed when buses took over:

> For pupils leaving School there was the ritual of throwing the hat out of the train window while passing a certain place between Kilmacolm and Port Glasgow.
>
> (Frances Graham and Ida McCallum [Diack])

Those going in the Bridge of Weir direction threw their hats from the train into the River Gryffe.

***Train girls, c 1964***

Back row: Elizabeth Chaffe, Rosemary Sim, Sally Hunter, Caroline Saul
Front row: Jane Cochrane, Carol Blackwood, Patricia Allan

*Chapter Nine*

# Edith Muriel Clark 1966-1976

Muriel Clark, BA, Dip Ed, came to St Columba's School in 1966 from Broughton High School for Girls, Salford. A strong and capable Head, she had, during her six-year headship of Broughton, steered that school from its position as a grammar school of 300 girls housed in a Victorian mansion to a 470-strong grammar-technical school in a new building, and left it ready to take its planned place in the comprehensive system at some future date.

***Miss Clark***

It was Miss Clark's aim to raise the academic profile of St Columba's, and there was a steadily increasing number of passes at SCE Ordinary and Higher Grade. Her honours degree from Liverpool University was in English, and she taught both English and Scripture – a half-timetable, no less – getting to know the girls as their teacher and not merely as their Headmistress. Her approach to discipline was very firm, but on a personal level she was responsible for many unobtrusive acts of kindness and generosity to pupils and staff.

Miss Clark's great love of Scotland was one of the things which attracted her to the St Columba's post, and her love of the countryside and its history, especially its spiritual history, was something which she wished to share with her new School. The pilgrimages to Iona, which culminated in the centenary year in a very special journey to the Saint's holy place, were started by her.

She could scarcely have foreseen all the challenges that lay ahead at St Columba's, but there could have been few headmistresses better able to lead the School at a time of political turmoil. On the School's seventy-fifth anniversary in 1972, Miss Clark addressed the St Columba's School Society and told them, 'It is a fact that the needs of St Columba's pupils are changing. Though a school may be "old", it dare not, on peril of its life, be old-fashioned.'

Miss Clark had a clear-sighted attitude to these changing requirements and faced them squarely, looking to the future of the School and the futures of the individual pupils in everything she did. Drive and determination were her hallmarks, and her energy was prodigious. These qualities brought about the most rapid expansion in numbers that the School had yet seen, and saw into being many innovations in school life.

Miss Clark left St Columba's in 1976, having reached the age of sixty, but, not yet ready to retire completely from teaching, she took up a post as assistant teacher of English at Paisley Grammar School.

## The Directors

Mr G N Ferguson took over the chairmanship of the Company from Mr John Tindal in 1966. His financial acumen and dedication served the Company supremely well until 1972, when he was given an affectionate farewell party by the School. He had been for many years Convener of the Company's finance sub-committee and the Company's representative on the Central Committee for Grant-Aided Schools in Scotland. He had been Chairman of the St Columba's local directorate since 1954, and over the years there had scarcely been a special occasion at the School which he had not attended, often accompanied by Mrs Ferguson.

*G N Ferguson*

He was succeeded as Chairman of the Company by Mrs Helen Mack, who served in this capacity from 1972 until 1977. The chairmanship of St Columba's local Directors was filled in 1972 by Mr Geoffrey Duncan, and he became Chairman of the Company in 1977 when Mrs Mack retired.

New to the local directorate, joining Dr Morag MacArthur and Mrs Jean Graham, were Mr J Michael Hepburn from 1972 and Dr Helen Laird from 1975, later to become Chairman of the Company.

Mr Gordon Wilson retired as Secretary in 1968 and Mr Robert Jackson took over this increasingly onerous job. He retired on health grounds in 1975. Both Secretaries had served the Company loyally and well.

## The big freeze

It was Miss Clark's lot to take the helm at a time of stormy weather, both meteorological and political. The School suffered damage in the notorious storm of January 1968, but that was easily put right. The political climate was at best unpredictable and at worst hostile. The maintaining of three grant-dependent schools in the late 1960s and 70s required a steady hand and a cool nerve on the part of the Directors and the Headmistresses.

In 1967 the Labour government had frozen the grant. They appointed the Public Schools Commission to report on how the grant-aided schools could become part of a comprehensive system. A delegation from the Scottish Sub-Committee of this body met representatives of the Girls' School Company in March 1969 and there was a discussion in which the schools were asked to justify their grant-aided position. There was plenty to be said on this subject, especially in the matter of benefits for pupils and parental choice, but there was a general awareness that this would count for little against the determination of the Government to build a monolithic education system. It came as no surprise when, in the spring of 1970, the Commission reported that the continuance of grant-aid must be dependent upon fulfilling a role in the comprehensive system. At the meeting of March 1969 both sides had agreed that it was very difficult to see how the Company's schools could integrate.

The election in June 1970 of a Conservative government, led by Edward Heath, postponed what had seemed the inevitable third act of the drama. Circular 600, which had imposed a comprehensive system, was withdrawn. The grant-aided sector enjoyed an unlooked-for thaw, with the restoration of grant, albeit based on only forty per cent of operating costs instead of the previous maximum of sixty. Rising costs and wage inflation meanwhile diminished the real value of that grant alarmingly.

The Directors used the reprieve from worry about the status of the schools to address the problems attached to the viability of each as an independent establishment. Informal approaches began to Laurel Bank School in Glasgow about a possible future merger with Park, and to Helensburgh's Larchfield, a fully independent preparatory school for boys, about amalgamation with St Bride's.

St Columba's had neither competitors nor neighbours with which to amalgamate, and demand for places was healthy. The problem was rather one of cost-effectiveness. The Scottish Education Department under the Labour administration had insisted that the cost per pupil must be reduced, saying that an 800-pupil school was the minimum number for operating at a reasonable cost level. The Directors were of the opinion that 600 was a desirable level. At Kilmacolm the demand for places made it conceivable that an additional hundred pupils needed to achieve this target could be found within a few years. There was room at Shalott to expand. With the enthusiastic cooperation of Miss Clark, the younger end of the School became the focus for expansion plans.

## The new Primary School

In Miss Clark's first year as Head, she and the Directors had already identified the need for more accommodation in the preparatory and junior schools as the main priority in the future development of the School. Six years later this aim had been achieved. The first stage was to devote the whole of Shalott to an enlarged preparatory department, which became possible with the end of boarding in 1970. Miss Clark was able at last to satisfy the big demand for places by admitting forty-five pupils to the reception class, in two streams, instead of the previous maximum of twenty-nine. A new teacher was taken on, Miss Helen Anderson, a former Head Girl of St Columba's. Gone were the old names of Kindergarten, Transition, Form I, and so on up to Form IV B, and in came the more straightforward Primary One to Primary Seven. Primary Five to Primary Seven (the Junior School) were still housed in Shieldhall and Westmarch.

The second stage of the development was completed in 1973, when the new wing of Shalott was opened, and the whole of the Primary department was for the first time united on one site.

The new building, which cost just under £60,000, was planned by Frank Burnet Bell and Partners. It was designed to be the maximum size possible within the limits of space, and the best building that could be managed within

***Shalott: the new hall***

***Planting trees outside the new extension of Shalott, gifted and organised by the SCSS, 1973***
Left to right: Dr Laird, Miss Margaret Birkmyre, Jennifer Barr and Lesley McGarva (planting the tree); the group at the far right are: Miss Wyllie, Miss Fyfe, Miss Reid

the constraints of budget. It has a steel framework with preformed panels fitted in between the steel beams, a 60-foot long hall with windows all along one side and six spacious classrooms and cloakrooms. Combined with Shalott it offered accommodation for 350 pupils. Shalott itself had a major refurbishment to comply with the latest fire regulations at a cost of £10,000.

A link, which became known as the Bridge, was made between the house and the new building:

> It was here that someone noticed a carved inscription on the outside wall of the old building. *Hope for the coming dawn,* it said.
>
> (Miss Margaret Croft)

The cost of these projects was offset by the sale of Westmarch, no longer needed for the Junior School. Shieldhall was retained as an arts and music centre until 1975, when it was sold, and Cargen Lodge, the property adjoining the main building, was purchased to serve this purpose.

## The big freeze: part two

The School opened in Miss Clark's first year with 441 pupils. The steady increase in numbers to 574 by 1973 was a significant achievement especially as an almost annual teachers' salary increase during these years had been accompanied by a corresponding increase in fees. The Heath administration, while giving the grant-aided schools a little breathing space in which to prepare for the future, had endowed the country with spiralling inflation. The economic freeze declared by the Government in 1972, in a futile attempt to control mushrooming prices and wage settlements, brought both a setback for the grant, which was cut to the 1969 level, with a supplement to account for increased costs, and also a temporary ban on increasing fees (doubtless a welcome respite for parents).

Running the schools in this climate was a struggle. With the election of a Labour government in March 1974 the pressing concern immediately became one of survival. The Directors, while painfully aware that too great an increase in fees would drive some pupils away and result in a decrease in revenue, nevertheless had to increase fees by twenty-five per cent in September 1974, with a warning to parents that a termly review of fees might now be necessary. The grant-aided sector prepared itself for an announcement that grants would be discontinued. But before this a further blow fell with the publication of the Houghton Report which recommended a thirty per cent increase for teachers' salaries backdated to April 1974. In January 1975 the double challenge of the announced withdrawal of grant and the Houghton Report necessitated an increase in the Company's fees for the second and third terms of fifty-six per cent. By June of that year twenty-three pupils had been withdrawn. In September 1975 the School reopened with just 507 pupils. Five years' worth of pupil increases had been wiped out and further reductions were to come.

## Hope for the coming dawn: the decision for independence

The phasing-out of grant faced the schools in this sector with a choice between independence or the possibility, depending on the wishes of the local education authority, of integration within the state sector. The comprehensive

***Miss Margaret Croft with Form II, 1967-68***
The same class two years later is pictured opposite.

***Staff at Miss Millar's retiral, 1968***
Miss Lakeman, Miss Weir, Miss Hagart, Miss Clark, Miss Millar, Dr Macdonald (with the school cat, Cindy Columba), Miss MacArthur, Miss Tytler, Miss Collet, Miss M J Walker

***Dr Sheila Macdonald's retiral presentation, June 1971***
Back row:
Miss M J Walker, Miss Fyfe, Mrs Cameron, Miss Jean Anderson, Miss Hutton, Mrs Couper
Front row:
Miss Reid, Mrs Scott, Miss MacArthur, Dr Macdonald, Miss Clark, Miss Millar, Miss Jenny Holmes

system was now being spread like a fire-blanket across Scotland, and there was no place for diversity in this new scene. The Scottish grant-aided schools were required to decide by September 1975 whether to offer to integrate or to accept a reducing grant for the years 1976/7 until 1981/2 and full independence thereafter.

The Directors had given thought to this question since the late 1960s, and they had canvassed the parents' views in 1969: the majority had made clear their preference for independence over the alternative. In September 1975, at a meeting with the Director of Education for Strathclyde Region, the Directors of the Girls' School Company were told that, of the three schools, only some of the St Bride's buildings would be accepted by the state sector. Soon afterwards the Directors informed the Scottish Education Department of their decision to opt for independence for all three schools. About eighty per cent of the UK's grant-aided schools took this course. The merger between St Bride's and Larchfield went ahead without delay, and the new independent school was named Lomond School. At Kilmacolm the Directors began to think about co-education.

## Changes in staff and curriculum

One problem the Company's schools did not have to contend with in this period was work-to-rule and strikes by teachers, which disrupted the schooling of most of the country's children in 1974. The St Columba's staff were as loyal and flexible as ever, some of them transferring between the Senior and Junior Schools when the need arose. Between 1973 and 1975 the art and music staff also had to make daily journeys between Shieldhall and the main building. The acquisition of Cargen Lodge brought the art and music departments back onto the main campus.

***Miss Kathleen Weir with Form III A, 1969-70***

Back row: Judith Blair, Lesley Bryan, Eileen Gillan, Fiona Best, Alison Brodie, Penny Clark
Second row: Jane Burt, Fiona Forrest, Elaine Holmes, Alex Hunter, Josephine Eden, Sandra Harvey, Marian Austin
Front row: Patti von Gliszczynski, Janie Aitchison, Caroline Golding, Ann Houston, Miss Weir, Jean Donald, Alison Best, Ann Coates

Miss Kathleen Weir, who had been Head of the Junior School, was appointed Deputy Headmistress in 1971, on the retiral of Dr Macdonald. The rearrangement of the Primary School in 1973 coincided with further staff changes. Miss Margaret Croft, hitherto head of the Preparatory School, became the Head of the new Primary School, and Miss Sylvia Pollock was made Assistant Head. They replaced Mrs Pearl McLean and Mrs Margaret Mackintosh, both of whom retired in 1973. Mrs McLean had come to St Columba's in 1962, originally to teach in the Senior School, but had transferred to the Junior School when she was needed there, becoming its Head in 1971. Mrs Mackintosh, who had also been on the staff since 1962 and taught in both Senior and Junior Schools, was her Deputy from 1971. Both had served the School with great energy and dedication at a time of change.

The School had for several years operated an A-Level curriculum in sixth year, and in Miss Clark's headship several subjects were added to this, including chemistry and physics, with an increasing number of girls choosing to add some A-Levels to their Highers. From Miss Clark's first year she encouraged the trend of increasing interest in science, and it became possible to opt for three sciences. Mrs Phyllis Notman taught biology from 1961 until she retired in 1977, achieving excellent results with a growing number of pupils. Mrs Anne MacInnes, who came to the School in 1957 as Miss Kellagher, taught mathematics and general science but later specialised in physics, raising the standard of results in this subject, and left her full-time post in 1974. She took responsibility for the careers department, and in her last year was made Principal Teacher of guidance.

## Men!

By the late 1960s the Americans were preparing to put a man on the moon, and it could not be long before there would be a man or two in Duchal Road's staffroom. The first full-time male teacher at St Columba's was Mr Tom Walton, who came to head the music department in 1967. He was followed

*Staff, 1970*

Back row: Mr Anderson, Mrs Buchanan, Miss Wyllie, Miss Govan, Mrs Lees, Mrs Martyn, Mrs Nicol, Mrs Jamieson, Miss Allison, Miss Neill
Second row: Mrs McLean, Mrs Craib, Miss Ritchie, Mrs Couper, Mrs Keanie, Miss V McInnes, Mrs Mackintosh, Mrs Woodward, Mrs Notman, Mrs A McInnes, Miss Shearer, Miss Macdonald
Front row: Mr Jamieson, Mr Campbell, Mr Forgie, Miss Nicol, Mrs Crowther, Dr Macdonald, Miss Clark, Miss Weir, Miss Walker, Miss Gillies, Mr T Walton, Mr Wyllie, Mr McAulay

in 1968 by Mr Ian Jamieson, teacher of history. These pioneers were joined in 1969 by three more: Mr William Forgie (classics), Mr Colin Campbell (science) and Mr Gordon Wyllie (art). It was a hugely popular development. In October 1969 a debate was held on the motion 'That there should be Male Teachers in an All-Girls School':

> This was extremely successful, attendance reaching the 200 mark, and audience participation was great. The motion was carried, the audience favouring the policy of St Columba's by a great majority.
>
> (School Magazine 1969-70, p. 28)

Male staff made an important and distinctive contribution to school life, helping to inaugurate some new events such as the Burns Supper and the St Valentine's Day debate, when their participation gave zest to such motions as 'That women will only be liberated when Playboy magazine is destroyed' (carried) and 'Frailty thy name is woman' (defeated).

Mr Campbell was succeeded by Mr Morris Banks as Principal Teacher of science in 1973. Mr William McAulay came to head the mathematics department from 1969 until 1973, and Mr John Spinks came to the School in 1974 and was Principal Teacher of mathematics from 1975. Mr David Craig arrived to assist Miss Avril Blythe in the art department in 1974, and Mr Derek Fry joined the music department in 1972.

A harbinger, perhaps, of what was to come, Kenneth Walton joined the sixth year in 1975-76, in order to take A-level music, and had the interesting experience of being the only boy in a school of 500 girls. He had a successful year both musically and academically, and at the end of it someone remarked to Miss Clark that Kenneth was a good advertisement for co-education.

## Music and drama

The extremely high standard of music at the School in its first seventy years had been achieved almost entirely in piano and in singing, with some violin. In 1967 eighty-eight girls, one fifth of the School, were studying piano at school. The following year Mr Walton brought in some visiting instrument teachers, and assisted by Mr William Rennie, who taught violin from 1968 until 1972, he formed the school orchestra, mainly from junior pupils, comprising eight violins, two flutes, four clarinets, two horns and a trumpet. The orchestra was greatly enjoyed in that first year, when:

> . . . it competed successfully several times with the singing at morning prayers, and was received with great enthusiasm.
>
> (School Magazine 1968-69, p. 35)

Mr Harry Morrison taught clarinet from the early days of the orchestra, and has enjoyed a long association with the School as a visiting teacher; but it proved difficult to find many other instrument teachers with the same commitment, and, after Mr Rennie left, the orchestra suffered a slight hiatus, during which the music department concentrated on building up the school choirs.

With the coming of Mr Walton to St Columba's the School enjoyed a new era of fine musical productions, akin to the era of drama under Mrs Jones. Mrs Jones's last production for the School, and Miss Clark's introduction to

*The orchestra, 1969*

Romeo and Juliet, *1967*
*Sally Rentoul as Romeo*

*Karen Ruse and Kitty Hill as Juliet and Nurse*

*Barbara Penrose and Isabel Tolhurst as Lord and Lady Capulet*

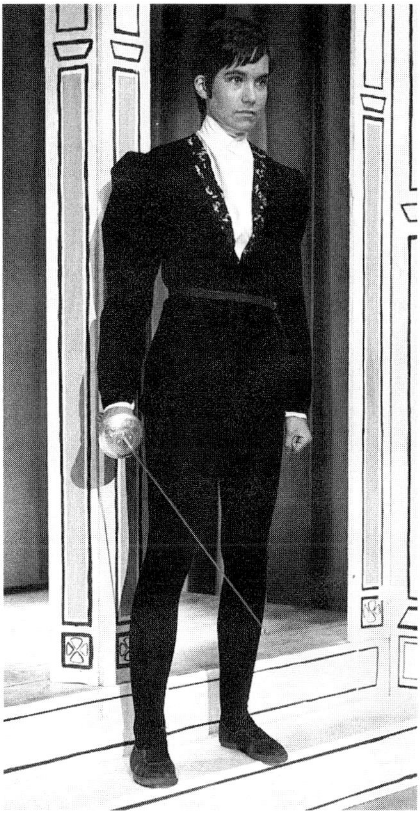

*Anne Marshall as Tybalt*

**Noye's Fludde,** ***1970***
The Gossips flee from the Ark as the flood approaches

drama at St Columba's, was *Romeo and Juliet* in 1967. It delighted its audience and won critical acclaim in the local press, especially for Karen Powell (Ruse) as Juliet.

In the following years Mr Walton was musical director of several outstanding productions. In June 1970 in partnership with Miss Kathleen Weir, then head of the Junior School, he produced Benjamin Britten's *Noye's Fludde*, the most ambitious production the School had ever undertaken. It was performed in St Columba Church, and the orchestra, mainly composed of junior pupils, was supplemented by some seniors as percussionists, playing drums, cymbals, triangle, tambourine, tam-tam and chime bars. In addition:

> . . . the string-mugs, representing rain-drops, provided some amusement amongst the audience. Of course, the orchestra would not have been complete without the generous and professional help of a string quintet led by Louis Carus, two buglers and a professional recorder player.
>
> (School Magazine 1969-70, p. 33)

Louis Carus was Head of strings at the Royal Academy of Music. The parts of Mr and Mrs Noah were played by Mr Stanley Sinclair and Miss Eileen Witherow, members of the Greenock Philharmonic Society, of which Mr Walton was conductor for twenty-one years. Several old friends of the School also took part, including Archie Shearer at the organ, and Parker Nicol as the Voice of God from his hiding place behind the organ pipes.

Mr Wyllie considered his design for this production the best work he had ever done. Assisted by Mrs Joanna Craib, he made a magnificent set, representing the ark, sun, moon, stars and the rainbow. The rainbow was revealed by an ingenious design like that of a venetian blind. They also made heads for all the animals and birds played by members of the Junior School. The dramatic effect of the design was heightened by the black and white used for the ark and all the costumes except those of Mr and Mrs Noah. Miss Gillies of the physical education department choreographed the dances of the raven and the dove, and the art and home economics departments designed and made the costumes. It was a remarkable performance, tremendous fun for all who took part, and never forgotten by those who saw and heard it.

The Christmas concert of 1970 featured Carl Orff's *The Christmas Story*, produced by Miss Jean Nicol, Old Girl and Head of the English department from 1967, with Mr Tom Walton as musical director. The following year the choir performed *The Christmas Story* by Heinrich Schütz in Paisley Abbey and then at St Columba Church, Kilmacolm. In 1973 the morality play *Everyman* was performed, as part of the Christmas concert, with music composed by Mr Derek Fry.

In October 1972, to celebrate the School's seventy-fifth anniversary, another ambitious performance was staged. Purcell's *Dido and Aeneas*, with Mr Walton as musical director and Miss Nicol as producer, featured Jennifer Barr in the part of Dido and Margaret Borland (Houston) as Aeneas, with Louis Carus and his string quintet again lending professional support. The Junior School's contribution to the birthday celebrations was the pageant *One Came From Erin*, depicting the life of St Columba. It had first been staged in 1963, to commemorate the 1400th anniversary of St Columba's landing on Iona, and no one who had seen it on that occasion forgot it. Now produced for the second time by Miss Weir, an equally memorable performance was a fitting celebration of the life of both Saint and School.

When Mrs Heather Woodward left at Christmas 1973, the School lost a member of staff who had been stage manager or otherwise involved at a practical level in every drama production during her twelve years at St Columba's. Mrs Woodward, who had been Miss Collins when she came in 1961, was a well-loved teacher of modern languages and Principal Teacher of guidance.

In February 1975 Lionel Bart's *Oliver!* was given an enthusiastic and spirited performance. It may have been 'an unusual choice for a girls' school', as one critic remarked, but it had a strong cast, including Janette Needham (Giffin) who made Fagin wholly believable, Julia Stevenson (Massey) as Nancy, and Evelyn Jamieson, one of the School's prize-winning elocution pupils at the Renfrewshire Music Festival, in the title role.

Mrs Patricia McTavish (Williamson) was visiting teacher of solo singing from 1967 until 1977. An Old Girl of the School, she had taken first prizes for singing at the Royal Scottish Academy of Music, and after her marriage went to Hong Kong with her husband, where she had her own radio and television programmes. Her professional name was Patti Duncan. Mr Walton expressed the regret of staff and pupils when she left:

> Her coloratura cadenza, her endless energy, her sparkling smile and her zest for yoga gave the staff and pupils of Cargen Lodge a bright start to many a bleak Monday morning.
>
> (School Magazine 1976, p. 20)

Three girls from Miss Clark's period were successful Silver Tablet candidates: Jennifer Barr in 1974 and Catriona Crawford (Jacobs) in 1975 on the piano and Janette Needham (Giffin) as a singer in 1976.

Both junior and senior departments of the School competed each year in the Renfrewshire Music Festival, always with success in several categories. By the end of Miss Clark's headship the range of entries was wider than ever, and in 1976 the high standard put St Columba's among the top overall prizewinners, with six firsts in the Primary department, and five in the Senior School. In that year Mr Fry's music-making group from Primary Six and Seven won first place in this category and had their performance broadcast on radio; the following year they won another first. In 1971 Primary Six's performance of 'Delaney's Donkey' in the Action Song category had all but brought the house down, and won them first place and the St Mary's Girls' School Trophy. The teacher responsible for this triumph was Miss Vivien McInnes, teacher of piano and class singing from 1968 until 1972.

Many of the successes at the Renfrewshire Music Festival were in elocution: in the 1970s one-sixth of the School studied diction. Miss May Sharp taught speech and drama from 1973 until 1977, and her teaching bore fruit in the dramatic performances from the hall stage as well as at the Festival. She formed a Drama Club in 1973, whose first performance was *Everyman* ; this was followed by *Frost on the Rose* by T B Morris in 1974.

**Dido and Aeneas, *1972***
Antonia Parish, Jennifer Barr (Dido), Margaret Houston (Aeneas), Susan Ferguson

**Dido and Aeneas**
The death scene

***Janette Giffin as Fagin***

**Oliver!**
Evelyn Jamieson as Oliver, second from the left; centre: Jane O'Neil as the Artful Dodger, Julia Massey as Nancy

***Renfrewshire Music Festival, 1969***
Unconducted and unaccompanied ensemble, winners of the Mary Graham Memorial Trophy and an honours certificate
Back row: Patricia Smith, Gillian Tweddel, Patricia McCall
Second row: Kathryn Williamson, Irene Johnson, Mr Tom Walton
Front row: Fiona Elliott, Sarah Lawson, Louise Garner, Sheena Graham, Mr Henry Havergal (Festival adjudicator), Hazel Stuart, Bryonie Stone

**Delaney's Donkey, *Renfrewshire Music Festival, 1971***

***Singing class in the school hall, with Mr Walton, 1968***

***Under-15 athletics team, trophy winners at Renfrewshire Inter-School Sports, 1971***
Lesley Hathaway, Una Lyle, Andrea Semple, Anne Lester, Elizabeth Will

***Lacrosse, 1966-67***

***1st lacrosse XII, 1967-68, which drew 3-3 with St George's, Edinburgh, in the final of the Scottish Schools Lacrosse Tournament***

Back row: Gill Hamilton, Catriona Hill, Amanda Boal, Miss Gillies, Jane Fraser, Victoria Jack, Ruth Clay, Sarah Lawson, Lorna White
Front row: Marion Hay, Susan Walker, Irene Johnson, Patricia McCall.
G Hamilton, A Boal, J Fraser and L White were selected to play for the Scottish Schools' Lacrosse Team in a tournament at Dunfermline College of Physical Education.

***1st lacrosse XII, 1971-72***
Back row: Mary-Jane Fennell, Julia Critchley, Lydia Lang, Alison Coghill, Christine Cowan, Nicola Aitkenhead, Vicky Payne
Front row: Una Lyle, Alison Duff, Patricia Lang, Sandra McDougall, Joanna Craib

## Games

The playing fields were improved in 1969, with new tarmac tennis courts, two winter netball courts and an area for volleyball and rounders. The physical education department was under the inspired and energetic leadership of Mrs Veronica Sandeman (Vickie Gillies), an Old Girl, from 1966 until 1972, and in the 1969-70 session she entered a team from the School for the Renfrewshire Inter-School Sports Day for the first time. In 1971 at this event the St Columba's team won the Lady Lithgow Trophy for under-15 girls' events.

The Principal Teacher of physical education from 1972 until 1976 was Miss Patricia Rodger. There were many successes in lacrosse, under both Miss Rodger and Mrs Sandeman, with several girls during this period being chosen to play for Scottish Schoolgirls' teams, notably Alison Band (Coghill) and Una Lyle. From 1973 onwards Miss Rodger took the First XII to Merton, London, to participate in the annual All-England Schools' Tournament. Early in her headship Miss Clark had proposed the re-introduction of hockey as a second major game, but the lack of facilities for play meant that this was delayed. In 1972 Miss Rodger introduced it at junior level. She was also responsible for an expanded athletics programme, including the shot putt, javelin and hurdling. She began teaching badminton and involved the School in the Renfrewshire Badminton League, and she started a school swimming club.

Many girls achieved local success in sport, and a couple in the international arena. Carol McDonald (Blackwood), who left school in 1969 to continue her schooling and skiing in Switzerland, won two gold medals for skiing at the Commonwealth Winter Games of 1970. In 1972 she went to Japan as a member of the British Olympic Ski team. Maureen Richmond (Walker) won the School Golf Championship, the West of Scotland Girls' Golf Championship and the Scottish Girls' Golf Championship in 1969. She retained the Scottish Girls' title in 1970 and 1971 and took it again in 1973. In 1972 she won the Girls' British Open Golf Championship, and in 1974 she was chosen for the Curtis Cup team. She left St Columba's in 1972 to take up an English Speaking Union scholarship in the USA, and returned to Scotland to study medicine the following year.

## Innovations

One of the most well-loved and lasting of the annual events started by Miss Clark was the Burns Supper. It was inaugurated in 1971, with Mr William Forgie, teacher of classics, in the chair, and the event proved to be both an annual showcase for outstanding talent among staff and pupils, and a vehicle, lubricated with humour, for the social mixing of senior pupils and staff. It could also be on occasion an opportunity to express deeply held feelings about the life of the School, as when Miss Clark proposed the toast to the School in her final year and was received with a standing ovation. Mr Forgie was always associated in everyone's mind with the Burns Supper, and there was sadness at his death within two years of his retiral.

There was a proliferation of school societies. An Arts Club was started in 1968. Mr Campbell founded the Scientific Society in 1969. A Scripture Union

***The library, 1968***

branch was formed in 1970 by Miss Sylvia Pollock. The Debating Society was active every year, with Mr Forgie taking over from Mrs Keanie in 1970, and then, from 1973, Mrs Janet Malcolm of the history department. In some years teams were entered for the Renfrewshire Schools Debating Union competition and the *Scottish Daily Express* Debating Union. In others inter-house debates were held. In 1972 a Music Club was formed, with the aid of Mr McAulay and then Mr William Robertson (Principal Teacher of classics, 1973-75). In 1973 came the Modern Languages Club. In 1975 for the first time a team from the School entered the Latin and Greek Prose and Verse Speaking Competition at Glasgow University: there was some success that year, and so much in the following that they brought home the trophy for the 'most distinguished performance by a school with a small classics department'.

The Preparatory School too had its extra-curricular activities and its successes: the Junior Branch of the British Wild Flower Society, led by Miss Conacher, gained third place in the national schools' competition in 1967, second place in 1968 and first in 1969 and 1970. In 'Plant a Tree in 73' year the children of the Primary School were responsible for planting 250 trees at Shalott, at their homes and elsewhere in the area.

In Miss Clark's headship, innovations made their mark on every area of school life. The art department began the teaching of pottery in 1967, and the following year Mrs Brenda Lenaghan arranged a fashion show as an end-of-term fund-raising entertainment. The clothes modelled were highly inventive:

> Materials ranged from sacking to silk, and drinking straws, rhododendron leaves and fish nets were used for some of the more exotic creations. Mr Walton gave the whole performance a very sophisticated atmosphere with his improvisations on the piano and his suave comments on the clothes.
>
> (School Magazine 1967-68, p. 23)

***Period piece: the prefects' room (Room 23), 1968, with petal-shaped purple coffee table and sunburst-yellow PVC armchairs***

In 1970 Mr Campbell acquired a car engine for the School and ran a very popular car maintenance course for senior girls. In June 1971 an art

***Prefects and Council members, 1975-76***

Back row: Fiona Best, Elizabeth-Anne McMurray, Mhairi Leishman, Janet Wanford, Shirley Farquhar, Annette Hardcastle, Inez Muir, Deborah Paton, Patti von Gliszczynski, Janie Aitchison

Second row: Fiona Gibb-Stuart, Karine Buchanan, Karen Stevenson, Valerie Lang, Janette Giffin, Janet Mack, Julia Massey, Grace Hendry, Rona Patrick

Front row: Lorraine Ingham, Rosemary Tainsh, Margaret McKinnon, Alison McMurray (Head Girl), Erica Martin (Depute Head Girl), Eleanor Pritchard, Jane McCready, Susan Heycock, Sandra McDerment

exhibition and musical evening were held in the School: the art exhibits were in various media. The cafeteria system for school meals was introduced in 1974, a development which proved popular with the girls, and reversed the drop in demand for school meals. A language laboratory was installed in Cargen Lodge in 1976.

Numerous new prizes were presented in Miss Clark's time. In 1970 the parents of Fiona Keyden, a pupil from 1953 until 1965, who had died in a car accident in 1970, gave a prize in her memory, to be awarded annually for outstanding service to the School. Miss Clark presented prizes for excellence in English when she left in 1976.

One of Miss Clark's most important new ventures was the annual visit to Iona, home of St Columba, the first of which was in June 1967. In 1969 and 1970 she took pupils from the third year to Whithorn where St Ninian built the first Christian church in Scotland, and each year from 1971 until 1974 she took third-year pupils to Holy Island.

There were many other trips to visit places of historical and geographical interest. Geography trips and field studies were organised by Miss Alice Macdonald, Principal Teacher of geography from 1967. Mr Banks took a party hill climbing each year, which Miss Clark enjoyed as much as anyone. There was a school visit to Paris in 1967, a holiday in Switzerland in 1973, and a

***Trip to Iona, June 1976***

***The new school hat, 1968***
Morag McNeil and Yvonne Morton with the school cat, Cindy Columba

ten-day visit to Wissant, Normandy, in July 1974 for third-year pupils, who appreciated some hitherto unnoticed qualities in their teachers:

> Miss Rodger should have been a nurse. She also runs around taking pictures of you. Miss Roberts uses her mathematical brain to keep our pocket-money intact. Miss Blythe explained in English about the pottery-making. Miss Ritchie keeps the peace. I've only one complaint – they laugh at night.
>
> (School Magazine 1974, p. 37)

In July 1976 senior pupils travelled to Caen and stayed with French families, coming together each day for tuition and excursions. In December 1975 some pupils joined a school cruise on SS *Uganda* to the Holy Land. The School's group was organised by Miss Ann Ritchie, teacher of modern languages from 1970 and Principal Teacher from 1971, with Miss Rodger and Miss Clark accompanying. It was a very successful first school cruise abroad.

If outward change is anything to go by, the biggest innovation was in uniform:

> The new headmistress, discreetly 'mod' herself, has made innovations, the most popular being the new hat; but she is sufficiently square to say firmly, 'hats must be worn all the year.'
>
> (*Scottish Field*, April 1968, p. 39)

*Into the 70s with 'Terylene', 'Crimplene' and 'Bri-Nylon'* trumpets the title of a 1971 leaflet about new school uniforms, which Miss Clark pasted into a school scrapbook, and few schools could resist such a call. Gone were the belted burberries and pudding-bowl hats; it was on with slimline coats and 'Jackie Stewart' caps in green corded velvet. In 1968 came the new summer dress designed by Mrs Lenaghan. Skirt lengths were fashionably short. On school trips Miss Clark permitted the wearing of casual clothes.

## An era of change

So many changes had taken place since the beginning of the 1960s, marvelled at by many of the Old Girls who received a copy of the school magazine each year: men in the staffroom, boys at the school dance, the baffling new system of naming classes, from Primary One to Seven and Senior One to Six (what could it mean?). An Old Girl who left in 1922 approves of what she sees in the photographs and reads the articles with interest, but expresses reserve on one subject:

> How Miss Waugh would have shuddered at the eating of 'crisps'!
>
> (Eleanor Murray [Morrison], School Magazine, 1975, p. 63)

The eating of crisps aside, Miss Waugh and the other Headmistresses doubtless would have approved of the way in which the Directors and Miss Clark had met every challenge and adapted the school to meet modern requirements. Miss Clark reminded an audience of former pupils at the School's seventy-fifth anniversary celebrations of the important changes taking place in the School:

> Senior pupils are staying on at School in increasing numbers. There

> is a marked and growing interest in and demand for mathematics and science. The girls, moreover, are career minded. So are their parents.
> (School Magazine 1972, p. 38)

There was an increased number of presentations for Highers and A-levels, and the majority of pupils left school to enter university. In 1972 the School held its first careers convention. The range of careers pursued by Miss Clark's girls go from medical research to industrial microbiology, from production management to computer systems engineering, from academic publishing to environmental health, and from market research to investment banking.

The first girl from St Columba's to be ordained into the ministry was Elizabeth Houston, who left school in 1971. Jill Hoyle (Tolhurst), Head Girl, 1969-70, made her career in merchant banking and was the first female director of Credit Suisse in London. Susan McConnell (Heycock), who left school in 1976, was elected President of St Andrews University Students' Union, and her contemporary, Eleanor Laing (Pritchard), was the first woman President of the Students' Union at Edinburgh University, where she took her law degree. While at school, Eleanor had distinguished herself in elocution and in the Debating Society, and it was no surprise to those who knew her in those years that she made a career in politics; she won the seat of Epping Forest for the Conservatives in the 1997 election. Jennifer Black, a multiple prize-winner at the Festival, and donor of the School's Cup for Drama, pursued a successful acting career, including a major role in the Bill Forsyth film, *Local Hero*. There have been many other outstanding successes, chronicled in the Former Pupils' section of the magazine.

At the seventy-fifth anniversary celebrations Miss MacArthur, as guest of honour, spoke of the many changes in the world and in society, which the School had not only survived, but absorbed. She paid tribute to the succession of Chairmen and Directors who had adapted the School to meet new educational and social needs, and she concluded by referring to the School's patron Saint:

> No one was more aware than Saint Columba that he had been shaped by his past and yet always he turned his face boldly towards every new challenge.
> (School Magazine 1972, p. 41)

'Boldly towards every new challenge' might serve as a motto for Miss Clark herself during these years. Having emerged from dark days of uncertainty, the newly independent St Columba's was justified in feeling hope for a new dawn.

*Chapter Ten*

# Sheila M Caldwell 1976-1987

Sheila Caldwell was Principal Teacher of geography at St Bride's when she was interviewed for the post of Headmistress of St Columba's. Her BA with Honours in geography was from University College, London. She had experience of teaching in a wide variety of schools: girls' and co-educational, boarding and day, direct grant and independent, public and state, English and Scottish. She had founded and been Headmistress of the Yejide Grammar School for Girls in Nigeria, and, having successfully established this school, she was invited to open and head the first state secondary school for girls in Lilongwe, Malawi (then Nyasaland).

*Sheila M Caldwell*

Under her headship St Columba's became co-educational. This was an immense challenge, successfully handled at a time when pressures were bearing down from many directions. Financial pressures meant that the School could not invest in its properties as the Directors believed necessary; educational pressures resulted from the changes nationally in curriculum and assessment, which were introduced in Scotland with uncertainty, delay and many last-minute revisions; and political pressures from the educational authorities in Scotland which in those years maintained a Kremlinesque coldness towards the independent sector, excluding it from discussions on the preparation of the new curriculum developments and other important matters. It was a period when several Scottish independent schools buckled under the strain and did not recover.

The need to maintain confidence in the School was of the utmost importance, and this Mrs Caldwell did, introducing many helpful developments. She saw the need for a Transitus class on the Senior School campus, and successfully put this into operation, as she did the nursery class on the Primary site. Mrs Caldwell was known for her careful preparation and attention to detail: in both these major changes, as in the introduction of co-education, her meticulous planning ensured that everything went smoothly.

In order to further the benefits to the School that more parental involvement might bring, she made St Columba's the first school in the West of Scotland to introduce open days for parents. She also gave her enthusiastic support to the new Parents' Association. She instituted biennial careers

***Senior School Staff, 1981-2***
Back row: Mrs Campbell, Mrs Miller, Mr Fry, Mr Wright, Mrs McGoldrick, Mr Spinks, Mrs Morrison, Mrs Hammond
Second row: Mrs Wales, Mrs Johnson, Mrs Duncan, Miss Blythe, Mrs Marr (Nelson), Mrs Smith, Mr Robb, Mrs Gunn, Mr Banks
Third row: Mlle Levy, Miss Willox, Mrs Lymburn, Mr Anderson, Mr Craig, Mr McMahon, Mrs Jacobs, Miss McLean
Front row: Miss Allison, Mr Walton, Miss Weir, Mrs Caldwell, Miss Nicol, Miss Macdonald, Mrs Scott

***Primary and Senior School Staff, 1987***
Back row: Mrs McKenzie, Mrs Judge, Mrs Lymburn, Mrs MacDonald, Mrs Allen, Mr Banks, Miss MacArthur, Mr Fry, Mrs Hammond, Mrs Robertson, Mrs Campbell, Mr Spinks, Mrs Buchanan
Second row: Mrs Willox, Mrs Jacobs, Mrs Morrison, Mrs Brown, Miss Conacher, Mrs Marr, Miss Blythe, Mrs McGruther, Miss Neill, Mrs Keanie, Mrs Somerville
Third row: Mr Morrison, Mrs Urie, Miss Weir, Mr Craig, Mrs Lockhart, Mrs Smith, Mrs Chambers, Mr Clark, Mrs Crampsey, Mrs Murray, Mr McMahon, Mrs Holms
Front row: Mr Walton, Mrs Nicol, Miss Allison, Mrs Johnson, Mrs Caldwell, Miss Pollock, Miss Paton, Miss Nicol, Miss Macdonald

conventions and her hard work and forethought ensured that, in this time of ever increasing competition for good university places, pupils were given the best possible preparation for their post-school careers.

Mrs Caldwell taught geography at all levels in the Senior School. She derived particular satisfaction from getting to know each pupil as an individual, enabling her to write a frank and knowledgeable assessment of each when the time came for university applications. She served on the committee of the Secondary Heads Association of Scotland for several years.

## Staff and curriculum

At times of great pressure the strength of a school is tested to the utmost, and St Columba's was fortunate in having a loyal and talented staff (see Chapter Eleven). Mrs Caldwell faced the rigours of her new post well supported both in the Primary and Senior School by two long-serving and dedicated teachers. Miss Margaret Croft retired in December 1981, after thirty-three years on the staff, seventeen of them as Head of the Preparatory School and eight as Head of the Primary. Miss Kathleen Weir had also been at St Columba's for thirty-three years when she retired at the end of the same session: thirteen of those years were spent in charge of the Junior School, and eleven as Deputy Headmistress. Both had been pupils of the School, and both are remembered by generations of pupils for their outstanding qualities as teachers and leaders.

On Miss Weir's retiral in 1982, Mrs Allison Johnson, who had taught mathematics at the School since 1977, was appointed to replace her as Deputy Head (see Chapter Eleven).

The academic standing of the School continued to be strong in all departments. The results obtained in the SCE Ordinary and Higher Grade examinations were very good, with a high percentage of passes at grades A to C. It was, as always, the School's policy to present for examination all pupils who had completed the course of study. From 1981 onwards some pupils were presented for O-Grade French in the third year.

Computing was added to the curriculum, taught by Mr John Spinks, Principal Teacher of mathematics from 1975, who was one of the first teachers in Scotland to gain the CNAA Diploma in computer education. In the sixth year, pupils were presented for A-Levels and Scottish Certificate of Sixth Year Studies in a full range of subjects, as well as for additional Ordinary and Higher Grade subjects. Most leavers went on to degree courses at universities, including Oxford and Cambridge.

## Assisted places and the running of the Company

From 1977 onwards there were annual increases in fees for the Company's two remaining schools, partly to offset the annual decline in grant which was to pave the way, however uncomfortably, to full independence. All the schools in this sector were preparing themselves for the grant to end at the end of the 1981-82 session. The Thatcher government, elected in 1979, had promised to restore it. In the event it gave a modest increase for two years, and rescheduled the phasing out over five years from 1981, announcing its replacement with the assisted places scheme, under which parents could apply for a means-tested contribution towards fees.

*Geoffrey Duncan*

At the beginning of the 1981-82 session eighteen pupils, only two of whom were new, had taken up assisted places at St Columba's. Although the financial benefits for the schools in the scheme were indirect, the scheme undoubtedly benefited families who qualified for it, and brought to the School pupils who might otherwise not have come. At most around forty-five pupils at any one time attended the School under the scheme. It was phased out from 1998, following the change of Government in the previous year.

Mr Geoffrey Duncan, who was Chairman of the local board of Directors for St Columba's from 1972 until 1982, was also Chairman of the Girls' School Company from 1977 until 1990, a time at least as demanding as any in the history of the Company; few people over the years can have put more time and effort into the running of the Company and St Columba's School than Geoffrey Duncan. In the early 1980s he steered the School smoothly into co-education and the introduction of assisted places.

Mr W Stewart MacFarlane was convener of the Company's finance sub-committee from 1980, when the phase-out of grant, together with high inflation and economic recession, made the task of budgeting an extremely tough one. Two other members of the finance committee, Mr James Higgins and Mr Colin Brown, were also local Directors for St Columba's. Mr Geoffrey Duncan was succeeded as chairman of the local board of St Columba's in 1982 by Mr J C (Ian) Ritchie. It was Geoffrey Duncan, Ian Ritchie, their fellow Directors and successors, who laid the basis for the increasing success of St Columba's in the later 1980s and 1990s. The School was put on a sound financial footing, the long-standing budget deficit at St Columba's (which had been balanced by profits at Park) was eliminated, and the annual increase in fees was gradually reduced.

A sub-committee of the Company for the overseeing of repairs and renewals to the fabric of the buildings was set up in 1980, with Mr Michael Hepburn (a local Director for St Columba's from 1972) in charge of the St Columba's side. Mr Ian MacConnacher took on this job in 1984, giving the School the benefit of his enthusiasm and experience in dealing with properties, a task which he continued to carry out for almost fifteen years with great financial benefit to the School. In those early years, when there were no resources for any but the most essential projects, it was a rather frustrating business. Cloakrooms for the boys were installed at the Primary School in 1982 and at Senior School in 1983. The sale of Allanbank in 1982 helped with this. The only other investments of note during this period were the replacement of the original language laboratory of 1976 with a superior new system in 1984, and the upgrading of a science laboratory in the following year.

Forces of destruction necessitated extra expenditure. The storm of December 1979 did serious damage to the roof of the science block, and anti-vandal precautions had to be taken at Shalott after damage in the grounds, with a caretaker living in for several years and floodlighting installed around the building. In 1981 the Company took out riot insurance – a sign of the times.

## New developments for the Girls' School Company

With the departure of St Bride's from the Girls' School Company in 1976, the Directors of the two remaining schools felt that it would be prudent to make new alliances with similar schools. In July 1976 St Columba's, the Park School, Laurel Bank School and Westbourne School for Girls formed the West of Scotland School Company, Limited, to act as an administrative body for the four schools. The governing bodies of all the schools saw the economic advantages in sharing common costs in administrative affairs, and also the possible future benefits of an even closer relationship, should circumstances make this necessary. The Board of the West of Scotland School Company was made up of representatives from the boards of all four schools, which continued to govern themselves in matters of policy.

The West of Scotland School Company was dissolved in 1991, when Westbourne School amalgamated with Glasgow Academy. The three remaining members continued to employ Mr Norman Floyd, who had been Secretary of the Girls' School Company since 1982, and the same office staff. This arrangement terminated in 1996 when Laurel Bank and the Park School merged to become the new Laurel Park School. Mr Floyd continued as Bursar for St Columba's until his retiral early in 1998.

It was in June 1987 that the Girls' School Company officially changed its name to The Park and St Columba's School Company, in recognition of the co-educational status of St Columba's.

*Language laboratory, 1985*

## Opening the doors to boys

The decline in numbers sparked off by the events of 1974 and 1975 had continued (see Chapter Nine). As numbers fell from a high of 570, and the grant was reduced, fees had to be further increased, and the result was that, in the 1981-82 session, there were fewer than 380 pupils at St Columba's.

It was clear that co-education was the way forward, but there was already a preparatory school for boys in Kilmacolm, Dardenne, and the Directors of St Columba's had no wish to trespass on its territory. But by the end of the seventies Dardenne was struggling to survive. Its offer in 1977 of places for girls (they wore boys' caps minus the skip!) was not successful in attracting many. The governors of Dardenne did not wish to amalgamate with St Columba's, and so St Columba's made its transfer to co-education independently and on its own terms. Dardenne closed in 1982.

The admission of boys to Primary One began in 1978. It boosted the numbers a little, but it was not until the Company announced a commitment to offering a full education for boys up to Senior Six that the tide began to turn. The announcement of co-education throughout the School came in 1981. It proved to be a turning point in the School's fortunes, but the Directors and Mrs Caldwell were concerned that it should not take on the aspect of a revolution, and for this reason the introduction of boys was made from the Primary School upwards. The introduction of boys to a girls' school was an unusual enough development, but the acceptance of boys by way of the Primary School rather than the Senior School was unique in Scotland. The gradual easing-in facilitated the full integration of boys to all aspects of school life, and the School had time to adjust to their presence. In becoming

*Primary One, 1984-85*

Science laboratory, 1985

co-educational St Columba's strengthened its character as a family school, in which brothers could now join their sisters.

The new boys were fitted in at Shalott with the minimum of fuss:

> Around this time alien things like goal posts began to appear in the sunken garden. Footballs rolled around on the playground and, in the words of one teacher, school was noisier and dirtier, but otherwise much the same.
> (Miss Margaret Croft)

Miss Croft and some of her staff could remember teaching boys in the preparatory department many years before. The School had been without boys for a little over two decades.

In the 1983-84 session the first class containing a sizeable group of boys entered the Senior School. The Directors and Mrs Caldwell viewed the crossing of this hurdle as an important indication that their unique method of introducing co-education was succeeding. St Columba's was no longer a girls' school.

*Home economics, 1985*

*Playtime at Shalott, 1985*

To coincide with the arrival of the mixed Senior One classes in 1983, the Primary Seven pupils were brought up to Duchal Road from Shalott, and took their place in the Senior School as the new Transitus year. Mrs Joyce Keanie, teacher of Primary Seven, came with them, and was the class teacher of Transitus for six years until her retiral in 1988. The move enabled the Transitus classes to be taught by Senior School staff for half of their timetable, during which they were introduced to the use of the science and language laboratories and computers, and to the rest of the senior curriculum. It was one of Mrs Caldwell's major innovations, requiring complex timetabling arrangements, carefully planned and successfully carried out.

## Opening the doors to pre-school children, parents, and others

The nursery, or preparatory, class was started in 1985. A large classroom which looked out into the garden was made available in Shalott, and fourteen children in their pre-school year moved in with their nursery teacher, Mrs Carol Crampsey, and nursery nurse, Mrs Susanne Allan. There was never any lack of pupils and the venture was a great success. Mrs Caldwell was delighted to see children coming through into Primary One 'with a song in their hearts', fully prepared for what school had to offer.

St Columba's has always been fortunate in having parental support, and in the spring of 1983 a Parents' Association was formed. The first task the parents set themselves was to organise bus transport to and from Paisley to replace the discontinued train service. Numerous social occasions raised useful sums of money for the School, and much practical help was given at various school functions. Parents had for many years organised a sale of second-hand school uniform, and donated the proceeds to the School.

The first open day for parents was held in November 1981. The open day became an annual event, and, from 1982, every second year it was combined

*School's out, 1985*

*The preparatory class, 1985*

with an evening careers convention. Miss Marjorie Willox, Principal Teacher of guidance, had also organised careers evenings in 1978 and 1980. Representatives from various professions and industry were invited, as well as staff from colleges and universities. Some parents and friends of the School also had expertise to offer. These evenings were very successful, and helped to guide pupils through the maze of proliferating courses and career options.

Mrs Caldwell was keen to see pupils make good use of their time in the last few weeks of the summer term, and in 1983 the staff planned a programme of activities after the SCE examinations. Beginners' Italian, dance, car maintenance and photography competed for pupils' attention with interview techniques, computing, typewriting and bridge. The reaction from pupils was favourable:

> . . . hte t6ping was xery educational. Since the karate there has been a distinct lack of whole pencils. My mother had not had a puncture in 20 years. Since we were taught how to remedy this ailment, I've had to diagnose and treat two!
>
> (School Magazine 1982-83, p. 26)

After repairing parental punctures, students could presumably move on to dealing with those in cars. The alternative activities programme became a regular fixture at the end of each school year.

The first work experience programme was in the summer term of 1985. Many employers offered places, and valuable experience was gained. The magazine listed the widely varied organisations which took on students from St Columba's:

> Greenock Police; British Airways; Glasgow University Veterinary School; Possilpark Farm Site; Paisley Daily Express; Playtex Ltd; Boswell, Mitchell and Johnstone (Architects) . . .

and many more.

***1st lacrosse team, 1980-81***
Back row: Sarah Barlow, Fiona Hamilton, Diane Fisher, Tammy Davis, Gillian Barclay, Jill Carnduff
Front row: Julie Paterson, Claire Willis, Valerie Gallacher (Captain), Kirsteen Cameron, Caroline Kerr

***1st hockey team, 1978-79***
Back row: Fiona Stirling, Marion Armstrong, Morag Masson, Susan Galbraith, Jan Frankgate, Corrine Martin
Front row: Alison Hirst, Barbara Hardcastle, Gail Cunningham (Captain), Marion Craib

## Games and physical education

'The amount of activity in this department is really quite astounding,' reported Mrs Caldwell in 1987, and this might have been said of any of the preceding ten years. By the end of the 1970s it was becoming more difficult than ever to arrange fixtures for lacrosse, which very few schools in Scotland now played. In the 1979-80 session, hockey was made the main winter game for girls, and lacrosse became a club activity. It continued to be very popular and was still played to a high standard, with the School providing players for the Scottish Schoolgirls' team most years: Gillian Barclay was selected two years running, Fiona Stirling captained the Scottish Schoolgirls' team in 1979, and Valerie Gallacher, who had also been selected in the previous two years, was Captain in 1981. The School took lacrosse tours to the North of England in 1982 and 1984, hockey/lacrosse tours to York in 1985 and 1987, and a tennis tour to the Lake District in 1984. Strong first and second XI hockey teams were established: in the 1983-84 session, for example, the PE department was able to report seventy-five per cent of matches won or drawn. In most years, girls were selected to play hockey for the Renfrewshire and South West Scotland teams.

Other new developments were a senior netball team, two gymnastics clubs, and a cross country club which was very successful in 1976-77, its first year. Rugby was an entirely new departure. Rugby and football fixtures were played with other schools in the 1982-83 session. Enthusiasm was there from the start and expertise was gradually built up.

Mrs Carole Marr was appointed Principal Teacher of physical education in 1976, and was assisted by Mrs Marjorie Martin (then Miss Flockhart) until 1981, and then by Mrs Lorna Urie (Miss McLean). Mr Stuart Clark came in 1985. Other members of staff gave time after school and on Saturdays to coach and supervise games, and Mrs Caldwell in her 1984 Report to the Directors paid tribute to 'a dedicated, able and enthusiastic PE staff for whom nothing is too much trouble'.

***Hockey practice, 1985***

***Rugby club, 1984-85***
Back row: Iain Adam, Stuart Murray, John Burns, Thomas Lang, Craig Mackinnon
Second row: Scott Schoenleber, Barry Corkindale, Carlo Palombo, Jonathan Dunn, Fraser Simpson, Ian Currie
Front row: Graeme Clark, David Russell, Martin Drummond, Jonathan Eadie (Captain), David Clark, Angus Munro, Blane McDougall

## Making records and breaking records

With the encouragement of Mrs Caldwell and under the musical directorship of Mr Tom Walton, choral singing at St Columba's conquered new peaks. Mr Walton and Mr Fry built up the choirs from the mid-seventies. Entry was by audition, selection was rigorous, and there was great competition to get in:

> But we never said to anyone 'You can't sing'; we said, 'Come back next time'. In fact one girl who in the Primary could not pass the test, kept coming back, and by the time she was in sixth year she did solo singing, and she was one of the strongest members of the choir.
>
> (Mr Tom Walton)

At the Inverclyde Music Festival St Columba's School set many new records. The Cuthbert Foster Memorial Trophy, for the most meritorious performance of a choir at the Festival, was held by the School for twelve successive years (1979 until 1990). These were heady years. At the Festival of 1982, St Columba's provided one-sixth of the total number of musical entries, and brought home a great haul of trophies. First in their class were:

> . . . the Primary and Junior Choirs, Junior and Senior Ensembles, the Gilbert and Sullivan Choir, and also the Senior Music-Makers. This . . . group of singers and instrumentalists were invited back on the last night of the Festival, . . . and at the end of our performance, the adjudicator shouted 'Encore' above tumultuous applause. Once again it was our Senior Choir which won the trophy for the most

> meritorious performance of the whole Festival. When he stood up to adjudicate the class, [the adjudicator] said, 'I have nothing more to say to this choir. I have run out of expletives to describe them'.
> (School Magazine 1981-82, p. 19)

This was one of the occasions on which a St Columba's choir was awarded the highest mark (92 for each song) ever awarded at the Festival.

Mr Walton, amazed at their ability to memorise so many pieces, and worried that it might be too much – some senior girls might perform in ten choir or ensemble competitions, singing two pieces in each, besides solo events, during the two-week festival – announced that he would cut the number of entries. He and Mr Fry were met with a deputation in protest, and gave way.

In December 1979 the senior choir was chosen to represent the STV region in the ITV Youth Choirs Competition. The St Columba's choir was among the final twelve invited to London. A few months later the senior choir competed in the Strathclyde International Festival in Glasgow, and won the trophy for the best under-18 girls' choir as well as the special award for the most meritorious performance of the whole Festival. In 1984 the senior choir was one of the two Scottish youth choirs which won through to the regional finals of the Sainsbury Choir of the Year Competition. Their performance of Benjamin Britten's *This Little Babe* at Hopetoun House was televised.

***The senior choir at the Sainsbury Choir Competition at Hopetoun House, Edinburgh, October 1984***

**Rejoice and Be Merry**
The senior choir, 1978, with Mr Fry and Mr Walton

*This Little Babe* was one of the pieces sung by the choir for two programmes recorded by BBC Radio Scotland, one of which was broadcast on Christmas morning, 1982. When the senior choir sang it at the Festival a few weeks later, the marks awarded broke another record. Fifteen years later a choir of former pupils, conducted by Mr Walton, sang it to a spellbound congregation at the School's Centenary Christmas Carol Service in St Columba Church. Having come together at short notice and having had the barest minimum of rehearsal time, their polished performance was testimony to their superb training by Tom Walton many years before.

Many concerts and performances were given at various venues for charity. At the School an annual informal concert, based on the Festival repertoire, was staged each year for parents.

A record of choral music for Christmas, entitled *Rejoice and be Merry* was made in 1978, and another record, *Perfect Young Ladies,* in 1982.

A Silver Tablet performance was given by Elizabeth Boyd on piano in 1982, and a joint performance by Gail Hawthorne, soloist, and Marjorie Gibb Stuart, pianist, in 1983. Alison Campbell gave a Silver Tablet clarinet recital in 1984, and Helen Butter and Caroline Thaung gave piano recitals in 1985 and 1986 respectively.

***Primary School orchestra, 1985***

Mr Walton and Mr Fry were kept busy each year arranging music and rehearsing singers and orchestra for the school shows. Music was, of course, part of everyday school life, especially class music and class singing. For many pupils and teachers music at St Columba's is one of their strongest memories, even in the Primary:

> . . . scales and arpeggios from the piano pupils mingled with violin, flute and recorder, while class singing, choir and orchestra practice could be heard floating from the hall to lift the spirit and gladden the heart.
>
> (Miss Margaret Croft)

Miss Croft also remembers the Primary School children walking from Assembly each morning to the accompaniment of Mr Walton's rousing march; on occasion he amused himself by:

> . . . increasing the tempo to such a speed that the pupils were torn between maintaining the decorum which they felt was expected by Miss Croft or obeying the urge to break into a run, which the piano seemed to dictate.
>
> (Miss Margaret Croft)

## Some ladies of Shalott

Miss Sylvia Pollock was made Head of the Primary, with Miss Elma Paton as her Deputy, on the retiral of Miss Croft at the end of 1981. Miss Pollock left in 1991. They were assisted by several long-serving members of the Primary staff, including Old Girls Miss Elizabeth Conacher from 1953 until 1990 (see Chapter Seven) and Mrs Marjory Holms (Harrison) from 1966 until 1997, who taught in the room in which she had boarded many years before. Miss Flora MacArthur taught from 1967 until 1988, and Miss Jean Neill from 1969 until 1989. Mrs Joyce Keanie arrived in 1966, originally appointed to teach some English in the senior School, as well as a Junior School class; as the teacher of Primary Seven, she transferred to the Senior School when it became Transitus, and she retired in 1988. Mrs Jennifer Chambers (Weir), a former pupil, came in 1973 and left in 1997, having taught Primary Five, and, in recent years, French throughout the Primary School. She continues to work with senior pupils for the Duke of Edinburgh's Award scheme. Mrs Sarah Marr (Howse), another Old Girl (see Chapter Seven), returned to teach from 1973 until 1983 at the Primary School and also took senior pupils for physical education and games for some of these years. To catalogue all that they, and their other colleagues, did for the School would take many pages; there was among them an outstanding amount of talent, particularly of the artistic and dramatic kind, and all, typically of the St Columba's teacher, gave many hours of their time to extra-curricular activities.

*Shalott*

***The Russia trip, 1987***

**Trial By Jury,** ***one of the Senior School entertainments put on by Fifth Year in June 1977***
Back, standing: Alison Wright (Usher), David Craig (Judge)
Foreground, standing, centre: Anne Houston (Plaintiff); seated: Ann Pinkerton (Associate), Hilary Brown (Defendant)
Foreground, right, seated: Evelyn Jamieson (in wig, Counsel for the Plaintiff)

***The Cobbler, June 1979***

## Other activities

A dedicated and enthusiastic modern languages staff, headed by Mrs Janette Nicol (Jinty Wither), took many school trips abroad. German exchange trips were organised with a school in Nürnberg for the first time in the summer of 1977, and they continued most successfully for the next ten years. Two St Columbans, Jill McNeilage and Caroline Baldwin, having been introduced to Germany in this way, later settled there. There were many trips to France, in some years one for second and third years, and another for seniors. Skiing trips were regular features, both to the Highlands and abroad. In partnership with Paisley Grammar School, St Columba's pupils went as far as Rome and Greece. In June 1987, Mr and Mrs Nicol and Mrs Rosemary Hammond, Principal Teacher of home economics, took a party to the Soviet Union.

Mr Morris Banks, Principal Teacher of chemistry, organised an annual hill climbing expedition: Ben Venue, the Cobbler and Goatfell were among the peaks conquered. Mr John Spinks and Mrs Carole Marr, among others, led the annual sponsored climb of Ben Lomond to raise money for the Royal Commonwealth Society for the Blind.

School productions flourished under the directorship of Mr David Craig, and included *The Boyfriend*, *Salad Days*, *My Fair Lady*, and *Lady Winderemere's Fan*. In 1986 Mrs Joyce Keanie organised a production of *Joseph and the Amazing Technicolour Dreamcoat* by pupils from Transitus to Senior Six, and Mrs Elspeth Buchanan, teacher of diction, produced a musical version of *Tom Sawyer*.

**Salad Days, *1982***
Left to right: Christine Sandilands, Alison Irvine, Karen Wilson, Gillian Barclay, Karen Allen
(With thanks to Walter Alexander, photographer)

*Fashion show, June 1977*

***The school fete, 1977***
The staff, left to right:
Mr Walton, Mr Fry, Mr Spinks,
Mr Miller

The fashion show became an annual event eagerly looked forward to, organised and compered by Mrs Rosemary Hammond assisted by Mrs Helen Jacobs. Each year an audience of over two hundred was entertained to a parade of garments made by pupils in school. A brief resumé recalls not only changing fashions, but the changing style of St Columba's:

> . . . a white towelling anorak . . . and a multi-coloured bib-top skirt (1978), jeans . . . to three-piece suits (1979), quilted jackets (1981), 'Lady Diana' blouses and ra-ra skirts (1982), Transitus boys wearing training tops (1984), Primary boys modelling butchers' aprons and carrying a real pig's head down the catwalk (1986).

Mr Dave Anderson, the School's science technician, often provided expert jazz accompaniment on the piano, and most years there was an exhibition of work done in the art department or the home economics department.

## Achievement and reward

After the sudden death in 1979 of Sheila McGill, a pupil from 1955 until 1967, the Sheila McGill Memorial Prize was endowed, on the initiative of her former classmates, by the St Columba's School Society, to be awarded annually to any pupil in the Senior School showing special initiative and progress in any area connected with school life during the session. A scroll was designed and executed by Mr David Craig. A similar scroll, designed by Mr Craig and hanging in the school hall, lists the winners of the annual Tricia Scott Award for services to drama in the School, presented by her parents in 1986 (see Chapter Seven).

The Doris Arthur Tyrrell Scholarship for music was presented by Mr G H Tyrrell in 1981. Doris Arthur had been a distinguished pupil and had gone on to a career in music and education (see Chapter Four). This valuable prize is awarded on merit to a school leaver intending to go on to a career in music.

News of interesting careers in many areas continued to be gathered in the Former Pupils' section of the magazine, as well as some notable academic successes. There was news from Marjorie Mann (Munro) of her successful completion of the Whitbread Round the World Yacht Race in 1989-90, in which she was part of the crew that won the cruiser class; from Caroline Heycock of her first in modern languages from King's College, Cambridge, and her assistant professorship at Yale University, and lectureship in linguistics at Edinburgh; from Caroline Knox (Fowler) of her Ph D from the University of Padua and her career in medical research; from Julia Butt of her work as news editor for BBC Radio's *Today* programme, and other work for its news and current affairs and its drama departments. There are of course many others: the story of the achievements of former pupils is a chapter without an end.

## Success to build upon

When the time came for Mrs Caldwell to retire, she and the Directors had some justification for feeling that they had completed the ascent of the Hill Difficulty, even if they had not yet reached the Plain called Ease. The integration of boys had been a success, a fact which was reflected in the school roll. Already at the beginning of the 1985-86 session boys made up a quarter of the roll throughout the School.

The 1986-87 session was the first year of full independence from grant. Schools in receipt of grant had been prevented from running a surplus; its discontinuation freed them from this constraint. The Company was now able to save funds from a budget surplus and start to build up reserves. The annual fee increase for the following session was the lowest for many years. The number of pupils had started a slow climb in 1985, and at the beginning of her last session at the School Mrs Caldwell was able to report a roll of 401, not including the nursery class, which increased throughout the session; in September 1987 there were 425 pupils and an additional sixteen in the nursery class. In 1986-87 also a Development Appeal was started to help to provide a good financial start for Mrs Caldwell's successor.

The many pupils who had passed through the School under Mrs

Caldwell's headship, the great majority to go on to higher education, had reason to be grateful for her eleven years' conduct of the School as a happy place where the highest standards were maintained. Mrs Johnson, Deputy Head, summed it up:

> Over the years many hundreds of pupils came to know Mrs Caldwell and she displayed an individual concern for them. This genuine interest in her pupils, and indeed in everyone connected with the School, must be the hallmark of Mrs Caldwell's headship.
>
> (School Magazine 1987-88, p. 14)

*Chapter Eleven*

# Andrew H Livingstone FROM 1987

Andrew Livingstone was brought up and educated in Campbeltown. The son of a local businessman, he imbibed the principles of sound business management very early in life, along with a love of the West Highlands, 'the long lochs and the burns and bens' and the sea. He gained his BSc Honours in mathematics from Aberdeen University and Dip Ed from Glasgow. Always a believer in broad horizons, when he embarked on a teaching career he also joined the Royal Naval Reserve as a navigator, and for fifteen years gained valuable training and experience at sea and in and around naval bases. He taught at Glasgow High School under Mr David Lees and at Paisley Grammar School under Mr Robert Corbett, finding inspiration for his own teaching career in these notable Heads of two of the foremost schools in the West of Scotland. After five years as Assistant Rector of Williamwood School, he returned to Paisley Grammar as Deputy Rector.

When he came as Rector to St Columba's in 1987, Mr Livingstone had a clear idea of what was needed to continue the ascent in the fortunes of the School which had begun just two or three years earlier. He planned to carry forward the drive for academic excellence, thereby making the School a place of first choice for male as well as female students. After a period of about fifteen years when it had been impossible to make any investment in the fabric of the School, he planned to nurture the gradually increasing numbers and generate extra funding to improve the resources of the School. He saw the need to enhance the important extra dimension added to school life by music and sport. The increase in numbers would fund investment in sport, music and teaching facilities, and so attract yet more pupils.

*Andrew H Livingstone*

In partnership with an active and able team of Directors, Mr Livingstone has seen all this achieved. The school roll has increased from 425 to over 600. St Columba's is one of the leading co-educational independent schools in Scotland, with academic results regularly among the highest in the country. Success in sport and music continues to be harvested every year. Improved playing facilities and a new games hall have given new heart to the sporting side of school life, and by the end of 1998, as part of the long-term strategic development plan, the School will have a new arts, music and technology building on the site of Cargen Lodge.

Mr Livingstone's objectives on taking the helm were to sustain the School's family atmosphere and happy environment for learning and working, and to maintain its tradition of educating the whole person and of valuing the full range of contributions to school life. The standards of courtesy and consideration, always remarked on by outsiders who came into contact with the School, would not be permitted to slip.

'An educationalist who has become a business and marketing man' is how Mr Livingstone, with a certain sense of amusement, describes himself now. He embraces the professionalism which has, in the past eleven years, entered the business of funding schools. The challenge he set himself and the School in 1987 – 'invest and develop, or die' – was a wholly serious one. The story of how that challenge was met is one of the most exciting chapters in the history of the School.

## Progress on the ground – and higher!

Under Professor Sir David Mason, a Director of St Columba's from 1981 until 1992, a development appeal raised enough money, in the 1988-89 session, for the implementation of the first phase of Mr Livingstone's plan to use space more efficiently. A new school kitchen was built adjoining the school hall, which itself was redecorated and, with portable furniture, used for dining. The significance of this extended beyond the provision of better cooking and serving facilities, welcome though they were. It meant that on the ground floor, where the old kitchen and dining room had been, three additional classrooms were gained, including a technology room, and a room for secretarial studies, accounts and computing. The other big project funded by this appeal was the construction of a blaes pitch for hockey at the school

*The opening of the games hall, January 1993*

Rt Hon Ian Lang, Stella Smith (Deputy Head Girl), Mhairi Reid (Head Girl, in background), Dr Laird, Mr Livingstone

playing fields and the upgrading of the tennis courts. The provision of better facilities for the music department was a plan for the future, but in the meantime Cargen Lodge was improved by, among other things, the knocking together of two ground floor rooms to make a large music room. The art department was also given a larger room in the main building.

It was at this time that the Directors introduced a new scheme to provide regular funding for development, in the form of a designated termly payment by parents. The first results of this were an extra rugby pitch to supplement the one small pitch at Birkmyre Park used by the School (now there are three), the rehousing of the preparatory class in a large room at Shalott (the former dining room of the boarding house), and the division of the large geography classroom at Duchal Road into a working and an informal staffroom, which freed for teaching the two rooms previously used for these purposes.

To raise money for the next phase in the development, the Rector and Directors approached trusts, local industries and former pupils. The result was a new games hall in the grounds of Shalott, opened in January 1993 by a former pupil of St Columba's Preparatory School, Lord Lang, who was Secretary of State for Scotland at the time. The games hall, which was built and equipped at a total cost of £468,000, provides facilities for badminton, volleyball, netball, basketball and indoor hockey, as well as gymnastics. The D W T Cargill Trust was a particularly generous contributor.

Among the many improvements made in the School during the summer of 1994 was the installation of a new language laboratory.

Miss MacArthur had once remarked that she did not see how the school building could be extended unless it began to soar heavenward. In 1996 that is just what happened to the science block, where (at a cost of £300,000) a third floor was added, providing two new biology laboratories. In the same year the old gymnasium at the Senior School was converted into a large classroom for Transitus. At Shalott a modular music room was erected. These developments were paid for out of the School's own resources, the fruits of several years of pupil increases.

## The end of an era for the Company

The local boards of Park and St Columba's had, throughout the 1980s, continued to constitute the Board of the Girls' School Company, and, from 1987, the Park and St Columba's School Company. In 1990 the St Columba's School Company was established, and the two schools became independent of each other: Lord Muirshiel remained Honorary President of the St Columba's School Company for a further two years. It was the end of one era, spanning 110 years, and the beginning of a new one. In 1996 the Park School amalgamated with Laurel Bank School to form Laurel Park School.

The new Chairman of St Columba's School, taking over from Mr Ian Ritchie in 1989, was Dr Helen Laird, OBE, a former Head Girl and gold medallist of the School. She had been on the Board of the Girls' School Company and the local board of St Columba's since 1975, and at the same time served on several other important committees and councils, notably the Board of World Mission of the Church of Scotland, the Board and

Management Committee of the Scottish Council of Independent Schools, and the World Association of Girl Guides and Girl Scouts, of which she was Chairman, and later Chairman of Fund Development at World level.

Sir Donald Miller, then Chairman of Scottish Power, accepted appointment as Honorary President in 1992. The Board of St Columba's School, with permanent sub-committees dealing with finance, education, buildings and development, expanded to include several more industrialists, businessmen and professional people, some of whom also knew the School as parents. Mr Norman Floyd brought his experience as Secretary of the GSC to serve the new Board. Their thoroughly professional approach to fund raising was reflected in the appointment of a development officer to run the Development Campaign (the School's first fundraising appeal for ten years), an approach to fund raising being introduced by other independent schools in the West of Scotland at this time. The Development Campaign, 'Building for the Future', was officially launched, under the chairmanship of one of the Directors, Mr John Wylie, to coincide with the School's Centenary; it seeks funds from trusts, foundations, the corporate sector, parents and former pupils. A Centenary Committee was formed under the leadership of another of the Directors, Mr William Biggart, to plan and coordinate a year-long series of events, involving everyone connected with St Columba's.

In 1996 St Columba's gained membership of the Headmasters' Conference, the premier association for independent schools; and the Rector is a member of West of Scotland Heads, a group within which Heads and staff of independent schools work together to further their common interests. One of its current projects, which has attracted interest and imitation from independents elsewhere in this country, is to pool advertising resources and to cooperate to increase the market share for the independent sector.

The Rector liaises closely with the Parents' Association, as does the Head of the Primary School, Mr Alan Maclean. The Parents' Association has worked very hard over the last ten years, raising money for various projects and giving practical help of various kinds.

The Former Pupils' Association is active and helpful, with steadily increasing membership. It has been instrumental in preparing for the School's Centenary celebrations, and it has a key role to play in helping the Development Campaign to reach its target.

## Staff

Mr Livingstone acknowledges his debt to the loyal support of the excellent team of staff from the beginning of his headship. Several were veterans of St Columba's, such as Mr Tom Walton, who retired as Principal Teacher of music in 1989 and returned to teach part-time for several years.

Mrs Janette Nicol (Jinty Wither) was a distinguished former pupil of the School, having come from the Park School on the outbreak of War. She was Head Girl of St Columba's in 1946-47 and gold medallist in 1946. She taught, first in the Junior School, from 1967, and was Principal Teacher of modern languages from 1979, 'a dedicated, inspiring teacher' who earned the affection and gratitude of hundreds of pupils during her career. She retired in 1990 and her death the following year was a matter of sadness to all: it could be said of her that she had given a lifetime's service to the School. She loved the School and served it in many different ways, running her department with unflagging determination to achieve the highest of standards, and, often with her husband, she organised and led a quite astonishing number of school parties on trips to Europe, sometimes two each year.

Miss Jean Nicol was another who made the transition from desk to staffroom at St Columba's, and was Principal Teacher of English for twenty-five years until her retiral in 1992. She was Senior Mistress for seventeen years. Her loyalty and commitment to the School made their mark on many areas, not only in her department, (Mrs Caldwell said, 'no other school could boast such a record of achievement' in English), but also on the school stage, where she directed; in the magazine, which she edited; in the library, which she organised; and in public speaking, which she developed and encouraged. In her retiral she continued to be a source of strength to the School, in her capacity as President of the Former Pupils' Association and as one of the orchestrators of the Centenary celebrations.

Miss Marjory Willox was Principal Teacher of guidance and teacher of French from 1975 until 1992. She made a valuable contribution to the house system, social education, careers conventions and the work experience programme, aspects of school life which became increasingly significant during her time. She was yet another example of the multi-talented staff member, and gave her musical and dramatic talents freely for the School.

Mr Morris Banks was Principal Teacher of chemistry from 1972 until 1990, 'a character and a gentleman' as the tribute paid him at his retiral said, and the leader of many an expedition into the hills with 'not a pupil lost' in fifteen years. His part-time colleague in the department was Mrs Sheila Campbell,

***Fifth and Sixth Year, 1987-88***

Back row: Kay Findlay, Linda Kennedy, Audrey Hepburn, Fraser Glen, John MacDonald Gaunt, David Clark, Melanie Somerville, Jane Lyle
Second row: Pamela Robinson, Sarah Ferguson, Susan Thomson, Melanie Todd, Helen Tidswell, Sarah Noble, Jane Rowand, Caroline MacLean, Nicola Forrester, Nina Carmichael, Jillian Adams
Third row: Catherine Harbon, Carol Fisher, De-Hanne Caldwell, Fiona Russell, Jennifer Brown, Kirsty Taylor, Bethany Williams, Jane Calvert, Alison Freebairn
Front row: Judith Church, Jane Collin, Shona Thomson, Nicola MacRae, Alison Welch (Head Girl), Emma Ritchie, Lindsay Johnson, Tracy Dunn
(Absent: Julia Currie, Stuart Murray, Jane Kellock, Claire Stewart, Julie Brown, Margaret Twaddle)

who spent twenty-six years on the 'chemical advancement' of her pupils and assisting them with numerous other activities besides, retiring in 1997.

Miss Avril Blythe was Principal Teacher of art from 1971 until 1989. Her skill was in evidence in the beautiful stage sets she painted for the school productions, as well as in the school hall at the Christmas dances and in the art classroom. Mrs Rosemary Hammond was Principal Teacher of home economics for twenty years until her retiral in 1997; she was assisted by Mrs Helen Jacobs from 1979 until 1997. Both contributed to the School in countless ways, from designing and making costumes for the school shows, to taking groups of Transitus and Senior One pupils to France for culinary adventures on *cuisine française* trips. Thanks to their encouragement, there have been many enthusiastic young cooks at St Columba's, who have taken part successfully in national competitions and who eagerly look forward to the visits of Jeff Bland, professional chef.

Mrs Allison Johnson taught mathematics from 1977 and was Deputy Head from 1982 until her retiral in 1997. She has been an enthusiastic supporter of the Duke of Edinburgh's Award Scheme, to which she has devoted much time and energy. Mr Livingstone paid tribute to her 'twenty years of selfless devotion' to St Columba's:

> . . . an excellent mathematician and first-class teacher, an organiser and administrator par excellence – meticulous to the last detail, but above all a friend and supporter to countless numbers in their times of need.
> (School Magazine 1996-97, p. 6)

***The class of '97***

Back row: John Dunn, Andrew Watson, Kevin Stevenson, David Madden, Christopher Armour, Alasdair McDonald, Craig Begbie, Boyd Gawish
Second row: Christopher Hansell, Shona Watson, Jennifer Mair, Debbie MacDonald, Emma Wilson, Catriona Young, Lynsey Robertson, Joanne Stevens, Preeti Ravangave, Katherine McCullough, Scott Gemmell
Third row: Gregory Wilson, Laura McConnacher, Sarah Black, Anna McGeachie, Russell Christy, Sally Lindsay, Sharon Mungall, Susan Ritchie, Susan Gibb, Stephen Blair
Front row: Niall Glen, Amanda Williams, Julie Hunt, Robert Leckie, Mrs Johnson, Mr Livingstone, Abigail Flinders, Cameron McNair, Erika Lucas, Nigel Jamieson
(Absent: Alan Black, Fiona-Anne Lynn, Rona Sutherland)

The Centenary year must count as a time of need, if anything does, and Mrs Johnson's organisational skills are still being used for the School. Indeed, to celebrate it without her, would seem a very strange thing.

The Revd Bernard Lodge, Minister of the Old Kirk, acted as School Chaplain until 1998, when he was given an affectionate farewell by staff and pupils, grateful for his help and guidance over the past seventeen years.

Several members of staff who have taught since the 1970s have made their mark on the School in a number of ways. Mr John Spinks, Principal Teacher of mathematics from 1975 and Senior Master from 1992, and Mr David Craig, Principal Teacher of art from 1989, joined the staff in 1973 and 1974 respectively. Mrs Carole Marr has taught games and physical education for almost as long. It is fair to say that St Columba's would not be the school it is, had it not been for their creative and devoted efforts over the years, assisted by numerous colleagues.

Several others have taught under both Mrs Caldwell and Mr Livingstone: Mrs Zena Morrison joined the mathematics department in 1978; Mrs Carolyn Miller has taught biology from 1977, initially on a part-time basis; Mrs Isabel Smith has taught history from 1981; Mrs Marion Somerville, now Principal Teacher, came to the English department in 1983. All have given to the School much more than their expertise in their subjects.

Keeping everything running smoothly is the job of the office staff, of whom Miss Beth Allison was the longest-serving, having given her skills in the Senior School since 1957 (where for many years she was the only secretary), transferring on a part-time basis to the Primary in 1991, until her retiral in 1998. Mrs Caldwell described her as 'the epitome of the all-remembering, highly organised personal assistant.' Generations of pupils have cause to remember with gratitude her pleasant and helpful presence; her compendious knowledge of the School and the people who have passed through it was a much-used resource. In 1998 her services to education were publicly recognised with the award of MBE.

## The Primary School

Mr Alan Maclean succeeded Miss Sylvia Pollock as Head of the Primary School in 1991. Numbers are higher than ever before, with a roll of over 250, which is still rising and near maximum capacity. The Primary has seen several changes in the past few years, not least the adoption of the 5-14 curriculum in language work, mathematics and environmental studies. The recent national Guidelines and Assessments were taken on board and integrated with the School's own distinctive approach.

The Primary prides itself on the range of its teaching. From 1992 all classes, from Primary One upwards have been taught French, in several short sessions each week. Music is of course at the heart of St Columba's Primary School, reflecting Mr Maclean's own musical interests and ability, and members of the Senior School music staff visit to give lessons, as does Mrs Elspeth Buchanan to teach diction. There is an orchestra at Primary Six level, and all pupils leaving this class can read music and play at least one instrument.

Physical education staff from the Senior School visit to teach both boys

***Morning assembly at the Primary School, 1997***

***The moment of victory for Transitus boys in the final of the Centenary Tournament, 1997***

and girls. Rugby at the Primary School has been greatly developed over the past few years, and boys from Primary Five and Six play fixtures against other schools. There is a new cafeteria system which has proved highly popular. The new modular music room provides extra space for music making and other functions.

The Primary School has been fortunate in its contingent of excellent and long-serving teachers, many of whom, having retired during this period, are mentioned in Chpater Ten. Others are still at work: Mrs Mary MacKenzie has taught since 1974 and Mrs Barbara Murray since 1983. Mrs Fiona McGibbon (Carter), a former pupil, has taught since 1988. Miss Elma Paton has been a mainstay of the Primary department for very many years. She came to St Columba's in 1973, and she has been Deputy Head to both Miss Pollock and Mr Maclean. She is in charge of the youngest children, up to Primary Three level, and, as a qualified learning support teacher, she is responsible for this aspect of teaching up to Transitus level.

*Miss Elizabeth Conacher with pupils, 1990*

Back row: Miss Conacher, George Leggat, Rona MacDonald, Tai Alvis-of-Lee
Second row: Erin Anderson, Ian Woodcock, William Ritchie, Leonie Scott, Bruce Fraser, Hazel Elliott
Front row: Lindley Stuart, Iain MacDuff, Polly Turner, William Shaw, Kerry Lyons, Thomas Maclay

## The curriculum and the house system

Several new subjects have been added to the curriculum since Mr Livingstone's arrival, including secretarial studies, accounts, computing, word processing, Spanish, classical studies, modern studies, management and information studies, craft and design, and graphic communication.

It has always been St Columba's policy to admit where possible all the members of a family at Primary level; once admitted to the Primary School, pupils normally continue into the Senior School. Excellent results are achieved not by rigorous selection but by good teaching and individual attention to each pupil. Language support, learning support and the use of computer notepads are forms of extra help given to pupils who need it.

Mr Livingstone came to St Columba's at the time when Standard Grade curriculum and examinations were being introduced to the Scottish curriculum after more than one false start. The story of curriculum development in the eighties and nineties is not one of the more glorious episodes in the history of the Scottish Education Department. The repeated revising of syllabuses at Standard Grade and Higher level, and the unrealistic expectations in many areas, notably in Primary testing and in the administration of courses, led to unprecedented pressures on the teaching profession and an unfortunate decline in morale in many parts of it. Acutely aware of the need to preserve goodwill among staff, the Rector and the Board have done all in their power to rationalise the demands. Careful thought is given to priorities when considering the introduction of new courses and procedures. The introduction of the long-delayed Higher Still awards at Senior Five and Six levels have presented significant challenges for the staff and the Board.

The house system has come a long way since its inception in 1932. Professional guidance and social education were unknown in those more spacious days; home background and school discipline were usually

***First XI hockey, 1991-92***

Back row: Penny Anderson, Fiona Fairbairn, Lesley Robertson, Linsey Knowles, Jennifer Morrice
Front row: Mhairi Reid, Lynne Corkindale, Nicola Morrice, Gillian Soutar (Captain), Victoria Knowles, Nicola Baillie, Joanne Lindsay

***Scottish caps, 1994***

Cameron McNair, Under-15 Scottish Rugby Cap
Andrew McAlindon, Under-16 Scottish Athletics Cap
David MacKay, Under-16 Scottish Rugby Cap

***Scottish Honours, 1996-97***

Back row: Christopher Scott (weight lifting), Kenneth Morrice (Under-18 hockey), Mark Ferguson (Under-16 cricket)
Front row: Rhona MacKinnon (Scottish Schools' Athletics Team, gold medal in 300m), Sally Lindsay (Scottish Schools' Athletics Team, bronze medal in 300 m)

sufficient to equip those young women for all that society would demand of them. In the much more complex and fractured society which forms the background of children's lives in the late twentieth century, pastoral care given by school can make an important difference to their educational and personal development.

In the past few years Mr Livingstone has transformed the house system into an effective mechanism for this personal attention. Mr Stuart Clark, as Principal Teacher of guidance, has the overall responsibility for this, assisted by the other heads of houses: Mrs Zena Morrison, Mrs Carolyn Miller and Mrs Janet Stevens. Within the house system there is access to guidance, social education, work experience, careers interviews and the preparation of UCAS forms for university entrance. House staff know each member individually, and parents can with confidence bring matters of a personal nature to their attention. Inter-house competition is a focus for effort and enjoyment for the pupils. Each house is headed by both a male and a female student, just as the school is headed by both a Head and Deputy Head Boy and a Head and Deputy Head Girl.

## Games and physical education

Rugby has been built up over the past ten years, from Primary Six to First and Second XV level, and the 1996-97 Captain was able to report that, 'rugby at St Columba's is becoming more of a way of life and the senior school is able regularly to field six teams on Saturday mornings.'

Several players have been selected over the years for Glasgow Schoolboys' teams, and Cameron McNair was selected for the Scottish Under-15 team and David Mackay for the Under-16 team and the full Scottish Schoolboys' team in 1994. There have been rugby tours to Dumfries and Dundee. The 1996-97 season saw the First XV win fourteen out of its nineteen fixtures, and play host for the second time to a touring side from Wesley College, Perth, Australia, scoring a decisive win. This season put the teams in good heart for their very successful Centenary rugby tour of Canada in July 1997. Mr Brian Manson, Principal Teacher of physical education, is assisted with rugby coaching by Mr Stuart Clark.

Lacrosse sticks were regretfully put away for the last time in 1988, St Columba's bowing to the inevitable consequence of the absence of competing schools in the West of Scotland. Hockey then became the major winter game for girls, and it was perhaps some consolation that in the previous season, in the lacrosse and hockey tour to York, the St Columba's team won all their hockey matches. Several girls have been selected to play for the South West of Scotland and Renfrewshire teams, and the School has been strongly represented at District and County level every year. Gillian Soutar and Jennifer Morrice were selected for the Scottish Schoolgirls' Under 18 teams in 1992 and 1994 respectively. From 1989 onwards the School's new blaes pitch and floodlighting enhanced the playing of the game, as has the sole use on Saturday mornings of the astroturf pitch at Linwood. By 1994 nine teams were regularly being fielded. Hockey tours to Aberdeen, the Lake District, and Chester became a regular feature of the season, and in the Centenary year thirty-two players went to Canada on the School's rugby-

***Some of the Inverclyde Music Festival winners, 1995***

***Senior mixed choir, 1992-93***

Winners of the Cuthbert foster Trophy for the best school performance at the Inverclyde Music Festival, 1993

***Senior orchestra with Mr Fry at the Inverclyde Music Festival, 1991***

***First XV rugby, 1991-92***
Back row: M Crawford, A Hosie, R Aitchison
Second row: M Wheeler, I Anthony, J Lamb, D Owens, R Sanga, I Munro, Mr B Manson
Front row: A Anderson, I McAlindon, B Corkindale, D Mories (Captain), S Wilson, I MacFarlane, J Simpson

hockey tour. Mrs Lorna Urie, long-standing member of the PE department, assists Mrs Carole Marr with hockey.

A Junior cricket XI was started in 1989, and the School fields teams from Transitus upwards each season. Cross country running is a popular sport from Primary onwards, and the School makes a very creditable showing at District and at Divisional level.

St Columba's is also well represented at the Inverclyde Athletics Championships and the Renfrew District Championships, and often too in the Scottish Schools Championships, where medals have been won by Andrew McAlindon, Alistair McDonald, Sally Lindsay, David Eccles, Jonathan Clayton, and William Shaw. In the T S B Thistle Award's Scottish Competitions of 1995 the St Columba's After School Athletics Club gained third place. In 1995 and 1996 Sally Lindsay represented Scotland in athletics. Tennis, badminton, and basketball are all played with enthusiasm.

The new games hall gives facilities for many indoor games, and an opportunity for hockey practice when the pitches are unplayable. But the School's upgrading of games facilities is not yet complete: Phase Two of the current development plan includes the astroturfing of the playing fields to give a new hockey pitch and seven tennis courts.

## Music

St Columba's reputation in music is as high as ever. There is enormous enthusiasm for singing and music-making of all kinds. The music department, under Mr Derek Fry, is now just as strong in the orchestral arena as in the choral. Around fifteen visiting teachers give instruction in a range of

*The cast of* **Koppelberg Hill,** *spring 1992*

**The Mikado,** ***February 1994***
Back row: Colin Adam, Sally Flinders, Julie MacDonald, Douglas Clark, Derek Hutcheson
Front row: Elizabeth Scott, Morven Wilson, Simon Thirde

**The Boyfriend,** ***1996***

instruments, as well as in the traditional subjects of singing and piano. The senior orchestra has been built up over the past ten years, and there is also a junior band, composed of members of the Transitus to Senior Two classes. A strings group was started in the 1997-98 session. The orchestra has won first prize in its class at the Inverclyde Music Festival several times. Several pupils play in the West of Scotland Independent Schools' orchestra.

There is now a senior mixed choir as well as a senior girls' choir. The choirs give great pleasure each year at prizegiving, the Festival concert and the Christmas carol service, as well as to wider audiences. The choirs and ensembles continue to have outstanding success at the Inverclyde Music Festival. Such is the reputation of the choirs that there have been many invitations to perform in public in the last ten years. In 1993 BBC Radio 2 recorded pupils and staff at the Old Kirk for their Easter broadcast, and Radio 4 Scotland broadcast a live service. In December 1994 the two senior choirs made a live broadcast with GMTV from Princes Square, Glasgow. On two occasions the junior choirs joined the John Currie Singers and Orchestra at Glasgow's City Hall, in 1995 in a performance of Bach's *St Matthew Passion*, and in 1997 for the Monteverdi *Vespers*. At Christmas 1996 a choir of pupils from Primary Five and Six sang at Paisley Abbey. The visit to Iona and walk to Kilmacolm of June 1997 gave BBC Radio Scotland an opportunity to make live broadcasts of the school choir at Iona and Kilmartin, and the choir also appeared on BBC television's 'Songs of Praise' from Iona.

None of this is achieved without very many hours spent in rehearsal, time which can be difficult to find in the crowded school day. Nor would it be possible without a dedicated and talented music staff, both full-time and part-time. There is considerable musical talent among the staff generally, and choral pieces by a staff group at Christmas services and on other occasions are always very much enjoyed.

Mrs Elspeth Buchanan has taught diction at the School since 1967. Over the years hundreds of pupils have done credit to her teaching, not only at the Festival, where St Columba's pupils are always prominently represented among the prizewinners, but also on the school stage and in many other places where the spoken word is valued.

The tradition of broadening the horizons of music students at the School continues: inspiring visits have been made by David Fanshawe, composer of *African Sanctus*, and by members of the RSNO and the Scottish Chamber Orchestra, to lead workshops and perform.

The music department has been heavily involved in almost all the school productions since 1980. Mr David Craig has been responsible for most of these productions, assisted by Mr John Spinks and many other members of staff. *Dracula Spectacula* was staged in 1988, and George Bernard Shaw's *The Applecart* in 1990. These have been followed by *Trial By Jury*, *The Mikado* and *The Boyfriend.* Mrs Patricia Gulbransen, Principal Teacher of biology, produced *Oliver!*, *I Remember Mama* and *Oh What A Lovely War!*, a revue performed by the junior drama group. In the 1990s male roles have been played by boys: *The Pirates of Penzance* in 1991 was notable for their debut on the school stage. The Primary School has staged four operettas especially written for it by its Head, Mr Alan Maclean: *Koppelberg Hill*, *Gypsum's*

*Journey*, *Cuckoo Time*, and, for the Centenary year, *The Scottish Crossbill*.

The Centenary carol service at Christmas 1997 in St Columba Church was a high point in the musical life of the School, which will be forgotten by no one. A professional tenor and parent of a former pupil, Mr John Treleaven, returned from Germany to sing, beautifully complementing the young voices. Between the traditional processional 'Once in Royal David's City', with a boy soloist singing the first verse, and the recessional 'Still the Night', were many items of outstanding beauty, both spoken and sung.

## Enterprises and adventures

The school magazine is now a handsome publication, with lively writing and fine illustrations. Mrs Sandra McGruther was the editor for several years until 1992, and her successor Mrs Lindsey Duncan has maintained the high standards. A new venture in 1994 was the annual Sixth Form Yearbook, a record of the highs and lows of life in Senior Six, which they finance by finding sponsorship from local companies or by their own fundraising efforts, gaining an insight into some aspects of financing a project.

Even more business sense is learned by the senior pupils who have run mini-companies each year from 1993 under the Youth Enterprise Scheme. Projects over the last few years have included the production and marketing of T-shirts, Christmas cards, Centenary mugs and golf balls, the running of several discos, and the attempted sale of red roses on St Valentine's day. Unfortunately for the mini-company, few of the youth of St Columba's turned out to be romantics after the style of Rabbie Burns.

But Burns is celebrated in style on his own day, the Burns Supper having been revived in 1988 by Mrs Marion Sommerville. In 1993 the haggis was for the first time piped in, rather than fiddled, by a pupil, Gregor Campbell. This laid the foundation for the establishment of the school pipe band, which now makes rousing appearances at important occasions in the school calendar.

Public speaking is still pursued with enthusiasm. The participants regularly surprise and delight at the Burns Supper, and have a chance to

***The school magazine committee, 1992-93***

Faisal Nazir, Gillian Thomson, Claire Grimble, Alastair Bell, Derek Hutcheson

*English Speaking Union public speaking team, 1990-91*

Miss Nicol, Julia Reid, Sarah Saxton, Carlo Palombo, Lois McNeilage, Jill Rae

display their talents before a wider audience at the annual English Speaking Union competition. Various members of staff put in much time and energy to the arranging of debates and training the team.

There are regularly three or four trips abroad each year for various age groups, providing cultural, linguistic or character-forming opportunities. Destinations have included Italy, Greece, the Rhine valley, locations in France including the Ardèche (for descent by canoe), Russia, and various ski resorts. There are also many excursions closer to home, and two notable innovations are exclusively for the benefit of Senior Six: a weekend at the start of the session for leadership and team-building activities, and several days touring Mull and Iona in June after the examinations.

## The Duke of Edinburgh's Award Scheme

> The Duke of Edinburgh's Award Scheme is a test of morale, strength, skill, judgement, team work and how much water your feet can soak up!
>
> (School Magazine 1994-95, p. 50)

St Columba's began participating in the Duke of Edinburgh's Award Scheme in 1961, and in 1986 interest in it was revived and it became an important extra-curricular activity. Under the leadership of Mrs Carole Marr many pupils have taken part in dozens of activities which would otherwise have been left untried. Participation was offered first to third and fourth year pupils, many of whom gained the bronze and silver awards, and from 1990 onwards some pupils each year have worked their way through to gold standard. Over 200 bronze awards have already been achieved, ninety silver and thirty-nine gold, an impressive record for a school of St Columba's size. A range of skills, services, and physical recreations are pursued, together with a demanding expedition at each level; gold candidates are also required to take part in a residential project. Within the Scheme, valuable service is given to the local community, at, for example, the Kilmacolm Day Centre. Over the

***Duke of Edinburgh Gold Award Presentation, 1993***
Gillian Soutar, Lesley Robertson, Michelle Sangster, Nicola Morrice, Alison Lamb, Victoria Wright, Robbie MacDonald, HRH the Duke of Edinburgh

years not only staff but also many parents have willingly given much help with the Scheme, notably Mr Stephen Hampson, Mr Barry Stoddard, Mr Joe Knowles and Dr Ian Morrice.

The expedition section can be a truly character-forming test of independence and initiative. As a way of combining this with the service section, and to mark the School's Centenary year, a group of gold award holders, and supporters, walked from Iona to Kilmacolm in June 1997, raising £9000 for three children's charities.

What it does for the pupils is perhaps best summed up by the words of one of them:

> I believe the Award has given me the courage to do things I wouldn't have thought possible.
>
> (School Magazine 1993-94, p. 74)

## Recognition and reward

An innovation of which Mr Livingstone is particularly proud is the introduction in 1993 of Achievers' Ties. They are awarded to students who demonstrate outstanding achievment, whether in the academic field, sport, music, drama, art, or the Duke of Edinburgh's Award Scheme. The Achievers' Tie awards reflect something which has always been part of the St Columba's style: encouragement to strive for excellence and the recognition of effort and talent in many different spheres.

## A tradition upheld

A school must change as the needs of its pupils change, as Miss Clark once said. Over the past century St Columba's has done that, but each Head has recognised the important elements in the School's traditions and handed them on. Each has of course also brought something distinctive and individual to the School.

With an experienced navigator as Rector St Columba's is on course for continuing success, with a clear vision of its future. The School is publicly recognised as one of the leading independent schools in Scotland; in sending almost every leaver into a university course or other form of higher education it has few rivals. Facilities have been steadily upgraded, and plans are in place for further developments in the areas of teaching and sport. The tradition of the School as a family-based organisation where each individual is known and nurtured is something distinctive, and something hard to achieve in larger establishments.

St Columba's has remained true to its motto: *orare, laborare, literisque studere.* The Christian tradition, the importance of work and of learning, are still as strong as ever within the School. The beginning of the Centenary year coincided with the fourteen-hundredth anniversary of the Saint's death, and the walk from Iona to Kilmacolm focused attention again on the civilising and scholarly attributes of Columba. Each Head in turn has found room for the spiritual in school life, and this has been a prominent and formative influence on pupils throughout these hundred years.

What has emerged from the vision and confidence of the original subscribers to a school for girls at Kilmacolm, is an outstanding co-educational establishment which is loved and respected by many hundreds. The past and the present meet when the former pupils visit the School and maintain links with it through a strong network of formal and informal meetings and encounters. The School has been a source of opportunity and inspiration for so many, and they care intensely about its future. The spirit of St Columba's has much to do with giving: the giving of themselves by teachers and Heads, the giving of time and expertise by Directors, the often sacrificial giving by parents, and the giving of their best – whether on the sports field, in the classroom, on the stage, or in expeditions further afield – by students. And it also has to do with receiving – quite simply – the best that a school can offer.

***Duke of Edinburgh Award winners, 1988***

Back row: Emma Ritchie, Benjamin Hillier, Kirsty Wilson, Catriona Muirhead, Jonathan Dunn, Kirsty Jamieson
Front row: Helen Campbell, Jane Collins, Kathleen Kyles, Gillian Scouller, Fiona Tehrani

**Laburnum Grove, *1937***
left to right:
Quita Broadfoot,
Barbara Innes,
Hugh Semple

**Alice-Sit-by-the-Fire, *1934***
Back row, standing,
left to right:
Ethel Lakeman,
Margaret Maclaurin,
W C Reid,
Betty Fyfe,
Lilla Stuart
Seated, left to right:
Jim Cuthbertson,
Barbara Innes
Seated, front:
Katherine
MacArthur

***The library, 1938***

*Chapter Twelve*

# The St Columba's Former Pupils' Association

## Foundation

The St Columba's School Society, as it was named, was formed in October 1906, with Miss Waugh as Honorary President, Milly Twist as President and Katherine Wood as Secretary and Treasurer, and a committee of members each representing one year since the School's foundation. The programme of meetings in the Society's first year featured a play reading, a progressive games party, and a dramatic entertainment. Pupils in the highest forms were invited to the meetings, and prizes were offered by the Society for special competitions.

Anne Marshall (Fullarton), an original pupil of the School, was President at the time of the Society's first dance in 1912, and closely involved with the Society in its early days. She was Secretary in 1914, when the Society resolved to devote its efforts to fund-raising for the War. The Society sponsored a bed in the military hospital in Rouen, and the School had three beds named after it in the Scottish Women's Hospitals. In the next few years, after their efforts had raised a total of £125 for the Red Cross and the hospitals, both School and Society were asked to name four more beds. Meetings were few and far between during the War, with most of the members engaged in some form of war work.

When the School needed funds for its new playing fields in 1921, the Society assisted with a subscription dance, stalls at the school fair, and a gymkhana organised by the Old Girls and Old Boys. Another lasting benefit for the School was the establishment in 1926 of prize medals, funded by the Society, a gold medal to be awarded annually to the best scholar in the Upper School and a silver medal for the best in the Lower School.

## Plays and anniversaries

To mark the thirtieth anniversary of the School's foundation, a reunion weekend for former pupils and Mistresses was held in December 1927. The Old Girls came 'in their hundreds', and, at a dance on the Saturday evening:

> . . . the Old Boys were present in tremendous force and outnumbered the husbands and fiancés, though often they filled a dual role!
>
> (School Magazine 1927-28, p. 17)

The Reverend Foster Franklin, the school Chaplain, preached at a service in the school hall on the Sunday.

From then on reunions took place about every three years, and the pattern for these highly enjoyable gatherings attended by scores of Old Girls and Old Boys was set. A reception hosted by the Headmistress opened the weekend's proceedings and a service in the School conducted by the Reverend Foster Franklin concluded them. A tennis tournament or lacrosse match against pupils was sometimes part of the programme, but the highlight of the weekend was the play: *Lord Richard in the Pantry* in 1930, *Alice Sit-by-the-fire* by J M Barrie in 1934, and J B Priestley's *Laburnum Grove* in 1937. Plays had also been staged in the mid-1920s, and, high as the standard of production was, their attraction went beyond the mere entertainment:

> To begin with, the actors are mostly old friends and those who are not are at least the friends of old friends. We have known the greater number of them probably since kindergarten days. We remember, for example, one of the actors on the programme playing Humpty Dumpty at a very tender age, very solemn, very intriguing, and we know that, to this day, he has kept the gift for throwing himself into his part. We recollect also, perhaps, that one of the girls was in the same class as ourselves, and how we shared many an inky scrape together. In short, we can exchange reminiscences about nearly everyone in the cast, and we know them in the effortless and satisfying way associated only with friends of our childhood.
>
> (School Magazine 1936-37, pp. 18-19)

In 1929 the Society presented Miss Waugh with her portrait, painted by Norah Neilson Gray (see Chapter Three). Miss Waugh in turn presented it to the School. Elsie Cuthbertson (Hislop), who retired as President at that time, served the Society as Secretary several times over a period of about fifty years.

## The Library

When the School's extension of 1936 was opened, with its new dining room, the large room that had served this purpose was freed for an important new use:

> 'Literisque studere' – so ends the School motto, and in what better place can study be done than in a library? In a school of the size and importance of St Columba's it is surely a real necessity that there should be within the building a suitable room set apart for peaceful reading, a quiet and beautiful room secluded from the rush and bustle of the class-room.
>
> (Janie Marshall (Wood), School Magazine 1936-37, p. 28)

Thus did the Old Girls, at a Cake and Candy Sale, launch their appeal for funds to give the School a library more gracious than the bookshelves in Miss Nicolson's top-floor sewing room, which had served the purpose until then. The former pupils responded handsomely, and Mr Frank Burnet donated his architectural skills. The room was panelled in walnut, chairs and tables to match were bought, and a stone fireplace was installed. The Directors met the cost of oak flooring from Company funds. Rugs and curtains were purchased, and a fine glass door bearing the school crest completed the transformation. Books flowed in from former pupils and friends of the School. The opening ceremony was performed by Sir Alexander Taylor on prize-giving day, 1938.

All meetings were suspended between 1939 and 1945, and the school magazine became the means by which members kept in touch, with an extended section of news, edited by Norah Hislop and Miss Lakeman, reporting the various kinds of war service and work being done by St Columbans.

## The Jubilee

In 1947 the School reached its fiftieth anniversary, and in October of that year many Old Girls, Old Boys and staff converged on Kilmacolm to revive interrupted friendships and celebrate the School's Jubilee. The jubilee committee was headed by Mona Laird, President, Elsie Cuthbertson (Hislop), Secretary and Margaret Brown (Burnet), Treasurer. A reception and dance began the weekend's festivities. The next day's lacrosse match was won by the Old Girls, who counted four trialists for the Scottish team in their side, as well as Joan MacRobert, who at that time played for Scotland. At a concert in Shalott three Old Girls who had become professional musicians performed for a large audience: pianist Catherine Kneebone (Shanks), soprano Amy Fryers, and violinist Hannah Wishart (Dorothy Jones).

Later in the weekend Barbara Innes produced a version of *Pride and Prejudice* on the school stage. Four performances in all were given, for friends, pupils and parents. To conclude the reunion, the Reverend Dr Franklin and the Reverend Robert McNeill conducted a commemoration service in the Old Kirk. The only shadow over what had been a very successful celebration was that Miss Waugh was not there to see it: she had

***The four Headmistresses, 1947***
Miss Young, Miss MacArthur, Miss McMurtrie, Miss Waugh

died earlier that year. A tribute to her appeared in the small book produced for the Jubilee.

The Society's gift to the School to commemorate Miss Waugh was a system of bell and clocks. It was presented on behalf of the Society by the President, Quita Paterson (Broadfoot), at a ceremony in June 1950.

## Old Boys

The Jubilee provided a reminder of a significant cohort of the School's supporters: in proposing a vote of thanks, Helen Laird, the Head Girl, referring to *Pride and Prejudice*:

> . . . reminded her audience that the Old Boys of St Columba's were apt to be forgotten but on that evening their importance had been realised.
>
> (*Jubilee Book*, p. 27)

Many Old Boys who remained in the Kilmacolm area, some of them married to Old Girls, were active in their support of and interest in St Columba's. Others moved away and lost touch, and, because they spent only four or, at the most, five years at St Columba's, the School could claim only a small part in the honours they achieved afterwards. Still, it took pride in those whose fame spread back to Kilmacolm. Among these were R B McCallum, a pupil from around 1904, who was Master of Pembroke College, Oxford, from 1955 until 1967. Patrick MacArthur, the brother of Dr J Morag MacArthur, Old Girl and a Director of the Company, was awarded the OBE in 1969 for services as a Consultant Paediatric Physician. Rear-Admiral Wilfred Graham, C B, son of W Bryce Graham and Jean Graham (Jackson), both former pupils themselves, was Captain of HMS *Ark Royal* from 1974 until 1976, and later Port Admiral of Portsmouth; he also served as Director of the Royal National Lifeboat Institution. Ian Lang, Secretary of State for

**Pride and Prejudice, *1947***
Left to right:
Joan MacRobert,
Elaine Andrew,
Jean Haddow,
Barbara Innes

Scotland (1990-97) is another former pupil of St Columba's Preparatory School. There are doubtless many other distinguished Old Boys whose subsequent careers have not found a place in the annals of the School. Since the advent of co-education to St Columba's, men begin to appear in those annals again, and in increasing numbers.

## Growing branches

In 1929 a London branch of the SCSS was formally opened, with Miss Macindoe as President and Margery Reid as Secretary. Miss Waugh attended some of the meetings, which were ususally in Miss Macindoe's flat, and the dinners held in London. Temporarily extinguished by the War, the London branch was reconstituted in 1949, by Mrs Douglas (Miss Peterkin) and Miss Bowie. Over the years its fortunes fluctuated: it was set up again in 1957, after some time in abeyance, by Miss Sutton along with Nancy Spells (Harrison) as Secretary, and Miss MacArthur made a point of visiting it each year. It was disbanded in 1970, but in 1977 over forty members met for a reunion attended by Miss MacArthur, Miss Clark and Mrs Caldwell, and London reunions were again held in 1982 and 1987. These meetings, as well as the recent House of Commons visit, were organised by Mrs Heather Woodward, who has for many years done the important job of keeping the members living in London in touch with their old school.

An Edinburgh branch was formed after the War, with Miss McMurtrie, living there in her retirement, as its President and Betty Cowan (Mories) as Secretary. It carried on meeting once or twice a year until 1961, but after the death of Miss McMurtrie, who had been its mainstay, it ceased to be an official branch. From around 1983 an annual coffee morning or meeting was held in Edinburgh; many of the coffee mornings were hosted by Margaret Moodie (Andrew), and others by Miss MacArthur.

**Bonaventure,** ***1951***

Left to right: Margaret Brown, Hugh Blair, Jim Lester, Margaret Maclaurin, Barbara Innes, Margaret Croft, Kathleen Weir, Hector MacLean

## Reunions and celebrations

After the War triennial reunions continued to bring members flocking back to Kilmacolm, where they were always entertained graciously at the School by Miss MacArthur. The plays had become a much-loved institution: *Bonaventure* produced by Barbara Innes in 1951, *Milestones* produced by Betty Fyfe in 1954, *Treasure Hunt* directed by M V (Bill) Service in 1957 for the sixtieth anniversary of the School. Margaret Brown (Burnet) was thanked for her term as President. The reunion on this occasion was attended by 220 members.

In 1959 Jean Graham (Jackson) formally opened the newly panelled entrance hall, made possible by the sixtieth birthday fund established by the Society. The Society instituted, in 1964, the B S B McMurtrie Memorial Fund, to provide an annual scholarship to be granted to a senior pupil who showed ability or promise, who otherwise might not be able to continue her education at St Columba's. After the death of Miss MacArthur in 1987, a fund in her memory was set up, and the donations which poured in were added to the Memorial Fund to increase the value of the scholarship.

*Island of Sirens* was produced by Phyllida Bowser (Blackater) in 1966, unique among SCSS productions in having an all-female cast. A new feature of the reunion on this occasion was an art exhibition, which included work by Freda Gentleman (Harrower), Norah Neilson Gray, Alison McKenzie, Chica Munro (MacNab), Muriel Marskell (McKenzie) and Ann Sanders (Meade).

Some meetings were held in Glasgow, in the form of dinners at various venues such as the Trades House and restaurants. At the autumn A G M and spring meetings members were often entertained by an Old Girl sharing her recent experiences, travels or professional expertise, or giving a musical performance.

**Milestones, *1954***
Left to right:
Joe Russell,
Joan MacRobert,
Sarah Marr,
Margaret Maclaurin,
Margery Haddow

***The 75th anniversary lunch, September 1972***
The top table, clockwise from left: Miss Clark, Margaret Renwick (Daisy Lang), Miss MacArthur, Wieda Russell, Helen Laird, Jean Graham, Morag MacArthur

The next major event was the celebration of the School's seventy-fifth birthday in 1972. The reunion weekend was very well attended, and members were entertained to a 'Musical Evening, 1897' and the third act of *Pygmalion*. The Reverend Dr Jack Barr, the school Chaplain, conducted a service, after which lunch was served in the school hall. Miss MacArthur and Miss Clark spoke of the School past and present. The following year's autumn meeting was held at Shalott, to enable members to view the new extension, and the Society voted to donate chairs and a table for the stage in the new hall.

In 1974 Mary Ure (Gourlay) was thanked for several terms of office over a period of many years; and among the many other faithful supporters over the years were Margaret Marshall (Graham), President for 1975-77, Hazel Gibb (Cuthbertson), Secretary for 1976-79, Muriel Gibb, Treasurer for 1982-86 and Margery Baird (Tough), Treasurer for 1986-88.

The eightieth birthday reunion was marked by a variety show produced by Mrs Rita Jones, who had for many years been active in the Society. In 1984 Nancy Scott (McKinlay) took over as President from Janette Nicol (Jinty Wither), who was thanked for all the work she had done over many years as editor of the Society's section of the magazine, as Treasurer and as President.

The ninetieth anniversary celebrations in 1987 coincided with Mr Livingstone's first term as Rector. The Society presented the School with a wall hanging, each square embroidered and appliqued by a member, which hangs facing the entrance of the School. An art exhibition was a feature of

***Presentation of wall-hanging for 90th anniversary, 1987***
Mr Livingstone, Nancy Scott, Ann McGarva

this celebration. Among the works on display were some by Mairi Hedderwick (Crawford), the illustrator and author, who had left St Columba's thirty years earlier. The new President elected in 1987 was Ann McGarva (Ross), who had long been an active member of the Society. Miss Muriel Clark, who succeeded Clare Robertson (Morrison) as Secretary, gave much time and effort to up-dating the files of members, an enormous task now that the membership numbered around a thousand.

## Into the Centenary

In 1991 the Society was formally renamed the St Columba's Former Pupils' Association. During the next few years it held several enjoyable functions: a ceilidh in Shalott, School versus Former Pupils hockey and rugby matches, and October dinners where guests were entertained by the David Craig Ensemble, Morrison Haddow, and Seona Anderson (Laird).

The names of members – over 1400 of them – have been put onto computer discs. The former pupils have a major role to play in the Development Campaign, launched in 1997, the first project of which is the construction of the music, arts and technology building on the site of Cargen Lodge, to which they have generously contributed. This building will commemorate the work of Tom Walton, Sophie Tytler and other music and art teachers who have given so much to the School. The support and financial backing of the former pupils is a key element in the School's future as a place where the finest facilities for study will be available.

Events to mark the School's Centenary had been planned by the committee, under the presidency of Jean Nicol, for many years. In November 1997 a Centenary reunion for former pupils was held in the Churchill Room of the Houses of Parliament, followed by a tour of both Houses. Eleanor Laing, MP, (Pritchard) hosted the event, Mrs Heather Woodward organised it, and it proved to be a most memorable and enjoyable occasion.

A most successful and enjoyable reunion in April 1998 included a reception and lunch at the Senior School, lacrosse, rugby and hockey matches at Birkmyre Park, a boarders' reunion in Shalott, and a celebration dinner and ceilidh at the Glynhill Hotel in Renfrew; on the following day a commemoration service in the Old Kirk was taken by the Reverend Elizabeth Houston, a former pupil of the School, with music provided by former pupils, including, under the direction of Mr Walton and Mr Fry, a choir of Old Girls. Their rendition of Mozart's *Ave Verum* and *Laudate Dominum* brought back memories and stirred many hearts.

The Association takes great pride in its many members who have reached the heights of their professions in the academic, medical, business and scientific spheres. Others have excelled in the world of music, art, television and drama. It receives correspondence from artists in the USA, farmers in Australia, nurses in the Middle East and doctors in South America and Bosnia. The list appears endless.

The nature of St Columba's ensures that most pupils put down deep roots at the School. The Former Pupils' Association is the strong and healthy tree that grows from them, a source of joy to its members and of strength to the School.

*The Canada Rugby Tour party with Craig Chalmers*

*The Canada Hockey Tour party with Craig Chalmers*

*The Iona Walk party pictured with TV personality Jimmie MacGregor*

*Postscript*

# The Centenary Year

**by Adrian Miller**

The thirteenth of September 1997 marked the successful completion of one hundred years of education at St Columba's. On that day, and indeed for several months before and after, the school celebrated the achievements of its first century. It was fitting that these celebrations represented each of the three components of the school's motto *orare laborare literisque studere* (to pray, to work and to pursue learning). Centenary events consequently reflected a school balancing academic, non-academic and spiritual pursuits. The spiritual element was perhaps best symbolised by the broadcast from Iona. In this founding Centenary event, a party of twenty students and staff commemorated the 1400th anniversary of St Columba's death with choral contributions to two radio shows and to the BBC's "Songs of Praise". The visit to Iona also provided the Rector with the opportunity of meeting Irish President Mary Robinson to whom he gave a school umbrella! The group was presented with a piece of the specially-woven St Columba tartan, blessed by the Bishop of Argyll.

One week later, the school's enduring connections with Iona were reinforced. A party of twelve Duke of Edinburgh Gold Award holders, led by television personality Jimmy MacGregor, raised a massive £9000 for three charities by walking from Iona to Kilmacolm. With them they brought the Centenary Flag and were welcomed by the Inverclyde Provost Cathie Allan at Cornalees Bridge. Upon their arrival in Kilmacolm, the group was piped through the village to the finish at Shalott. Even the harsh weather conditions did not detract from the enthusiasm of the pipers and exhausted walkers.

This emotional journey was followed by adventure abroad as St Columba's expanded its horizons and sent fifty-nine pupils and seven staff on a seventeen-day rugby and hockey tour of Canada. Participants played in the Calgary Olympic Stadium, experienced white water rafting, visited the gigantic Edmonton Shopping Mall and marvelled at the famous Calgary stampede. The tour provided fond memories for all involved and the results of the matches reflected the school's rapid development on the sports field.

This enthusiasm for fitness emerged again on the morning of the fourteenth of September, the Centenary Gala Day, when hundreds of pupils and other competitors displayed their stamina in one, four and ten kilometre runs and

***Runners embark on the Centenary Gala Day fun run***

Primary pupils released balloons in Birkmyre Park. Among those attending was Mrs Jean Graham, the school's oldest former pupil, who cut an enormous Centenary cake and raised the Centenary flag.

After officially completing one hundred years, the Primary School remembered earlier times with a Victorian day. Traditional attire, playground games and speeches by Mrs McGarva, a former boarder, and Miss Weir, former pupil and Depute Headmistress, provided an authentic look back at the educational environment of the present pupils' forebears.

The previous year's election of former pupil Eleanor Laing as a Member of Parliament allowed a November reunion of the St Columba's Former Pupils' Association in the House of Commons. Former pupils travelled from all over Britain to join Mr Livingstone and the Head and Depute Prefects for lunch in the Churchill room and a tour of the Houses of Parliament.

***Mrs Jean Graham cuts the Centenary cake***

***Mrs McGarva and Miss Weir share memories of the school with primary pupils***

***Primary pupils drill at Shalott on Victorian Day***

*Mr Livingstone and Dr Laird look on as Mrs Graham raises the Centenary flag*

November also saw the final rounds of the school Mastermind, Top of the Form and Young Musician of the Year competitions. Mastermind was hosted by Magnus Magnusson who brought with him the famous black chair and ominous music. A close competition was fought and fourth year pupil, Sarah Peggie, whose specialist subject was the First World War, emerged the winner of the trophy donated by the Holms family. The Young Musician of the Year competition was judged by Mr Tom Walton, Mr Donald Finlayson and the RSNO's Edwin Paling. Kathleen Erin Fitzpatrick's rendition of piano pieces by Gade and Groulez earned her first prize in a fiercely contested competition.

*Mastermind finalists*

*Top of the Form teams*

*Very stern primary staff*

Continuing this musical excellence, the 1997 Carol Service surpassed all expectations, thrilling over one thousand parents and friends. Contributions by professional tenor John Treleaven and harpist Rhona Mackay enhanced a magnificent programme which also included secular and religious readings, choral and orchestral recitals and the second public performance of the Centenary Fanfare composed by Mr Derek Fry.

*Once Upon A Century*

*Young Musician of the Year finalists*

As Christmas approached, the Centenary Ball, held at the Forte Crest Hotel in Glasgow, united staff, sixth year, former pupils and friends of the school in a spectacular event. The largest ever St Columba's Ball provided good food, music and dance for the hundreds who attended.

Following the success of Mastermind, Young Musician of the Year and the Centenary Cookbook (compiled by Home Economics teacher Mrs Helen Jacobs and Mrs Martine Ferguson) renowned Chef Jeff Bland hosted a Masterchef competition at the Senior School on the fifth of March. After demonstrating the culinary talents which have taken him from Cameron House to the Balmoral Hotel in Edinburgh, Chef Bland joined Mrs Mo Scott and Mrs Jo Kennedy in voting Jillian Currie the winner:

§ § §

Fillets of Lamb wrapped in Spinach and
Proscuitto, Wine sauce,
Colcannon Potatoes,
Caramelised Onions and Baby Carrots

~ ~

French style Strawberry Tarts covered
with a Caramel Cage

* * * *

*Centenary Ball*

*Judges Mrs Mo Scott, Jeff Bland and Mrs Jo Kennedy with the Masterchef finalists*

ST COLUMBA'S SCHOOL

KILMACOLM

*Menu*

STRATHGRYFFE OAK SMOKED SALMON
SERVED WITH RED ONION, CAPERS, LIME
AND A WHOLEGRAIN MAYONNAISE

◆

DUCHAL BROCCOLI AND
LEMON CREAM SOUP

◆

KILALLAN CHICKEN CABERFEIDH
NEW POTATOES WITH FRESH HERBS
MEDLEY OF FRESH VEGETABLES

◆

CRAIGMARLOCH CRANACHAN

◆

FRESH COFFEE WITH
WHISKY TRUFFLES

THE MENU HAS BEEN SPONSORED BY
J MCDOWALL & SON, FAMILY BUTCHERS,
191 GEORGE STREET, PAISLEY. 0141 889 2606

THIS EVENING HAS BEEN ORGANISED IN CONJUNCTION
WITH ST COLUMBA'S SCHOOL PARENT'S ASSOCIATION

In celebration of the outstanding successes of previous school shows, 1998's *Once Upon a Centenary* revisited some of the best. The first half recreated moments from 1950's *A Midsummer Night's Dream* through to 1997's *The Boyfriend*. The second half reaffirmed the school's affection for the work of Gilbert and Sullivan in a performance of *The Zoo*.

**O What a lovely War!**

***The Zoo***

*The lacrosse players*

The weekend of the fourth and fifth of April provided former pupils with their opportunity to participate in the Centenary celebrations. Despite inclement weather conditions, a rugby '10s' tournament, a 1st XI vs Former Pupils hockey match and a game of lacrosse were played on the Saturday morning. Only hours after victory in the rugby match, many of the former pupils visited the Senior School. Displays of photographs and memorabilia had been arranged in the classrooms to commemorate the stewardships of past Headmistresses and of the present Rector. The large turnout for this reunion conveyed the durability of these former pupils' affection for St Columba's. That evening the Centenary Dinner and Ceilidh for three hundred people was held at the Glynhill Hotel in Renfrew.

*Centenary weekend rugby players*

Speeches were delivered by the Revd Norman Drummond, Chairman of BBC Scotland and by Miss Jean Nicol, President of the Former Pupils' Association, who had been responsible for the skilful organisation of the weekend. The following afternoon a church service to give thanks for the ongoing success of St Columba's was attended by many with happy memories of the school. Mrs Eleanor Laing MP, Dr Helen Laird, Miss Jean Nicol and Mr Livingstone all delivered readings. Musical performances were provided by soloists Gail Hawthorne, who sang

*The reunion*

*Bist du Bei Mir* and Luke Williams, who played two trombone pieces. The former pupils' choir performed *Laudate Dominum* by Mozart and *This Little Babe* by Britten, conducted by Mr Tom Walton and accompanied by Mr Derek Fry, past and present Heads of music.

*Centenary Dinner*

On the fourth of May, Primaries Five and Six travelled north for a five-day stay at Nethybridge outdoor centre. During a packed week, they participated in many activities, including an adventure course, abseiling, climbing and raft-building. A day spent canoeing on Loch Morlich proved particularly popular and contributed to an exciting educational trip.

Later in May, the school hosted a large number of French students as part of the exchange programme, inaugurated this year. Twenty-seven second year pupils, accompanied by Mrs Smith, Mrs Johnson and Mme Bretaudeau had already visited their foreign correspondents in February. This excursion had taken them to a town called Bron, near Lyon, in the East of France, where they stayed with local families. This hospitality was returned when the French pupils travelled to Kilmacolm. During their stay here, they explored the surrounding area and enjoyed a cycle round Cumbrae and especially the

chance to try Scottish dancing at a vibrant ceilidh in the Senior School on the final night of their stay. Shortly before their departure, the French visitors were treated to a performance of current hit songs by a group of second year Spice Girls. They had promised to return, keeping the Auld Alliance strong and departed to the tune of *Will ye no come back again?*, played by the school pipers.

The Former Pupils' reunion provided the inspiration for the school's major charity contribution of the year. Jane MacDonald, a former pupil had been given a dog by the charity Dogs for the Disabled. Consequently, the school decided to raise the money to provide a disabled person with a helping dog and an appeal ran from December to May. Generous donations at the Carol Service, contributions from former pupils and monthly class collections raised the £5000 required to train and support a dog. A representative visited the school with a trained dog in May and brought the pleasant news that a suitable owner had already been found for the school dog, Columba.

*French exchange*

*Primary pupils hand over a cheque to fund 'Columba', helping dog for the disabled*

*Rafting at Nethybridge*

***Provost Cathie Allan presents a commemorative silver plate to Mr Livingstone, Dr Laird and the Heads of School***

On the 21st of May, as national examinations neared completion, Provost Cathie Allan hosted a Civic Reception for the school at Greenock Town Hall. Representatives from all areas of school activity and development were entertained by a varied musical programme in which Kathleen Erin Fitzpatrick, Jennifer McLachlan and Kirsten Blackie, finalists from the Musician of the Year competition, performed. In addition, two hit songs by Boyzone and The Spice Girls were sung by Almost Angels, a group of six third year girls. Provost Cathie Allan proposed a toast to the school and wished St Columba's every success for the next hundred years.

The music of St Columba's played across Europe in early June when the pipers, the orchestra, the choir and Susan McDowall, our highland dancer, embarked on the Centenary Music Tour. Accompanied by Mr Fry, Mrs Slaven, Mr Murray, Mr Craig and Pipe Major Gordon Allan, the pupils enthralled audiences with lively classical pieces and traditional Scottish music and dance.

The music played on in Kilmacolm for the Primary School show in June. Every pupil from the preparatory class to Primary Six took part in a journey through one hundred years of music. The preparatory class took the circus as its theme and their rendition of Nellie the Elephant will long be remembered! Primaries One to Three's *Oliver!* recreated Victorian

***opposite: The Prep Clan - "Nellie the Elephant"***

***P2 Workhouse boys***

FRITS GEURTEN & ZN.
RIDE

NETHYBRIDGE
EMERGENCY EXIT

children's lives in song while Primary Four whisked the audience through ten decades of popular music. Mr Alan Maclean wrote, produced and directed *The Scottish Crossbill*, an operetta involving pupils from Primaries Five and Six which wove a magical tale of faries and humans and was hugely enjoyed by both participants and audiences.

On the fifteenth of June, a party of sixth year pupils, accompanied by the Rector, Mr Spinks and Mr Clark set off on the traditional four-day visit to Mull and Iona. This was a fitting conclusion to the pupils' final year, bonding them together in the special atmosphere of St Columba's spiritual home.

Later that week the first Leavers' Ball was held at Shalott. Staff, guests, parents and pupils mingled on the terrace before enjoying a buffet provided by the school's catering staff. Mr Livingstone bade the leavers a fond farewell and the dancing that followed a programme of entertainment, enthusiastically provided by the sixth year, was enjoyed by all.

***P4 music through the century***

***opposite: Dr Helen Laird, Chairman of the Board of Directors, takes her leave of pupils at Shalott***

**The Scottish Crossbill**

*Miss Beth Allison, MBE*

In the Queen's Birthday Honours List of 1998, Miss Beth Allison, secretary at junior school was awarded the MBE, having given forty years of service to St Columba's. The school's delight at this recognition of Miss Allison's commitment was reflected by the reception she received when she carried out her final duty: presenting prizes at Primary Prizegiving.

The twenty-fifth of June marked the final day of St Columba's Centenary year. The Former Pupils' Association made the inaugural presentation of specially commissioned celtic necklaces and Former Pupils' ties to the class of '98. Senior School Prize-giving was held at St Columba church and prizes were presented by Mr Philip Dry, President of the Law Society of Scotland. As always, there were reflections of the past and visions of a future as yet only half-revealed and promises to return from those for whom the time had come to move on. Dr Helen Laird became an honorary member of the class of '98, announcing at prizegiving her retiral from her position as Chairman of the Board of St Columba's School.

St Columba's Centenary year comprised an enormous number of events. The quantity and quality of these occasions conveyed the breadth of the school's talents. It also became clear that the motto, *orare laborare literisque studere*, is not something merely pinned to the blazer pocket but is, in fact, worn close to the hearts of all pupils.

This year was one of reflection, connection and animation. May saw the demise of Cargen Lodge, most recently the home of the music department. Its imminent replacement, a larger, more advanced arts and technology facility will prove highly beneficial to all future pupils of the school. The new building will house the Tom Walton Music Suite to celebrate and commemorate the much-loved and inspirational former Head of Music. Throughout the building, plaques will display the school's appreciation of the contributions made by former members of staff.

Over the past months, the media has made the wider community aware of the excellence of St Columba's achievements but, as the millennium approaches, the school will not bask in the reflected glory of the centenary year. Instead it looks to the potential of the future. Such is the strength of its tradition, however, St Columba's essential character will not change. The school is certain to remember, to appreciate and to remind others of its history and of the roots which provide its anchor.

***Architect's drawing of the new building***

***'Swan Song' for Cargen Lodge, conducted by Mr Tom Walton***

# Sponsors of this book

John and Helen Anderson
Beechwood Nurseries Ltd
F J Boyle FBCO, Optometrist
Anne, Allan and Ross Bradley
Central Garage, Johnstone
Clyde Coast Coaches
J J Cree and P Lunney, Dental Surgeons, Gourock
Miss J H Frederick BDS, Dental Surgery, Greenock
Gerard Removers
H T Developments, Ltd
Holland House Electrical Ltd
Mr and Mrs T Isherwood
Anne Johnston
John G Jones
KMA (Public Relations Consultants)
Kamscot Construction Ltd
Keppie Design Ltd
Kilbarchan Shuttle (Michael Black)
Kingsley Wood & Co.
Drs Jack and Katherine Leighton
The Lindsay Group
McDermid Decorators
McKenna Financial Services Ltd
R McLellan
Donald J Malcolm, W H Malcolm Ltd
Raymond and Letitia Miller
Kenneth D Mitchell (Lynton House Dental Surgery, Port Glasgow)
Lauren Morrell
Heather Mutch
Patterson Supplies Ltd
Pirie & Co. (Paisley) Ltd
Pride of the Clyde Coaches Ltd
Joseph Reilly, Artistry in Flowers
Blair and Helen Ritchie
Ian and Marcia Ritchie
Lesley and Olivia Robertson
Teknek Electroniks Ltd
Semple Cochrane plc
Strathclyde University, Faculty of Engineering
Threads
Irvine and Christine Watson
Weir Dental Surgery
The Weir Group plc
Wellmyn Holdings Ltd

# The Chairmen of the Girls' School Company

JLK Jamieson 1879-83
Professor Thomas Lindsay 1883-1914
John A Spens interim chairman 1914-17
Professor George Gibson 1917-29
A Peden Fyfe 1929-44
Norman Millar 1944-54
John Tindal 1955-66
G N Ferguson 1966-72
Mrs Helen Mack 1972-77
Geoffrey Duncan 1977-90
(from 1987 The Park and St Columba's School Company)

Chairman of St Columba's School 1982-1989
J C Ritchie

Chairman of the St Columba's School Company
(set up in 1990)
Dr Helen Laird 1990-98

# Head Girls

| | |
|---|---|
| 1902-03 | Edith Twist |
| 1903-04 | Mabel Brydie |
| 1904-06 | Janie A Wood |
| 1906-08 | Margaret Lang |
| 1908-09 | Lilias M Woodburn |
| 1909-11 | Margaret M M Graham Brown |
| 1911-12 | Katherine W S Adams |
| | Anne A Mowat |
| 1912-13 | Helen M Rae |
| 1913-14 | Katherine G Wood |
| 1914-15 | Alison C Todd |
| 1915-16 | Mabel A M Wilson |
| 1916-17 | Katherine C S Shankland |
| 1917-18 | Elinor Drinkwater Jackson |
| | Edith Helen Reid |
| 1918-19 | Agnes Margaret Macdonald |
| 1919-20 | Margery Fletcher Reid |
| 1920-22 | Elspeth Hope Duncan |
| 1922-23 | Frances Elizabeth Handasyde |
| 1923-24 | Mary Winifred Williamson |
| 1924-25 | Gladys Isobel Ledingham |
| | Elizabeth Mackie McCutcheon |
| 1925-26 | Elizabeth Mackie McCutcheon |
| 1926-27 | Euphemia Russell |
| 1927-28 | Agnes Watson Hamilton Brown |
| 1928-29 | Agnes Rona Morrison Mackay |
| 1929-30 | Isobel Marshall Hunter |
| 1930-31 | Jessie Cullen Cochrane |
| | Morag Dorothy Mackay |
| 1931-32 | Margaret Stevenson Watson |
| 1932-33 | Elizabeth Waddell Mories |
| 1933-34 | Kathleen Rose Macdonald |
| 1934-35 | Jenny Marianne Bridge |
| 1935-36 | Jean Archibald McGregor |
| 1936-37 | Hannah Dorothy Jones |
| 1937-38 | Sheila Anne Rutherford McBride |
| 1938-39 | Muriel Agnes Phillips |
| | Margaret Elizabeth Watt |
| 1939-40 | Muriel Mary Gibb |
| 1940-41 | Ann Weir Drummond |
| | Doris Christine Johnston |
| 1941-42 | Frances Katherine Snodgrass |
| 1942-43 | Jean Dickson Anderson |
| 1943-44 | Catherine Gordon McAuslan |
| 1944-45 | Margaret Allan McIntyre |
| 1945-46 | Margaret Isabel Pratt |
| 1946-47 | Janette Wither |
| 1947-48 | Helen Mary Laird |
| 1948-49 | Helen Mary Laird |
| 1949-50 | Marion Millar Baird |
| 1950-51 | June Ward Close |
| 1951-52 | Jean Liddell Laird |
| 1952-53 | Margaret Jean Thomson |
| 1953-54 | Eleanor Mary Ewing |
| 1954-55 | Helen Fionna McGregor |
| 1955-56 | Aileen Drummond Wilson |
| 1956-57 | Marilyn Pollock |
| 1957-58 | Margaret Bain |
| 1958-59 | Hilary Burnet |
| | Helen Anderson |
| 1959-60 | Helen Anderson |
| 1960-61 | Elspeth McW Reid |
| 1961-62 | Margaret McGregor |
| 1962-63 | Hilary Rouse |
| | Mary Balderston |
| 1963-64 | Patricia Gillies |
| 1964-65 | Anne Duff |
| 1965-66 | Catherine Cathrall |
| | Yvonne Howard |
| 1966-67 | Margaret Macaulay |
| | Isabel Tolhurst |
| 1967-68 | Catriona L Hill |
| 1968-69 | Bryonie F Stone |
| 1969-70 | Jill Tolhurst |
| 1970-71 | Fiona Hannah |
| 1971-72 | Sandra Macdougall |
| 1972-73 | Jennifer Barr |
| 1973-74 | Lesley Gow |
| 1974-75 | Lucy Holms |
| 1975-76 | Alison McMurray |
| 1976-77 | Margaret McKinnon |
| 1977-78 | Caroline Heycock |
| 1978-79 | Lesley Clark |
| 1979-80 | Susan McEwing |
| 1980-81 | Rosamund Muir |
| 1981-82 | Susan Johnson |
| 1982-83 | Laura Carmichael |
| 1983-84 | Lesley Tait |
| 1984-85 | Fiona Pottie |
| 1985-86 | Nicola Carmichael |
| 1986-87 | Jaya Rajoriya |
| 1987-88 | Alison Welch |
| 1988-89 | Sarah Ferguson |
| 1989-90 | Kathleen Kyles |
| 1990-91 | Lois McNeilage |

# Head Prefects

| | |
|---|---|
| 1991-92 | Victoria Knowles |
| | Stuart Wilson |
| 1992-93 | Mhairi Reid |
| | Robert Macdonald |
| 1993-94 | Jennifer Morrice |
| | Simon Thirde |
| 1994-95 | Sarah Russell |
| | Colin Adam |
| 1995-96 | Jonathan Clayton |
| | Kirsti McGibbon |
| 1996-97 | Abigail Flinders |
| | Robert Leckie |
| 1997-98 | Katie McNair |
| | Adrian Miller |

# Gold Medallists

| | |
|---|---|
| 1925-26 | Euphemia Russell |
| 1926-27 | Agnes Watson Hamilton Brown |
| 1927-28 | Agnes Rona Morrison Mackay |
| 1929-30 | Phyllis Mathewson Walker |
| 1931-32 | Jean Morag MacArthur |
| 1932-33 | Lillias Barbara Davenport Philip |
| 1933-34 | Kathleen Rose Macdonald |
| 1934-35 | Jenny Marianne Bridge |
| 1935-36 | Gladys Helen Law |
| 1936-37 | Hannah Dorothy Jones |
| 1937-38 | Mary Hunter Bruce |
| 1938-39 | Muriel Agnes Phillips |
| 1940-41 | Janet Isabel Speirs |
| 1942-43 | Beatrice Margaret Campbell |
| | Catherine Gordon McAuslan |
| 1943-44 | Catherine Gordon McAuslan |
| 1944-45 | Edith Elspeth Parkes |
| 1945-46 | Janette Wither |
| 1946-47 | Sheila Gordon McAuslan |
| 1947-48 | Helen Mary Laird |
| 1948-49 | Isabel Allan Hendry |
| 1949-50 | Jean Millar Wallace |
| 1950-51 | Jean Shelagh Tough |
| 1951-52 | Shirley M C Denholm |
| 1952-53 | Marielle Maud Hunter |
| 1954-55 | Joan Cameron Craig Sharp |
| 1955-56 | Myra Boyce Winter |
| 1956-57 | Tessa Harrow |
| 1959-60 | Elspeth McWalter Reid |
| 1961-62 | Morag G Webster |
| 1963-64 | Lorraine Cooper |
| 1964-65 | Kathleen McDowall |
| 1965-66 | Caroline Cooper |
| | Gillian White |
| 1966-67 | Pauline A Carrick |
| 1967-68 | Hazel M Stuart |
| 1969-70 | Susan Hunter |
| 1970-71 | Fiona Hannah |
| 1971-72 | Sandra Macdougall |
| 1972-73 | Jennifer Barr |
| | Sharon Stevenson |
| 1973-74 | Marianne Houston |
| 1974-75 | Christine Houston |
| | Irene Lyle |
| 1975-76 | Valerie Lang |
| | Eleanor Pritchard |
| 1976-77 | Inez Muir |
| | Patti Von Gliszczynski |
| 1977-78 | Caroline Heycock |
| 1978-79 | Sara Hornibrook |
| 1979-80 | Nina Buchan |
| 1980-81 | Jacqueline Lee |
| 1981-82 | Susan Johnson |
| 1982-83 | Marjorie Gibb Stuart |
| 1983-84 | Deborah O'Hare |
| 1984-85 | Sarah Ramsay |
| 1985-86 | Caroline Thaung |
| 1986-87 | Pamela Newlands |
| 1987-88 | Lindsay Johnson |
| 1988-89 | Sarah Ferguson |
| 1989-90 | Benjamin Hillier |
| 1990-91 | Lois McNeilage |
| 1991-92 | Katherine Ferguson |
| 1992-93 | Donna Boyd |
| | Stella Smith |
| 1993-94 | Nicola Bowd |
| | Shona Fraser |
| 1994-95 | Farya Nazir |
| 1995-96 | Kirsti McGibbon |

# Senior Dux

| | |
|---|---|
| 1996-97 | Robert Leckie |
| 1997-98 | Rishma Maini |

# Athletics Champions

| | |
|---|---|
| 1923 | Winifred A E Auld |
| 1924 | Elizabeth M McCutcheon |
| | Mary W Williamson |
| 1925 | Mary Scott |
| 1926 | Jean S Parker |
| 1927 | Rosie M Kerr |
| 1928 | Annie Laurie |
| 1929 | Annabella C Little |
| 1930 | Gladys M Coltart |
| 1931 | Morag MacArthur |
| 1932 | Margaret D Kennedy |
| | Vida A McKelvie |
| 1933 | Margaret D Kennedy |
| | Vida A McKelvie |
| 1934 | Jean F Lyle |
| 1935 | Jean F Murray |
| 1936 | Sheila Shaw Cameron |
| 1937 | Sheila Shaw Cameron |
| 1938 | G Joan Shanks |
| 1939 | Doris M McG Millar |
| 1940 | H Margaret C Smith |
| 1941 | Doreen Rose Hairs |
| 1942 | Doreen Rose Hairs |
| 1943 | Doreen Rose Hairs |
| 1945 | Patricia Mary Baxter |
| 1946 | Patricia Mary Baxter |
| | Joan Carswell Morrison |
| 1947 | Doreen Chapman |
| 1948 | Margaret Ann Meade |
| 1949 | Agnes Macfarlane Balfour |
| | Mary Smith Hunter Williamson |
| 1950 | Agnes Macfarlane Balfour |
| | Jean Mary Hamilton |
| 1951 | Edith Frances Harrison |
| 1952 | Nancy Anne Paterson Clarkson |
| 1953 | Gertrude Anne Pinkerton |
| 1954 | Gertrude Anne Pinkerton |
| 1955 | Margaret Isabel McLaren |
| 1956 | Elizabeth Anderson Angus |
| 1957 | Elizabeth Angus |
| | Leslie Blackater |
| 1958 | Joan Le May |
| 1959 | Joan Le May |
| | Norah Brown |
| 1960 | Norah Brown |
| | Lynne Gardner |
| 1961 | SusanTolhurst |
| 1962 | Sheila Carter |
| 1963 | Susan Tolhurst |
| 1964 | Sheena Hannah |
| 1965 | Sheena Hannah |
| 1966 | Gillian Hamilton |
| 1967 | Gillian Hamilton |
| | Judith Walker |
| 1968 | Gillian Hamilton |
| 1969 | Ruth Clay |
| | Patricia Smith |
| 1970 | Amanda Boal |
| | Jane Fraser |
| 1971 | Victoria Jack |
| | Jean Weir |
| 1972 | Sandra Macdougall |
| 1973 | Christine Cowan |
| 1974 | Alison Coghill |
| 1975 | Elaine McIntosh |
| 1976 | Rosemary Tainsh |
| | Janet Mack |
| 1977 | Elizabeth-Anne McMurray |
| 1978 | Fiona Stirling |
| 1979 | Corinne Martin |
| | Fiona Stirling |
| 1980 | Helen Giffin |
| 1981 | Valerie Gallacher |
| 1982 | Valerie Gallacher |
| 1983 | Stephanie-Anne Ritchie |
| 1984 | Fiona Pottie |
| | Kirsty-Jane Ritchie |
| 1985 | Kirsty-Jane Ritchie |
| 1986 | Lorna Reid |
| 1987 | Cameron Muir |
| | Sally Lyle |
| 1988 | Jennifer Brown |
| 1989 | Christine Dry |
| 1990 | Gillian Soutar |
| 1991 | Karen Lindsay |
| 1992 | Gillian Soutar |
| 1993 | Jennifer Morrice |
| 1994 | Jennifer Morrice |
| | Andrew McAlindon |
| 1995 | Katie Lindsay |
| 1996 | Angus Campbell |
| 1997 | Sally Lindsay |
| | Cameron McNair |
| 1998 | Rhona MacKinnon |
| | Kenneth Morrice |

# Silver Tablet for Musical Perfomance

| | |
|---|---|
| 1917 | Margaret G L McConechy |
| 1918 | Marie F E Cullen |
| 1922 | Lilias McCallum |
| 1926 | M Joyce Nicol |
| 1927 | Phyllis M West |
| 1928 | Greta E O S Riddell |
| 1930 | Doris S Arthur |
| | Phyllis M Walker |
| 1933 | Elizabeth W Mories |
| 1935 | Marjorie T Chalmers |
| 1938 | H Dorothy Jones |
| 1939 | Margaret W Pollock |
| 1940 | Dorothy S Howie |
| 1941 | Mercedes Margarita Park |
| 1949 | Moira Carlin Baird |
| | Mary Smith Hunter Williamson |
| 1951 | Violet Cooper Shearer |
| 1954 | Clare Lilias Mary Morrison |
| 1957 | Mairi T N Crawford |
| 1973 | Jennifer E Barr |
| 1975 | Catriona Jacobs |
| 1976 | Janette Giffin |
| 1982 | Elizabeth Boyd |
| 1983 | Gail Hawthorne |
| | Marjorie Gibb Stuart |
| 1984 | Alison Campbell |
| 1985 | Helen Butter |
| 1986 | Caroline Thaung |
| 1995 | Colin Adam |
| | Anne Ritchie |
| 1997 | Shona Watson |

# Carson Award for Art

| | |
|---|---|
| 1930 | Agnes M Anderson |
| 1931 | Isobel L Macfarlane |
| 1935 | Jean F Murray |
| 1936 | Elinor Anderson |
| 1937 | Iris E D Nicol |
| 1941 | Esmée M S Cousin |
| | Janet I Speirs |
| 1944 | Mary B Edwards |
| 1947 | Elizabeth M Gray |
| 1948 | M Ann Meade |
| 1959 | Ann E Finlayson |
| 1964 | M Elizabeth Hay |
| 1968 | Pamela Buchanan |
| 1970 | J Anne Critchley |
| 1971 | Janis G Anderson |
| 1972 | Lorna J Will |
| 1987 | Lois Girdwood |
| 1991 | Catherine L Fairbairn |
| 1993 | Kim A M Clark |
| 1995 | Sally McMaster |
| | Susan L Wharton |
| 1997 | Sarah Black |
| | Victoria C Saxton |
| 1998 | Pamela Graham |
| | Georgina McMaster |
| | Lindsay Wilson |

# Achievers' Ties

1993-94
Iain Anthony
Alastair Bell
Nicola Bowd
Fiona Fairbairn
Shona Fraser
Laura Gibb
Derek Hutcheson
Linsey Knowles
Susan Livingstone
Andrew McAlindon
Julie MacDonald
David Mackay
Cameron McNair
Jane Miller
Jennifer Morrice
Faisal Nazir
Amanda Paterson
Judy Stanley
Kim Russell

1994-95
Colin Adam
Nicola Begbie
Paul Clark
Barry Connelly
Sasha Gawish
Katie Lindsay
Lesley McDonald
Sally McMaster
Farya Nazir
Vicki Rae
Anne Ritchie
Isobel Ritchie
Sarah Russell
Christopher Scott
Pippa Shaw
Shona Watson
Susan Wharton
Andrew Wilson

1995-96
Jonathan Clayton
Russell Hosie
Emma Howard
Stuart Johnston
Nitish Khanna
Sally Lindsay
Kirsty Lyle
Kirsti McGibbon
Kenneth Morrice
Morven Wilson
Carolyn Young

1996-97
Craig Begbie
Sarah Black
Stephen Blair
Louise Clayton
Mark Ferguson
Abigail Flinders
Julie Hunt
Nigel Jamieson
Robert Leckie
Erika Lucas
Laura MacConnacher
Katherine McCullough
Alastair McDonald
Jamie McIlroy
Rhona MacKinnon
Georgina McMaster
Victoria Saxton

1997-98
Nicola Anderson
Clare Brown
Victoria Catterson
Jillian Currie
Kathleen Erin Fitzpatrick
Pamela Graham
Sarah Johnston
Joanna Lindsay
Alan Macleod
Jennifer Macmaster
Katie McNair
Rishma Maini
Adrian Miller
Sara Montgomery
Catherine Morrison
Ilaria Nardini
Sarah Peggie
Andrew de Rozario
Helen Russell
Catriona Semple
Victoria Stoddard
Julie Thomson
Lindsay Wilson

# Duke of Edinburgh Gold Award

| | |
|---|---|
| 1992 | Victoria Knowles |
| 1993 | Lesley Robertson |
| | Michelle Sangster |
| | Gillian Soutar |
| | Robbie MacDonald |
| | Victoria Wright |
| | Alison Lamb |
| | Nicola Morrice |
| 1994 | Nicola Baillie |
| | Alastair Bell |
| | Fiona Fairbairn |
| | Laura Gibb |
| | Annika Hampson |
| | Linsey Knowles |
| | Karen Lindsay |
| | Susan Livingstone |
| | Jane Miller |
| | Jennifer Morrice |
| | Judy Stanley |
| 1995 | Shona Fraser |
| | Sasha Gawish |
| | Fiona Glen |
| | Julie MacDonald |
| | Vicki Rae |
| | Pippa Shaw |
| 1996 | Nicola Begbie |
| | Nicola Gemmell |
| | Katie Lindsay |
| | Lesley McDonald |
| | Sarah Russell |
| | Morven Wilson |
| 1997 | Julie Hunt |
| | Deborah Lang |
| | Sally Lindsay |
| | Laura MacConnacher |
| | Mhairi Reid |
| 1998 | Robert Leckie |
| | Erika Lucas |
| | Alastair MacDonald |
| | Carolyn Young |
| | Catriona Young |
| | Nicola Anderson |
| | Clare Brown |
| | Katie McNair |
| | Jennifer Macmaster |
| | Helen Russell |
| | Victoria Stoddard |

# Staff 1997-98

## Senior School

RECTOR
Mr Andrew Livingstone, BSc (Hons), DipEd
DEPUTE RECTOR
Mrs Jennifer Wallace, Dip PE, Dip in Spec. Educ. Needs

TEACHING STAFF:
ART
Mr David Craig, DA, ATD
Mrs Maria Robinson, BA (Hons)
BIOLOGY
Mrs Patricia Gulbransen, BEd
Mrs Carolyn Miller, BSc (Hons)
Mrs Joan Andrew, BSc (Hons), DipEd
CHEMISTRY
Mrs Teresa Munro, BSc
Mr Kenneth Robertson, BSc (Hons)
CLASSICS
Mr Alan Milligan, MA (Hons), DipEd
ENGLISH
Mrs Marion Sommerville, MA (Hons)
Mrs Lindsey Duncan, MA
Mrs Janet Stevens, BEd
Mrs Pamela Wales, MA (Hons)
Mrs Maxine Jack, MA, DipEd
GEOGRAPHY
Mr James McDougall, MA (Hons)
Mrs Sheilagh White, MA
HISTORY
Mrs Isabel Smith, MA (Hons)
Mrs Joyce Scott, BA, Cert SL
MODERN STUDIES
Mrs Louise Eadie, BEd
HOME ECONOMICS
Miss Emily Baird, BA
Mrs Rosemary Hammond, Dip II
MODERN LANGUAGES
Mr Calum Ure, MA (Hons)
Mrs Véronique Bretaudeau-Eteiba, Degree in English Lang & Lit, Degree in Educ. Sciences, Lyon
Mrs Victoria Reilly, MA (Hons)
Mrs Anne Hunter, MA
Mrs Norma Smith, MA

Maths and Computing
Mr John Spinks, BSc (Hons)
Mrs Zena Morrison, BSc
Mrs Fiona Bruce, BSc
Mrs Jacqueline Marshall, BSc, MSc
Mrs Joan McMahan, BSc
Music
Mr Derek Fry, MA (Hons), B Mus, FRCO, LRAM, ATCL
Mrs Patricia Slaven, BSc, DipT (Mus), Adv Dip Ed, Dip SL
Mrs Anne Sutherland, Dip Ed (Mus), LTCL (Piano), LTCL (Voice)
Physics
Mrs Hilary Fraser, BSc (Hons)
Mr Alistair Meek, BSc (Hons)
PE
Mr Brian Manson, Dip PE
Mrs Carole Marr, Dip PE
Mr Stuart Clark, BEd
Mrs Lorna Urie, BEd
Mrs Jillian Bellew, BEd (Hons)
Mr Roderick Glen, Dip PE
Technical
Mr Archiebald Murray, HNC, Dip Tec Ed
Mr Alexander Philip, Dip in Educ Handwork
Business Studies
Mrs Kay Hamilton, BA (Hons), MSc
Transitus
Mrs Isobel Evans, DCE, ALCM
Extra Subjects:
Diction
Mrs Elspeth Buchanan, ATCL, ALCM (Eloc)
Clarinet/Saxophone
Mr Henry Morrison
Pianoforte
Miss Agnes Allison, DRSAM (Piano)
Solo Singing
Mrs Betty Kidd, MA, LRAM
Flute
Miss Fiona Chisholm, DRSAM
Brass
Mr Craig Anderson, DRSAM, CPGS
Violin
Miss Hilary Smyth, BA
Percussion
Mr William Glendinning
Guitar
Mr Michael Simons
Keyboard/Accordion
Mr Graham Laurie
Cello
Mr Harold Harris

Administration:
Mrs Dorothy Motherwell, Dip Sec Sc
Mrs Jan Greenan
Mrs Norma Syme
Mr Alan Rodger, BSc, LTCL
Company Secretary
Mr Norman Floyd, CA/ Mr Allan Gallacher, CA
Assistant Bursar
Mrs Barbara Gethin
Cashier
Mrs Lindsey Martin, HND
Technicians
Mr Robert Brown, HNC Chemistry, HNC Computer Systems Support
Mrs Flora Rodger, BSc
Library
Mrs Rosemary Reeves, MA
Auxiliary
Mrs Pat Shaw
Janitorial
Mr George Walton
Mr Kenneth Bassett
Kitchen
Mrs Pauline Young
Housekeeping
Mrs Lena Martin

## Primary School

HEAD OF PRIMARY
Mr Alan Maclean, MA, DipEd
DEPUTE HEAD
Miss Elma Paton, DCE, Infant Endorsement, Associate of the British Dyslexia Association

TEACHING STAFF
Mrs Eileen Black, DCE
Mrs Margaret Blackie, DCE
Mrs Yvonne Campbell, DCE
Mrs Sandra Clarke, DCE
Mrs Gail Henderson, BA
Mrs Karen Jamieson, BA (Hons)
Mrs Fiona McGibbon, DCE
Mrs Mary MacKenzie, DCE
Mrs Angela Moore, DCE
Mrs Barbara Murray, BEd, Cert Ed
Mrs Rosemary Nott, BA (Hons), Dip Ed
Mrs Sheila Swinnerton, DCE
FRENCH
Mrs Jean Clarkson, MA
NURSERY
Mrs Carol Crampsey, DCE, ACE, Nat Froebel Foundation Certificate
Mrs Alison Edwards, Cert Ed
ADMINISTRATION
Miss Elizabeth Allison
Mrs Jacqueline Ebner
Mrs Marjory Taylor
JANITORIAL
Mr Andrew MacGillivray
Mr Kenneth Bassett
KITCHEN AND HOUSEKEEPING
Mrs Anne Blakely

(Music, PE and Extra Subjects Staff from Senior School also teach in Primary School.)

# Directors

Chairman of the Board: Dr Helen Laird, OBE, MA, PhD, DL

Kenneth M Barclay, FRICS
William M Biggart, BA
Mrs Elizabeth Clark, LCST, LRAM, ANEA
Miss Allison Cook, MBE
William Harkness, LLB, CA, NP
William Hill, LLB, NP
Ron M Kennedy, TD, FCII, FLIA
Ian MacConnacher
Dr. Judy Semple, MBChB, DCH, FRCP
Robin W Wilson, CA
John A Wylie, MBE, BSc, CChem, MRSC

Honorary President: Sir Donald Miller, BSc, FEng, FIMechE, FIEE

Honorary Vice Presidents: Mrs J Graham
G C C Duncan, BL, NP
J C Ritchie

# Index

# ST COLUMBA

(Hymn written for St Columba's School).

One came from Erin to the Isle of Hy,
And showed the Christ, and sang his praise,
And lived His life of love, and went His ways
In clachans where the seagulls cry.

And soon the long lochs and the burns and bens
Had heard with joy the Blessed Tale;
And up and down the lovely land of Gael
Jesus was known in all the glens.

And God's high meaning for the lives of men
Dawned out of superstition's night;
And things of wrath and evil, in the light,
Gave place to holiness again.

Saviour, our school bears Colum's sainted name,
And we thereof would worthy be.
Help us in him Thy will for us to see,
And feel through him our hearts aflame.

Aflame with purity and truth and love,
Burning to succour others' need,
And wheresoe'er our path in life may lead,
To seek the things that are above.

So we, in homely round, or search of lore
Or quest of weal, or work of art,
In Jesus' name would play our patron's part,
Saints of today as he of yore.

Written for St Columba's School, Kilmalcolm

*Words by* Foster Franklin
*Music by* E Linford Holgate
1930-31